CW01160967

The Time Advantage

JOHN W HALL

This is a work of fiction. The names, characters and events are fictitious and any resemblance to actual events or real people is entirely coincidental.

Copyright of this book belongs to the author. All rights of the author are asserted. No part of this book may be reproduced, stored in any type of media or circulated in any form by any means without the prior consent of the author.

Published by Enstrata Ltd, Cambridge, England

Printed by Print On Demand Worldwide, Peterborough, England

ISBN – 9780956583307

Date of publication, July 2010

Contents

Introduction	Essential Reading	-	You have been warned!	v
Chapter 1	Setting the Scene	-	Not Ground Zero	1
Chapter 2	Minutes on a train	-	Hours to reason why	9
Chapter 3	Organisational Release	-	The boss's foot	23
Chapter 4	Levers for Gaining Time	-	Distracted Acronyms	31
Chapter 5	Branding Conversations	-	Perceptual Magic	49
Chapter 6	Event Management	-	Precision Planning	67
Chapter 7	Measures for Success	-	Visually Mighty	87
Chapter 8	Purposefully Engaging	-	The SCOPE test	109
Chapter 9	Choices to Change	-	Swanning around	127
Chapter 10	Smiley's Place	-	Energy and cats	155
Chapter 11	Successful Formulae	-	Capturing more	177
Chapter 12	Friday Morning	-	The Plumstone Connection	201
Chapter 13	Everything, but the pipe	-	Timely Performance	209
Chapter 14	The Tenth Professor	-	It only takes a laugh!	221
Chapter 15	The Turning Point	-	Time for change	239

Introduction

'Essential Reading —You have been warned!'

This book is designed for managers (or aspiring managers). The aim of the book is to introduce managers to some of the more effective methods in advanced time management and show that there is a way forward from simply knowing basic time management.

So what is advanced time management, apart from being for managers and a step up from basic time management?

It is a wide field, drawing upon strategies and techniques in leadership, management, and the use of productive time. There is a strong focus on managing purpose, getting perceptions right, including time perceptions, exploiting time levers, dealing with time bottlenecks, finding synergies and conducting standard approaches at a high level.

Someone once said that advanced time management was not simply working smarter; it was working on the smarter things. There is a lot of truth in this.

Advanced time management also places a lot of emphasis on people. That is why you will also find motivation and momentum techniques here as well. And, of course, it is about releasing the time to do the smarter working in a way that keeps you in control, improves your approaches and still allows you to have a life!

The book is in the form of a story. I emphasise the word "story". All the characters are fictional. However, the techniques described come from the real world.

The story itself is about how one manager meets a professor. This professor arranges for him to meet eight other professors, all of whom have a strong interest in time management. Three of them suggest that he meets another rather mysterious professor, who can offer him something that none of the rest can.

Each professor describes different techniques that make a significant impact on how the manager can best manage his time. There is a good chance these techniques could also have a beneficial impact on how you can manage your own time.

In addition to the techniques on time management, the story contains a number of intriguing connections between the people, places, and events. There are also real surprises as you get to the end.

These connections are designed to make the book more lively, more memorable, and more discussed. You will probably notice some of them, as you are reading; others you may be able to work out as you near the end of the book. It depends on what you know.

To give you an indication of what there is to discover, there is a list of challenges straight after the acknowledgements. The best thing to do is to read the list before you start and then return to the list after you have finished the last chapter.

To discover whether you have worked out a reasonable answer to a challenge that is not otherwise explained in the book, you will have to find, and then ask another reader. It may be interesting to see what they think, not only about the mystery connections, but also about the approaches and techniques to time management. In this way, I am hoping that the entertaining part of the book will promote discussion that focuses upon the usefulness of the rest of the content – the ways to help you manage your time.

Now, though, is the time to hear John Watson's story. He is a manager on the lookout for useful techniques and strategies that can take him beyond basic time management. John Watson is no pushover. He tends to challenge what he is told. To have a character that can do this in a book is a great asset. It means that you do not have to accept, as in many management books, what is put in front of you. By reading the challenges to the techniques and the ways to manage them, you can learn more about their validity and usefulness.

I hope that through this approach you will not only become more expert at time management, but also will enjoy it more.

John Hall, Cambridge, July 2010.

Acknowledgements

I would like to thank Thak Patel, MBA, CEO of THINKindia Ltd, based in Cambridge for inspiring me to take the time to write this book, when so many other distractions beckoned. During one pub lunch, the decision was made to settle down and start writing. Thak also kindly read the first draft and, with a number of promptings, the book grew ever stronger.

Writing a book takes a surprising time and much dedication. Very little else gets done during the writing. I would particularly acknowledge the support of my family during this period.

Challenges for you!

Below is a list of questions to help you discover some, but not all, of the mystery connections and challenging puzzles within the story. There are plenty of time management challenges too. Read the questions before you start Chapter 1 and then return after you have finished the book.

The questions are organised into **General Questions** and **Specific Questions**. For general questions there are clues **in** two or more chapters. For specific questions there are clues in just one chapter. You will come across more specific questions as you read the book. There are some readers notes at the end of most chapters to draw your attention to them.

General Questions

1. What sport does John Watson's favourite team play?
2. What is the relationship between John and Mary?
3. Which cities does John visit to meet each of the professors?
4. What is the connection between all the pubs that John visits?
5. What do the professors have in common apart from an interest in time management?
6. Can you think of better answers to the acronym puzzle?
7. Is there any relationship between the two restaurants John and Mary visit?
8. What is the 'plumstone' connection?
9. What do you learn about Jane before you meet her?
10. What activity is directly or indirectly referred to on each visit to a professor?
11. What is the historic connection to one of the characters?
12. Can you recall what each professor asked John to do?

Some Specific Questions

13. Why did an innkeeper place LEDs on the belt of a figure in the sign for his Pub?
14. What is the nature of the object that the bio-robotics expert finds beautiful?
15. What is the nearest underground station to Professor Holmes?
16. What is the relevance of the full name of Professor Holmes's assistant?
17. What is a chronosphage and where is the one mentioned in the story?
18. Where exactly did John and Jane go after they left first professor?
19. What is the guide that John and Jane discuss?
20. Who makes a fleeting guest appearance?
21. Why did John and Jane fall about laughing on top of a hill?
22. How was it possible to see the hippopotamus beside a canal in London?
23. Why would John ask a question relating to 'Eel pie and Ham'?
24. Where exactly did John have his turns?

Chapter 1
Setting the Scene
'Not Ground Zero'

Hallo. My name is John Watson.

I would like to invite you to read about an incredible, and strange journey, as I meet with ten professors, who advise me about managing my time.

I call it an incredible journey because I learnt so much, even when I thought I already knew a fair bit about time management. I call it a strange journey, because there are some coincidences that are just ...well... strange. There are also a couple of things linking the professors apart from their expertise in time management. I was not able to work out those links until the end. Perhaps you will be quicker than me!

But I am getting too far ahead. Let me introduce myself.

I am a mid career executive working for a company in South West London. Although I have my own specific role, I am also responsible for managing six other people. I regard myself as a working manager, who has to fit management activities alongside what I have to do operationally.

The nature of my job involves supporting customers with the configuration of the software for the equipment that our company sells to them. As a team we also align the relevant manuals and do some of the training. This involves co-ordination with other internal departments.

I have some friends who are also mid career managers, both in the public and private sector. Much of our time is spent in meetings with outsiders, with our peer group, and with our teams. We all have to make plans and stick to budgets. We are expected to manage all the corporate rules that we have in the organisation. We all tend to use the same tools –

mobile phone, laptop, diary.

In my case, my boss is not involved in any "hands on" work, so I mostly have to swim, or sink, on my own judgement and activity levels.

I live in South West London, as well as working there, although I originally came from the North West. My current home is about a mile from the (famous to some) "Stoop" stadium, where I watch my favourite sports team play. Nearby is an even bigger stadium where national teams play.

I did not have much time after work to take up any hobbies, but I was able to get down to my local pub "The Plough" about one night in two. Even when I was not officially working, I spent time thinking about work. From time to time, I had regrets that I was missing out on some aspects of life, by focussing too heavily on work.

I had done this job for five years. In one sense, I was thinking that it was time to move on to something bigger, and better. However, it did seem to me that the personal sacrifices increase as you work your way up the corporate ladder. Those sacrifices are already pretty large in my existing industry sector.

The tempo of my work is pretty high. Lunchtimes were not much more than a sandwich at the desk. There always is more to do, and, as my boss has continually been telling me, there is always more that I must achieve. Targets only seem to go upwards, and usually much faster than inflation! The end result was that I'm usually pretty shattered by the time I can get away, which was usually 6:30 pm., although it was occasionally later if there was a deadline to meet.

In practice, the way the week worked was that I battled, as best I could, during the days to get enough done and use the evenings to tackle any overflow. Fairly regularly, I had to catch up on the weekend for a couple of hours. Sometimes, it took much longer.

Occasionally, I experienced a complete overload. In such situations, my ability to manage time almost breaks down, and I become disorganised. This always creates a further difficulty as disorganisation seems to breed more disorganisation. It usually takes a monumental effort to bring things back into balance again. It is like being stressed in two ways. There is the stress of doing the work that you have to react to, and there is the stress of getting organised again. I wished that I could find a solution to this.

My staff were pretty good. They are competent, although sometimes they did not work quite as fast as I would like and they were easily distracted. The good news is that most of them had been with me for a while, and knew what I required of them. Thankfully, I have not had too much recruitment or training to do. This can be very time-consuming.

It is a good bet that someone will leave in a two year period. Everyone will wish that person well, but after they have gone, we will all have to bear the stresses of an extra load. Usually there is a recruitment gap and a training load, as the new person learns to make a contribution. I always like to make a good impression on someone new, but the double disorganisation of extra load, and training, does not help me feel as organised as I would like to be perceived. These periods have been quite stressful in the past.

I had read a training book on managing stress. The message to its readers was the more you do of what you have always done, the more you will get what you always got.

In some ways, that is where I was. My working methods had not changed much over the last few years. The work levels had increased and my resources had not. So the future suggested that I was going to have to up the tempo even more to meet even higher targets.

The stress training book did not give me many practical suggestions. It did make the point that if you did not want to relive the past, you had to change the future. I had reached the stage where I recognised that I had to find a different approach. I was open, before I even started this journey, to looking out for either a new role, or a better way of working my existing role, but I had taken no serious action on either of these.

As regards time management, I thought I already knew a fair bit about working methods and managing time. I had been on a one-day course on time management earlier in my career. I had also read a couple of books on the subject.

Before I take you on the journey, it is probably worthwhile giving you a snapshot of what I knew about time management at the starting point. This puts us all on the same level of knowledge. Some of these time management points may be useful to you.

Not Ground Zero – What I already knew about Time Management.

I have already mentioned that I had a standard corporate pack of mobile phone and laptop computer - *personal productivity tools* as my company liked to describe them. The laptop has a diary management system, an email agent, and normal office software. I could access documents on the company server from home. The mobile was fairly modern, and we were about to convert to an updated version with a faster processor, and better e-mail facilities in the next year.

My friends told me that the latest sophisticated mobiles just made them more available. They ended up being interrupted more, both at work and at home. It seemed that we needed some organisational protocols about how these new devices are to be used in my organisation. I suspected that we would just be told to use them appropriately – whatever that might mean! I was pretty sure that there would be little debate on personal intrusion and about which communication channel to use for which purpose.

The only other thing that I used was an A4 day book. This was simply an A4 notebook, with a side binding and tear out pages. I carried this around with me for all the things I had to note during the day, regardless of the subject.

The time management course I went to earlier in my career had basic messages. The points made to me, on the course, included: –

1. Make sure you are clear on your priorities. Every task should be categorised as either high priority (A), mid priority (B), or low priority (C).

2. Only work on those items that are important and urgent and not on those that are simply urgent.

3. Every so often keep a diary of your time, so you know what wastes your time.

4. Only attend to your e-mails twice a day. The objective is not to get trapped into waiting for the next e-mail, and then responding to it regardless of its importance.

5. Make use of your computer's diary management system. Learn how to set things up, and most importantly, learn how to change things once you have set them up.

6. Use "to-do" lists and reminders. Print them off your computer and have them in front of you every day.

7. Prepare for meetings and get some chairmanship skills if you are likely to be running them. Always object, if a meeting drifts away from the agenda.

8. Keep your desk clear. You can only work on one thing at once!

9. Handle each piece of paper once. Whenever receiving a written communication, you should take an action with it - file it, put it in bring forward system, destroy it, or send it to somebody else!

10. Take advantage of project management software if you have complex tasks. Also use wall planners as much as you can.

11. Do not procrastinate. Carry out the instruction 'do it now' at all times.

12. Learn how to say "no" politely. Perhaps, tell people you have to do something else, or offer to go and see them in their office so you can escape from a long unproductive conversation easily!

13. Make sure you know how your phone works. This includes setting up voicemail and being able to transfer calls. Have a good system for taking messages.

14. Make use of any time when you are likely to be waiting. For example, on trains, in hotels etc.

15. Delegate as much work as possible. Don't let work sit on your shoulders. Give it to someone and make sure they know the first thing to do with it.

16. Book time with yourself, if you get too busy!

17. Get to know, and use, some memory techniques.

18. Learn speed reading if you have a lot of papers to get through.

The course I attended had no real surprises, and their productivity methods were often more about saving seconds and minutes rather than hours or weeks. OK, I can accept that seconds saved each day can add up to hours saved over a year. What I find difficult to accept is that often, in saving seconds, you end up spending just as many seconds, if not more, in learning to do the new thing, telling other people you are doing it, and ordering the resources to keep it happening.

Virtually all of the time techniques sound logical and are common sense. I did practise most of them when it suited me. In fact on some occasions I found it difficult not to practise them.

Generally, I found most of the above techniques too simplistic. For instance, what may not be urgent or important to me is urgent and important to somebody else. To always do something now means you don't necessarily put sufficient thought into it. Memory techniques sound great but in practice your natural memory suffices and you don't need to use other techniques.

I did however believe that technology could, and can still, offer a number of benefits to saving time and it will continue to enhance information access, information processing and communications. This was where I hoped some greater productivity would come from in the future.

If you have detected that I treat my previous learning on time management as rather basic, then you would be right. Don't get me wrong. I am not contemptuous about it. It is all useful stuff but for me it was not going to bring about the revolution! I felt that there must be something else that would improve what I did.

Hopefully, that brings you up to speed with the general level of knowledge of time management I had, and my attitude towards it before I met the professors.

So, we can now move on to what happened to me. This is where the story really starts and I am going to tell you about it just as it happened.

Readers Note:

You already have some information, earlier in the chapter about John's favourite sport. Don't worry if you missed it. More clues follow later!

Chapter 2

Minutes on a Train

'Hours not to reason why'

Every day, several trains shuttle between Manchester and London Euston. It was a Friday and I was on one of the late afternoon trains out of Manchester. I had come up the previous day at fairly short notice to meet two particular clients and had managed to fit in another three on my visit. My purpose with the extra three clients was to ensure they were all happy with our previous services.

This trip had involved five distinct meetings, as well as a rush around Manchester to get to each meeting on time.

It was the end of the week and I was feeling particularly tired. The only luxury I had was a first class rail ticket and a reserved seat. Many other businessmen have the same thing on a Friday afternoon, and every seat in my carriage was reserved.

There were four seats either side of the carriageway. In my set of four, I had been the first to arrive, followed quickly by two other gentlemen, one sitting beside me, the other diagonally across from me. A lady, turned up a couple of minutes later, and after some shuffling around, she ended up sitting opposite me. There was a table between myself and those opposite me. Across the passageway, there was an elderly gentleman, facing the opposite direction to me and sitting opposite a much younger man. The other two seats, in that set of four, were reserved either for people who had missed the train, or who would join at Macclesfield.

As we pulled out of Manchester station, I performed the first part of the normal executive ritual, as did some of my travelling companions. We get out some papers to work on. In my case, it was getting out my daybook and a pen. Then comes the second part of the ritual which is to look outside the window, and not do any work, until we reach Macclesfield, in approximately a quarter of an hour.

I had made some basic notes during each of the meetings I had been to, and these now had to be expanded with extra points that I was not able to get down at the time. It was crucial to do this before I either forgot the point, or became confused on the detailed nature of what was required. I also had to decide what points required action, what points I recorded for posterity, what information I needed to give to colleagues in other departments, and what I needed to communicate to the various members of my team. I have been in this situation before. As you cannot easily write on a train, it meant that I would make some jumbled scribblings now, which would need to be typed up on my PC on Saturday morning. This enabled other company staff to work on the actions from Monday.

As the train left Macclesfield, I pulled my daybook towards me, I noticed that the young professional on the opposite side of the corridor was already typing into a computer notebook. My colleague beside me was filling in a form as best he could, given the train movements. The lady opposite was still staring out the window, and the gentlemen beside her had started reading a trade magazine. The thought occurred to me that I should be using my laptop for the visit reports, but it is a weight to carry around. I still found pencil and paper a good way to organise my thoughts. I also did not like using a laptop in one of my customer meetings. It meant that I was splitting my attention between operating the laptop and building a relationship with the customer.

After ten minutes, I was getting fed up with making notes in my daybook, so I glanced across to see what my companion on my right hand side was doing. He was still working with forms, but he seemed to be getting through them quite quickly. He ticked several boxes on the form and wrote a few snappy comments in other boxes. As he completed the form, he ticked a box on the bottom right-hand side, before moving to the next piece of paper.

He must have noticed that I was watching him. He turned towards me with a friendly smile, and said, "Meetings! I guess you have to contend with them too?"

"Yes," I said, tapping my daybook. "I could not help but notice you have some forms to record the results of yours. For my sins, I use a notebook."

"We used to do that too," said my companion. "Then we sat down and asked ourselves about the purpose of the record of the meeting. We decided that we could do a lot with tick boxes and short statements. We then designed some tick box forms, even to the extent that they include a tick box to show who has completed a form. This means I do not have to try and do a legible version of my signature." He smiled, and, after a short pause, went on, "This just about makes it possible to complete a meeting or a visit report on a train."

He put his pen down, stretched out his arm as if to release a cramped muscle, recomposed himself and then continued, "This way of operating reduces the stress of having to do the reports later. When I get back to the office on Monday, they will scan the form for me into our computer system, and circulate it to all concerned. The original will be filed on a hard copy file and I, of course, get one of the electronic copies, so I can follow through any actions. From my point of view, this is easier than using a computer notebook, although I suspect I will end up having to use one soon."

At this point, he looked across to the young professional on the other side of the passageway, who was happily typing on his notebook and seemingly oblivious to everyone else. "I wonder if he is typing into a form," my companion said to me. "The Electronics might improve the speed of distributing what he completes, but it is more important to think about the purpose of what he is completing."

"It could be the case," I said, "that he will have finished whatever he does and be able to e-mail it to whomever he has to, before he gets home tonight. I find that an upsetting thought. Tomorrow, I will have to spend a couple of hours at home doing my reports on my PC."

"OK, I accept the point that he may finish what he has to do," said my companion. "However, we must use technology wisely and not use technology for technology's sake, just because it exists. There may be better alternatives. My crucial point is that we must always challenge our ways of working and make them purposeful. Existing ways of working can become entrenched and difficult to change. Often they continue to continue, particularly if your boss designed the existing arrangement! Then it becomes the case that some staff say to themselves 'Ours not to reason why. Our's just to do and die!' That is what I used to do until fairly recently. I just did my best to do the work in the existing ways. Now I challenge everything. I suspect I upset some of my colleagues and my boss sometimes, but I have had my successes. One of them resulted in these forms. They certainly save us time compared to the old method."

The gentleman opposite my companion had been gradually taking more interest in our conversation, than in his trade magazine. He caught our attention by putting his magazine down on the table, and leaning forward.

"I agree," he said. "It is important to be clear on what you are aiming to achieve. There are several different ways to write minutes of meetings. For instance, minutes at my production meeting have to be very specific about the actions to be taken and they can probably be written in a shortened form, no more than two pages of A4. Minutes of the staff committee meeting are going to be read by the rest of the staff who were not at that committee meeting. They have to be written in a style which explains the situation being discussed. They are of necessity longer and more wordy. Management Meetings can also vary in their nature. Some exist to make decisions, some exist for consultative purposes, and some exist for sharing information. Much depends on the purpose of the meeting, and the purpose of the communications to be issued afterwards. Those purposes should govern the style of the minutes. My organisation tends to be pretty good at debating what is best to fit our communication purposes."

He then changed his gaze to look directly at my companion and pointed to his papers. "I like what you have done. It seems to me that you have distilled the purpose of the meeting into a 'tick box' form, and fitted the outcome, and your records, to that purpose." Then, turning to me, he went on "Using day books in meetings can still be appropriate. It does strike me that, if you have several meetings, and you have to write them up afterwards, this could become a chore. I think you should review whether there is a better way to do them and the best way to start is to be absolutely clear on the purpose of your record."

The lady opposite me leaned forward at this moment. "Perhaps, I can offer you an alternative approach," she said. "Directly after I have a meeting, I dictate the key actions onto a dictation recorder. At the end of the day, I give the tape to the departmental secretary and she transcribes them into the right form. In that way, I do not have to spend so much time on a computer, and I can use my time doing things that I should be doing. I believe it an important principle that lower value activities are carried out at the lowest cost. A friend of mine is a good example. He does not have a departmental secretary to look after him. He uses an outsourced secretarial company. He dictates into a dictation recorder that stores the information electronically. Then he sends, via e-mail, the audio to the secretarial company, who type it up, and return it to him within 48 hours. In practice, it is usually done very much quicker than that. He just proof reads the final version. He only uses them when he needs them and the cost is low and his time on write ups is also low, so he is pretty productive."

I noticed at that moment the elderly gentleman across the corridor was also taking an active interest in our discussion.

"Isn't it interesting," I said. "We all have different approaches, and I know some of your approaches are much more time efficient than mine. I will certainly be reviewing the purpose of what I do. I am wondering though if any of you have any other time tips that you might like to pass on."

"I have one for you," said the lady. "Do any of you get involved in multitasking up to ten projects at once?" All of our heads nodded.

She reached into to her thin briefcase beside her and took out a comb bound document.

It was immediately obvious that the comb bound document contained sections of different coloured paper. There was a red section, followed by an orange section, followed by a yellow section, then a green section, a light blue section, a dark blue section and finally a white section, and then the colours repeated themselves. "Each of these colours represents a different project or task," said the lady. "If you are working on a number of projects in parallel, you use a different colour for each project, and make your notes on that colour paper."

"I could do that in a ring binder, and split up each section," said my companion, as politely as he could. "So what is the advantage?"

"There are two main advantages," said the lady. "The first is that you can lay the whole document flat on the table. It makes it so much easier to work on. If you are right-handed working on the left page, the comb bind is a lot less in the way than a ring bind. The second advantage is that a comb bound document not only lays flat in use, but it also folds flat when you have finished using it. You can easily put another document on top. Ring binders tend to be very cumbersome, particularly if you try to stack them. You can get far fewer ring binders in your briefcase, than you can comb bound documents. The downside is that you need to get a special hole punch, but once you get in the swing of using comb bound documents, taking used papers out and putting blank pages in is relatively straightforward. For creative work on different tasks, I find this a very useful arrangement.

She stopped for a moment and looked at each of us in turn. "I will give you another example where they have value. If you have to go through a long single sided draft, then having your text on the right-hand page and a blank page on the left – the reverse of the previous right hand page - means that you have lots of space to write notes, or additions, to go into the text. Finally, I would mention that this arrangement is very useful for general notepaper. If you have to get rid of, say, old letterheads, or special marketing paper, you can simply put it all in a comb bound document. To make any old letterheads or similar marks on the paper less intrusive, you simply indicate on the front cover which is the right way up of the notebook, and ensure that any marks are put in back to front and upside down. Quite a number of the managers in my organisation make up their general notebooks in this way. It does seem a productive way to work, and, at the same time, use up old paper."

"That's neat," I said. "I particularly like the idea that you can write easily on the left-hand pages for drafts of long documents. Has anybody else a time tip?"

"I can offer you something," said the gentleman diagonally opposite me. "You see this trade magazine that I am reading. You probably receive professional and trade magazines too. What do you do with them all?"

"I mostly throw them away," said my companion on my right, "but I have to admit that those that I like to keep just pile up for two or three years. They then get thrown out 'en masse', because I have not got the time to go through them again."

"Then let me offer you this tip," said the other gentleman. "When you go through a trade magazine, you probably identify a couple of articles that you would like to read, and another couple that might be useful at some time. I read the articles that I want to read and, if they are any good, I rip them out of the professional magazine. I then staple the loose pages together. I do the same with those articles that I have not got time to read now, but may have a need to read in the future. Then comes the clever bit. I simply stuff the articles into a large 'self seal' envelope. On the back of the envelope, I write the heading of the article and the date I put it in. You can get at least 30 articles in a large envelope. I mark the top of the envelope with a date and the general nature of the content, and I file it with other envelopes with other articles."

He paused for a few moments. I had the sense that he was enjoying this. "Now, say that in ten months time," he continued, "I need to quickly research a particular subject. I know I have seen an article about it somewhere. I go to the envelopes, and you'll be amazed how quickly your eye can scan down the lists on the back to see if you have anything relevant. If you have, you simply take it out of the envelope, and mark on the envelope the date you took it out. This means that I don't have to read every article in a trade magazine that could be relevant to my work. If I need something, I have got most of the resources to hand. I still find this process useful today, in spite of the Internet. Professional magazines may only be archived for a limited period on the net, and yet some articles, particularly management articles, have a longevity of years. I do not know whether this is of any value to you, and I simply pass it on as my tip of the day!"

"Talking of keeping old stuff," said my companion on my right, "my tip of the day is to put a 'destroy by date' on any old file that you are not likely to use for some time, if ever. For instance, recruitment files, old projects. If you do that, it makes it much easier to throw out old documents. You can also adopt the same practice with e-mail folders, moving them into a 'destroy by...' folder. If you have not got an archiving policy, it is probably worth talking to your Finance and HR Department about what should be kept, and for how long. Archiving properly today, will either save you, or the company, significant time in the future."

We all nodded in acceptance of the point. I remembered spending hours in one company, clearing out somebody else's cupboard, which was full of incompletely marked files. All my companions now turned their attention to me.

"The only thought that I could offer you," I said, "is more of a verbal technique. I never like dwelling on mistakes. If they make me feel guilty, then I am less likely to concentrate on putting what is wrong, right! Sure, I like to learn from what I do, but after I have extracted the learning, I want to move on. If I'm discussing a problem with a colleague and I, or they, have made a mistake, I always say 'History has happened, now what have we got to do?'. This expression gets rid of the past, and allows us to concentrate on the future. I've used it over many years, and I can vouch for both its simplicity, and the effect it has on focusing us on what to do."

"I like that," said the lady opposite. "Not only does it stop you, or anybody else, feeling guilty, it also gets away from blaming somebody else for what happened. I'm sure a lot of time must be wasted in a 'blame' culture. You only have to blame someone unfairly and you'll get no productivity out of them for the next month!"

"I'm going to try that out on my boss to see how he reacts," said the man beside me. "I will have to put some tactful words around it, such as ' History has happened, I can't change it, but I can change how we operate in the future, what should we do?'. As I think more about it, I think I should use that expression after I have summarised back to him, his point of view and made sure that he has understood my point of view. You have got me thinking now."

"I am thinking that you will find a better way of using it than I have done," I said. "I am also thinking it be wonderful if we could collect all the ideas of every executive everywhere, and use them to help us all in managing time. A lot of tips may only be for particular situations, but it does seem to me that there are some real techniques out there. I would certainly like more expertise. If I have a dream, it would be to be always acting as time efficiently as possible, and be able to convey what I do to others. I think I'm a long way from this ideal!"

At this moment, the coffee came round. The conversation turned to sporting events that would be happening over the forthcoming weekend. The gentleman, diagonally opposite me, shared my sporting interests. This led to a long exchange of views about the potential of key players. My efforts to write more notes about my meetings were shelved!

After a while, the tannoy announced that we were approaching Watford, and the train started to slow. "This is my stop" said my companion on my right. "Mine too," said the lady opposite. "And mine," said the gentleman diagonally across from me.

"I am definitely London bound," I replied. "I would like to thank you though, for your earlier ideas. I am definitely going to review what I do. If we meet again, I will tell you the results."

The two of my companions, nearest the passageway, started moving to get their luggage off the rack above. As they were doing so, the lady leaned forward, and said," I hope that one day you may achieve your dream of being an expert on time management, and then you can help us all. Good luck with what you have learnt today."

She then got up, picked up her thin brief case, and moved to join the other two, who were queueing at the end of the carriage. They all looked back and gave me a cheery wave, which I returned.

The train arrived in Watford. I looked out the window and watched them disappear. I had no idea who they were or whether we would meet again. I smiled to myself. It would be nice to be a time management expert, but there was no chance of that happening. There was simply not enough time!

As the train was stationary, I decided I would quickly list down in my day book what I had learnt from them.

Meetings

- Write down the purpose of my meetings.
- Write down the purpose of the minutes of the meetings.
- Use a form with tick boxes to capture standard information from customer visits.
- Put the form on a laptop for completion and communication purposes, if appropriate.
- Use dictation if someone can transcribe it for you.
- Consider outsourced secretarial services.

Time Tips

- Capture interesting articles from Trade magazines and retain in a large envelope.
- Use comb bound documents rather than folders for ease of writing.
- Use different colour pages for each task if you are multitasking.
- Recycle redundant paper into comb bound day books.
- Mark stored material with a 'destroy by' date to save future time.
- Get advice on what really needs to be kept and archived.

As I reviewed the list, I could not help thinking about the way we had each described our approach to doing minutes. I seemed to be the laggard in efficiently using my time. The man on my right was ahead but was not using technology that could take him a step forward. I got the impression that the lady opposite seemed to engage in unstructured dictation, although benefited from not having to type it up. The man diagonally across seemed to know what he was doing, but did not divulge any special technique about minute writing. It struck me that the main outcome from our discussion was the need to be clear on the purpose for minutes or reports. After that, consideration needed to be given to how technology could efficiently help.

I had this distinct feeling that I was missing something and perhaps there was far more to managing time than gathering a few tips. We had only discussed minutes of meetings. I wondered whether there were time strategies as well as time tactics.

"May I join you," said a voice that cut through my thoughts.

I looked up to see the older gentlemen from across the passageway. The young professional with the notebook had disappeared.

"By all means," I said, thinking that he just wanted some companionship.

He slid his way into the seat opposite me. Looking up, he said, "you know you said that you wanted to gain time management expertise".

"Yes," I said, somewhat guarded, wondering what was coming next.

"Then I think I may be able to help you. Let me introduce myself." He pushed over a business card that showed him to be:-

Richard Holmes
Professor of Physics

His details showed that he lived in London, and not far from Euston. He had quite a number of qualifications behind his name. I looked at him. I was taken a bit by surprise. Not only was there a professor in front of me, who was offering to help me with time management, but that professor had clearly nothing to do with the study of time management. I wondered whether he had misheard our conversations. He did have a hearing aid.

"I can see your look of surprise," he said. "It is not what I have done. I am retired now. It is who I know that counts. Don't they say that in business? It is not what you know; it is who you know."

"That's true," I said. "Still, the study of physics is a long way from expertise in managing time in business."

"Not as far as you might think," he said, "and I am not talking about theories of time and space. It just happens that I know eight professors who have a lot of expertise in the management of time. It is not their main subject. It is not a subject they have published papers upon, or done significant research upon. It is very much an active secondary interest for all of them. They all have very different views on time management."

He had got my attention. "Are they likely to publish anything?" I asked.

"I have spoken to each of them in the last couple of months," said the professor. "We all agreed that it would be worth bringing their views together for some sort of publication. The difficulty here is that it needs someone to talk to each of them, to challenge their views with a reality check, and then write up and publicise the result. It really needs someone from business to do it. It seemed to me that if you take their views together, they could save commerce, industry, and the public sector, huge amounts of time and cost. If you really want to be a time management expert, I can arrange for you to spend an hour with each of them, on one proviso."

He looked at me, as if to check that he still had my attention. "Go on," I said, thinking to myself that this is where I learnt the catch.

"The proviso is that you write up what you learn and if you, as a businessman, believe it to have some value, then you publicise the results through business networks. Most business people will not read academic journals."

"Why don't you do it?" I asked.

"I am not a businessman," he said. "I may have done work in the past about prioritising and managing activities, but I'm rather removed from it now. The world has moved on, since I retired. It is better that someone who is active in business does it."

"Can't the other professors organise somebody else to do it," I asked.

"In time, they probably could. Their difficulty would be agreeing amongst themselves who it should be, then agreeing who should organise it and finally trying, probably without success, to find some funding for it. Bear one thing in mind, they have only just agreed that this is a good thing to do. If I suggested someone, who is prepared to do it without academic funding, they are more likely to agree to that someone. It is a potential opportunity for you. I have been listening to you, and it sounds to me that this could be an ideal arrangement. The question for you, is whether you would like to take the opportunity or not."

"I would have to agree that with my company," I said, "and I would have to think about whether this is right for me. On the positive side, my company does have a policy about releasing people for relevant training. On the negative side, visiting eight people, presumably spread around the country, and writing up the results would take a fair bit of time."

"That is the decision you have to make," said the professor. "You have the opportunity to pick up expertise which could help you tremendously with your own job as well as increase your stature in business, at the cost of only about eight days work. If you are at all interested, let me have your business card now, and then let me know by the end of next week, whether you would like to be involved."

The distance from Watford to Euston only took a few minutes and the train was already slowing as the announcement came that we were approaching Euston station.

"OK," I said, "Here is my business card. I will let you know by the end of next week whether I am interested. Both of us are taking a lot on trust. I don't know you, or these professors, and you don't know whether I'm really capable of both giving them a business challenge, and writing up the results in a way that can be distributed."

"That's true," said the professor, "but even a business challenge to what they think will be useful. The risk, for them, is in giving up an hour or two of their time. Most of them will be able to do that without too much difficulty, if we organise things three months or so in advance. The professor who will probably have to make the greatest sacrifice, is actually the greatest fan of this idea, so it might work. Get back to me by the end of next week. Also send me, if you agree to do this, an outline of yourself sufficient for me to talk to the other professors about you."

The train came to a stop. I looked at the professor and said, "Thank you for the opportunity. I will be in touch with you by the end of next week."

Readers Note:

You are about to learn in the next chapter a bit more about the first professor. You will also meet Mary. Her background is also important and she plays an important part in the rest of the story. A challenge is to work out her connection to John Watson.

Chapter 3

Organisational Release

'The boss's foot.'

I am always wary about meeting strangers and agreeing something, especially when I do not know anything about those with whom I'm making an agreement.

Richard Holmes was convincing as a retired professor. The manner of his speech, and the alertness in his eyes, suggested that there was a significant intellect at his disposal. Of course, I am not the best judge of this, but sometimes first impressions make an impact.

My first action on getting home that evening was to switch the computer on, and search for the professor on the Internet. He did not appear on the first few search engine pages, but I did find reference to him later on. I was then able to trace him through a couple of university sites.

He was a Cambridge graduate, and had been at Cambridge for most of his career. His field was quantum mechanics, and he also seemed to have a couple of interests in forensic science. I could not pretend to understand any of the abstracts that I found about his work. However, what I had ascertained was that he existed and he was a well thought of academic.

My first reaction to his proposal was to turn it down. My knowledge of time management suggested that these professors would not have too much to offer me. They may be privy to some research, about how executives spend their time, but they would not necessarily know much of practical value.

I said as much to Mary, when we went out to The Plough, our local pub, that evening.

Mary, I should explain, lives in the same part of London as I do. We grew up in the same northern town. She is slightly older than me and always had different friends. She married one of those friends – a certain Tim Evans, or to give him his full name Thomas Ian Mark Evans. Put his Christian names together and you have TIM and that is how he was generally known. His work, coincidentally, brought him down to my area of London. Their marriage, unfortunately, did not last. He went back up North and Mary stayed down south. Mary refers to it as 'her best learning experience'. She kept his name, mainly as she was known by it in her work for one of the London Boroughs..

Her response to my story of meeting the professor was immediate. "Think how that would look on your CV," she said. "Eight professors of time management want to consult with you."

"I am not sure it would do me that much good," I said. "I would find it hard to justify to a new employer why they picked me. It would just come out as pure chance."

"Why don't you consider what you might tell that employer about what you learnt," said Mary, "That is likely to be even more impressive."

"We don't know that yet," I said, "Professor Holmes said their work needed a reality check. It may not be worth any practical value at all."

"On the other hand," said Mary, "it could be worth a great deal if no one knows about it. If you found that just one of those professors gave you a good tip which saved you ten minutes a day over the next couple of decades, would that not be worth it? It would certainly be a return greater than eight days effort. Besides, you have said in the past, that you have an arrangement at work, whereby you can go on any relevant course for up to five days in any two-year period. You were telling me the other day that you had not been away for any general training for at least three years. Surely your company would support you in doing this? If you offered to circulate some of the information afterwards, they may be very happy to release you. What have you got to lose?"

"That policy works on the assumption that my boss will release me," I muttered. "She has been a bit grumpy of late."

"Nothing ventured equals nothing gained," said Mary. "Why don't you email the professor on Monday to say that you will be discussing it with your company, and could he let you know the names and locations of the professors that you are likely to meet. You could then do a little research on the Internet, and make a more compelling case to your boss. It might also help you decide on whether you want to do it."

"Yeah, that's not a bad suggestion," I said. "I will do that. OK, I think this subject is now over, and we can talk about how my favourite sports team will do tomorrow. I hope there will be less penalties than last time."

Our conversation drifted away from anything to do with work. Further friends joined us to make for a merry Friday evening.

On Monday morning, I did just what Mary had recommended. I sent the e-mail to the professor. I also got hold of my organisation's policy about training release.

The principles in the policy were clear, although there were some constraints. It had to be training that was relevant to the job in a general sense, that would cost less than £750 and the time of release has to be approved by my boss as non-detrimental to company operations.

It was that last constraint where I expected problems. My boss was very mean with training. She regarded training as an expense, as opposed to an investment. She had an MBA, and did not seem to understand that her investment into that qualification had got her the job with us. She was also quick to make decisions, from which she would be unlikely to back down. If she was ever challenged, her two strategies were either to say, if it was clear that she was wrong, that she had not been given the full facts, or alternatively, to say that any disruption to the present was worth it in terms of strategy for the future.

Her first opinion would probably harden very quickly and would be guided by what I put on the form that HR required me to complete. The form itself was fairly simple. Some of it simply asked the standard questions about what, where and when and how much. The key variable element on the form was the objectives of the release. I had to put down at least one bullet point about what the course would do for me, and two further ones for what it would do for the company.

During the week, I came up with the following: --

My objective

1. To seek out, and make routine, two new time management techniques that will save me direct time of one week a year.

Company objectives

1. To increase departmental productivity, by implementing new techniques in order to speed up completion rates of projects by at least one day a customer.

2. To increase customer satisfaction rates of my team's delivery.

3. To be a source of expertise on time management techniques, so other managers could increase their productivity.

Given the number of customers we had, that should pay for my time away and give a payback of a few months. If I could spread any know-how I picked up to other areas in the business that would reduce the payback to weeks. The risk was whether I would be able to discover and learn any new techniques.

An e-mail arrived from Professor Holmes during the week, which gave details of who the professors were, and where they were located. It went on to suggest that the meetings be arranged for either one, of two weeks about three months ahead. So, for a number of the HR questions, I was simply able to say refer to correspondence. I also placed, with the papers, a short profile of Professor Holmes that I had got from the Internet.

All of this went back to HR with a copy to my boss.

Unexpectedly, within two days everything was confirmed. My boss actually knew of one of the professors whom she called a highly paid marketing guru. She couldn't understand why he would want to see me, but when HR suggested someone else go to see the professors instead, she put her foot down and stated it was important that someone from her department went. Success!

That evening, I told Mary that I had received the all clear. We were in a different pub with a couple of friends. The pub was called the Great Bear, which always seemed a strange name to me for an urban pub. Our friends, who had not visited there before made a wide range of jokes throughout the evening about the poor chance of seeing any real animal in this part of London. Plenty of animal personalities were attributed to all sorts of people though! On one of the few quieter moments, Mary turned to me and said, "Given your success today, there is a good chance of one thing happening."

"What's that?" I asked.

"You are likely to stay with your current company, until you've seen those professors"

I had to admit that I was now committed!

On the following day, I confirmed by e-mail to Professor Holmes that I would be able to dedicate a week to make the visits and I hoped that he would be able to make the appointments for me, as he knew the professors.

He replied, later in the day, saying leave it to him, assume it is on, and he will confirm the details two to three weeks beforehand. His assistant, Ms. Farthing, would make sure everything is properly confirmed.

Time marches on. I did receive a letter, and the details, from Professor Holmes exactly when he said he would send them. However, I was too busy to take everything in. Fortunately, one of my team members was a running out of work. I asked him to sort out train tickets and accommodation for all the visits, and just confirm to each professor in turn that I looked forward to seeing them on the appointed day and time. I particularly asked the staff member not to put me into any city centre hotels, just quieter places in the surrounding countryside.

This he duly did, and passed back a folder to me, nicely sectioned with all the arrangements laid out on a daily basis, with copies of train tickets and accommodation reservations. I thanked him for doing the work so neatly, but I was unable to do anything other than glance at what he had done.

True to form, just like going on holiday, my boss generated a number of requests about strategy, plans and operational performance in my last week. This was on top of a couple of deadlines that had to be met. It was also important that activity was planned for my staff for the following week, whilst I was away.

I left the office at 8 pm. on the final Friday exhausted. I rang Mary when I got home to say that I felt like a night in. "We will go to the Plough tomorrow," she suggested," They are putting on some entertainment, and apparently we can sit back and be entertained by a promising star from up north."

"Fine," I said. I made myself a quick meal, watched some TV and went to bed after the TV news.

The weather on Saturday brought an end to our promised Saturday evening entertainment, which had to be cancelled. Thunderstorms and floods meant we would not be watching the northern star. However, we went to the pub anyway.

Saturday had been a good day for forgetting about work. Mary and myself had gone to a sporting event that had been played, in spite of the rain. We were able to stay dry, as we were in the stand! The best news. Our team won, in spite of our kickers not being on form!

Mary raised the subject of my visits to the professors towards the end of the evening. "Where are you going on Monday?" she asked.

This is where I had to remember the basic details of what I was about to do. I struggled at first to remember. "I believe I am going down to the south coast for a mid-morning appointment, so it is an early start. Then I am meeting another professor somewhere near South Kensington later in the afternoon. The week has been structured such that I meet two professors a day. As they are scattered at different universities, I will be out on Tuesday night and Wednesday night. I am not sure about Thursday night, but I do know that on Friday, in the afternoon, I will be meeting

Professor Holmes in his rooms somewhere near the Euston Road."

"And what are your expectations?" asked Mary.

"I have not really thought the matter through," I said. "I suppose that means that I have no definite expectations, just a hope to be surprised. I am sort of thinking there will not be too much new to learn. I have no plan other than turning up, spending an hour with them, and then moving on. Professor Holmes did say they have views so I will no doubt ask them what they are."

"A previous boss said to me on one occasion, when I said I had no plan" said Mary, " that a failure to plan, was a plan to fail'. That is a quote that I have always remembered."

"But I have a plan," I said, "and I have all the documentation in a neat folder."

"What you have," said Mary, "is a process without much purpose. I suspect a number of organisations have those. How about doing some research tomorrow? You can also remind yourself what you said to your company about what you are doing. Any good company would ask you to report on what you did, and it is an opportunity to make a good impression."

"OK, OK." I retorted. "I will do that. It sounds to me like you should be one of the professors."

"I would be happy to be," she said. "You can have an appointment with me tomorrow, and it can last all day provided you give some time to your research, as well as helping me with the gardening. I will even cook you a Sunday lunch."

"Done!" I said.

Readers Note:

Did you notice the names of the pubs John visited and the fact that he could not see a promising star from the North? As John visits more pubs you will discover a connection between them. You also have half of the name of Professor Holmes's assistant and will discover the other half later. This has a future relevance to another set of mysterious connections.

In the next chapter, you will be visiting one of the professors. Can you work out the city where his university is located? Also note the context in which a Mezzo mug is discussed.

Chapter 4
Levers for Gaining Time
Distracted Acronyms

I was up early on Monday morning to get to Victoria Station to catch the train to the south coast.

My research on Sunday was fairly minimal, and it did give me one panic attack. The professors that I would be seeing were not all associated with business schools. Some of them were associated with a technical discipline. This was the case with my first visit.

Professor Roland Tinker was based at the School of Engineering, and he had an interest in systems engineering. My panic reaction was that Professor Holmes had got the whole thing wrong, or perhaps, I had. I was interested in the management of time, not the management of systems. Mary pointed out that there could be parallels between the two and I should simply go along with it. His expertise could be about work flow, or sorting out the inputs and outputs of the system. She said it would be a good idea for me to think about the inputs and outputs of my job anyway.

My appointment was at the University. Travelling by train did give me the opportunity to write down inputs and outputs. So I got a notebook out of my trusty airline travel bag, which I tend to take everywhere, and started preparing. It became obvious, pretty quickly, that I was simply writing down my budget on the input side and satisfied customers on the output side. This was not really new thinking, but it was probably a useful thing to have done.

I reached the south coast in good time. The sun was shining in this city of piers and pavilions. I hesitated on whether I should go and have a quick look at the sea and walk out onto the shingly beach, but I quickly decided against it. It was simply too risky. I lingered around the station for a few

The Time Advantage

minutes and then took a taxi to the University which was a little way out of town. I could have gone by train, but the taxi would deliver me to the door and the company would pay for the expense!

The university was arranged around a campus on a slight hill. Most of the buildings were built in the sixties. The School of Engineering was a fairly square building some four storeys high.

I arrived about ten minutes in advance of the meeting and found the administrative offices fairly quickly. The good news was that I was greeted by name, and was told that I was expected. The staff must have done a course on customer focus!

One of the staff directed me to some waiting chairs, and gave me an envelope, together with the message that Professor Tinker would be about quarter of an hour. He had asked that I read the contents of the envelope and complete the document inside.

I made myself comfortable and opened the envelope. It contained one single sheet of A4 on which was written the following simple instruction:-

Welcome John,

I am expecting to talk to you about time management. To get us started, I would like you to treat the word "Time" as an acronym. Can you come up with three possibilities about what that acronym could stand for, from your point of view.

I look forward to discussing your thoughts.

Roland Tinker

My first reaction was that this was a test. I read the note a second time. The professor mentioned possibilities, and those possibilities could be from my point of view. This would suggest that there are no wrong answers. I am usually pretty good at defending my opinion, so that made me more positive about what I had to do.

So what could the acronym T I M E stand for. Time for some analytical thinking!

The 'T' probably stands for 'time'. 'I' must then stand for 'improvements' or 'increases' or some such word. So I could start with "Time improvements". The 'M' could stand for 'make' and the 'E' for efficiencies. Easy.

I have my first acronym. TIME stands for 'Time Improvements Make Efficiencies'.

It was pretty easy to get to the second meaning. I could have 'Time improvements mean Effectiveness'.

Now I am beginning to get stuck. I have a sneaking suspicion I could use the word 'energy' at the end, but I'm not too sure how.

I looked out the window and my thoughts centred on the building. For some reason, I thought about engineering and, out of the blue, came the statement 'this is mechanical engineering', but that is probably an indication that I am getting truly stuck. And then I cracked it. ME could stand for 'Management Engineering'. So I could have 'This Is Management Engineering', or even, 'Time involves management engineering', or even, 'Time inspires Management Engineering'. I like that! You can have business engineering, or re-engineering, so why not management engineering?

My thoughts were suddenly broken by a voice. "John Watson?"

I looked up, and saw a thinnish man, over six foot tall, wearing an open necked white shirt, with a light brown sports jacket. He had short mousey coloured hair and a moustache.

"John, my name is Roland Tinker. Come with me, and we can discuss what you have been doing."

We went down the corridor, up three flight of steps, along another corridor into a room marked Tutorial Room 1. He offered me a seat, and a mug of coffee using the standing vacuum flask in the room. He took a mug from a large collection by the vacuum flask, filled it with coffee and passed to me with sachets of sugar and a small milk carton. It was a solid mug in white, with what looked like a black abstract picture. I noticed the name written vertically on the mug – MEZZO. Most of the other mugs were from suppliers, and some of the names I recognized, but not this one.

The professor noticed my curiosity. "That is a rare mug," he said. "It is from a small supplier and you won't get many mugs like that. It is very green in application, even though it is white in colour. Look closely at the mug."

I did and then I realised what he meant. "Every traveller should take one of those," I said, and then with a smile, I went on. "I am afraid that I have not done that today."

"Commuters, as well as travellers, should think about these things. They do take more time though," he said, with a smile. "If you can fold them quickly, it makes a big difference." He took off his jacket and put it over a spare chair, whilst I sat down still looking at the mug. He continued, "We are here to talk about time management. How did you get on with the acronym?"

I passed over the piece of paper on which I had scribbled my suggestions.

"That is interesting," he said, looking at them. "Did anything happen between the second and the third possibility?"

I told him that I had looked out of the window for inspiration.

"You clearly found it," he said. "What you have done reflects life in general, and also time management in particular. Let me explain. It is often the case that we think along a particular track and we get into the habit of being on the track. It is only when there is a different input to our thinking, that we re-evaluate the track we are on. When you think of the way you manage your time, you probably exercise some distinct habits, and you continue with those habits providing everyone is happy with your work. If you come under pressure, then you may deal with the pressure by working in the existing ways for longer at a higher tempo, until your ways of managing time breakdown, or, worse still, you breakdown! It would seem to me that you were thinking along a narrow track with your first two acronyms, and then you picked up inspiration from something external, which led you to a completely different way of thinking. You can apply this principle to the way you manage time. If you are determined in your search for new ways to manage time, you are likely to find techniques that make you evaluate what you currently do. That will eventually lead you to manage time better. Actively search for inspiration is the first lesson." He smiled.

"That reminds me," I said, "of a management saying that I heard somewhere – ' Strive to be better'."

"That's good," said the professor. "In this case, it is better to say 'strive to manage better'. To simply say 'strive to be better' could be a case for working harder rather than working smarter. It is the process of how you manage that is important to review. This is the first of two major points to consider." He looked at me.

"And the second major point?" I asked.

"Implementation of any change," he said. "That does not come easy. You have to break old habits to start new ones. I would like to discuss a couple of new habits with you a bit later on, but first tell me about your situation to help me understand how I might help you."

Over the next fifteen minutes, I told the professor about the company, my position, my team and my customers. He asked a number of questions about the complexity of the work we do and how we process some of the work. He went on to ask me what changes to working practice I had introduced over the last few years. The answer was not many. The professor then focused on the turnover of my staff, their competence, as well as recent training that we had all undertaken.

"What you have described is a 'steady state' situation," said the professor. "I may be assuming too much, but there is little evidence of changed practices, and there is little in the way of introducing new thinking, either through staff turnover, or through training."

"I do network, and keep my eyes open," I said in a voice with a hint of protest.

"That's important," said the professor, "but even as a result of that, you have made very little change. Be aware that your department has properly settled into some distinct time habits. They may not be so easy to change. If you do consider a change, you will need to change your own approach first. It will require some stronger leadership than you may have been used to."

The professor then asked me a couple of crunch questions: –

1. How efficient at work am I at the moment?

2. How effective at work am I personally at the moment?

I struggled a bit with the first question, but was able to give some figures relating to throughput, and costs versus budget. I had to admit that I had no good answer for the second question. I heard myself lamely saying that as things got done, and we did not have too many problems in the team, I must be reasonably effective.

"Interesting," he said. "You may want to think about whether you have all the measures you need for efficiency. It seems to me that you have some processes which you just do rather than questioning whether you could do them better. I think one of your steps when you get back to your office is to write down all the processes you use and then determine whether they are time critical processes, in all senses of that expression. On the question of effectiveness, it is true that an absence of problems is a sign of recent effectiveness. However, you can probably get some feedback, from your customers, your boss and your peers about what they think of your team's outputs. That will give you a strong indication. You will also personally know whether you are coping or not. You will be seeing some my ex-colleagues later on this week, and they can discuss that with you. For now, I would like to discuss with you two general issues that tend to make departments more efficient and effective. What do you believe could make your department better at both of those things?"

"Work planning, perhaps more flexibility in the team, perhaps a review of processes," I suggested.

"A couple of other things might help you," he suggested. "Both begin with T."

"Technology," I guessed.

"That is certainly one of them," he said. "If we use technology well, it can help us formulate and distribute information much more efficiently as well as helping us come to wiser decisions. One of the interesting things I have noticed is that most people only exploit part of the technology that is available to them. It goes back to this question of habits. If you can produce work that satisfies a situation, you will not necessarily spend the time to learn more to help you become better, or faster, at it. There is a tendency towards just being confident enough with the tools at your disposal. There is an old management principle – the Peter Principle that suggests everyone rises to their level of incompetence. In other words they are confident below this level, but incompetent above it. This tends to happen with the more sophisticated technological tools. People rise to a level where they can get particular work done satisfactorily and they just stick at that level. This means there is usually some potential for extra productivity to be gained with extra learning, or a refresher on previous learning.

"Are we talking about business systems here or more general competence? I asked.

"More general competence," replied the professor, "although IT does give us splendid examples. These days, it is assumed that most people know how to use the standard office software packages, which are quite sophisticated. That can be a poor assumption. People might have taught themselves, or been taught when they first learnt how to use the software. However, unless they have actively used most parts of the software package, they will have forgotten how to use the least used parts, and they will not have explored extra productivity gains in the updates. This means that their work is done usually using older ways. Good examples of forgotten items are macros, editing other people's documents and outline documents. Does what I say make sense?"

"Yes," I said. "I have to admit that I'm not very good with macros, or form design, on the PC."

"One of the things you could do," said the professor, "is to list some of the functions on your office software that you do not use regularly and then relearn how they work. Alternatively, go through each function on each of the toolbars. If I was to ask you how many toolbars you have on your word processor package, and what they were, how would you get on?"

"Not well," I said.

"Is this something worth knowing?" asked the professor.

"Maybe," I said, "it depends on what they are."

"But you won't know they are useful, unless you learn what they are. Could this be an action point for you?"

"Definitely," I conceded. I suspected that, with all the upgrades to word processing software over recent years, I was not fully up to date. I could use the basics, but had not thought of discovering whether there were any other opportunities.

"It sounds to me like this is definitely something you should work upon," said the professor. "You may have to go in half an hour earlier in the morning, or stay a fraction later at night, to give yourself the peace and quiet to do so, but it could provide a new and interesting reminder of what you do know, and what you don't know. If you were to do this before reviewing any processes with your team, it might open up possibilities of using technology to help you with some standard processes. If you have an IT department, you should get them involved in giving you any necessary training. Don't let them excuse themselves on the basis that they just provide hardware, or that you must define what you want to do first before they can provide training. It is important that you know the potential of what technology you have. This will allow you to consider doing things differently. If you do not know of a particular application, it is difficult to specify that you want training on it. You need to know the potential of what you have first to determine whether that technology can help you."

"That's a good point," I said. "Our IT people just set up the hardware and disappear until we have a problem"

"Once you know the potential," continued the professor, "you can get your team together and discuss with them the standard activities that go on in your department. By knowing the standard activities, and knowing of the potential of the technology, you can more easily bring the two together."

"My staff might feel that I'm attempting to get rid of them if I push the technology button too hard," I said jokingly.

"I thought you had too much to do, from everything you said earlier," chuckled the professor. "You can give them something you do, if they run out of things that they have to do."

That remark caught me out. It is not often that I'm short of a quick reply. The professor must have noticed, as he continued.

"Seriously," he said, "you should consider what you do. Have you ever written down a list of all the tasks you all regularly do in your department?"

"I have started to write down some of the processes, and we have a couple operating under a quality regime" I said.

"Good," said the professor. "When you have completed the exercise, rearrange your list in order from the most complex to the most simple. If you do that, you can then approach that list with a couple of important analytical questions, such as 'How can I simplify the more complex items?' and 'How can I standardise the simpler items?'"

"Are not the complex items complex because they cannot be simplified?" I asked.

"When I discuss this with people," said the professor, "I regularly discover complexity is often surrounded by things that can be simplified. As an obvious example, if staff want to ask you about something complex, some of them are likely to ask simple questions about it. You can standardise the answers to those questions in a bank of frequently asked questions. Do you use this approach at all?"

I must have looked blank. It is true that we get asked an awful lot of simple questions by people outside the Department. If they could refer to a FAQ bank of questions this may save time.

"No, I have not yet," I replied, "although I think I am just about to, given your question."

"Let me now take you to the second 'T'," said the professor. "The second 'T' stands for training. How do people become more effective? One of the ways to do it is to become more competent. To increase competence you need training. Training works if it helps instil useful habits that you can use in an appropriate setting. For most people, reading books does not instil a habit. You actually have to do something for two or three occasions for a habit to be formed. Generally speaking, if you want to improve your personal effectiveness, then you should seek out training in the areas that would be most useful to you and then turn that training into personal habits."

"Training is not a subject that features strongly in our company," I said. "Budgets are normally tight, and training is the first thing to be dropped as soon as we hit a difficulty. That is the reality I believe in many organisations."

"That is the real world speaking," said the professor. "Yet there are groups of people who gather together at institutional meetings, or special interest groups where training can be practised. If you're really stuck, ask around. There is an expression that I have come across which says 'seek and you shall find: if you do not find, you have a business opportunity!'"

I just got the feeling he was about to go off subject. The professor paused and then continued, "The business opportunity would be to suggest a network meeting on the subject."

He looked at me to make sure I was still with him and then continued. "The power of training is often overlooked. There are different sorts of training, of course. If training can be directly linked to productivity, then you should bang the drum for it. You have processes you work through in your department. Training related to those should be a no-brainer. Training arrangements will be very important with any new staff you take on."

"You are preaching to the converted, professor," I said.

"So what have you done about it?" asked the professor.

"Apart from improving induction some while ago, I have done very little." I admitted.

"This could mean that your staff, as well as yourself, are probably working within the habits they have formed. It sounds to me like you need some innovation training to improve on those habits."

"That won't happen," I said. "The company does not pay for that sort of training either."

"It is plainly up to you," said the professor. "Part of your role is to improve what you do. Listen to Professor Richmond when you meet him later this week. Some of his techniques can show you how to break up existing habits and get the team suggesting their own ways of breaking them. Talking of habits, let me ask you whether you do much typing, personally?"

"I do type," I said "but it is mostly with two fingers whilst watching the keyboard."

"I believe that gives you a choice," said the professor. "You could invest some time in learning how to touch type, which means acquiring new habits. If you could type twice as fast, how much time would that save you?"

"I am not too sure," I said. "Possibly quarter of an hour a day, maybe more."

"Yet, as you have always been able to produce work without difficulty, you have not invested your time in saving any of that time. You have fallen into the habit of simply extending your hours to accommodate this inefficiency. The next time you sit at a keyboard, you should ask yourself whether you are happy with being inefficient. That question, repeated every time you sit down to do some typing, could well jolt you into doing something about it. One thing you could do when you leave here is to properly work out how much time this might save you, and your department. However, if I was to tell you that there is an easier way to at least triple your speed of typing, would you be interested?"

"As long as it did not cost me too much money," I said, "and it would have to be practical."

"Well, it would need an investment in a piece of software that will cost you between a £100 to £200 per person, may be less, if you shop around. The time to learn how to use the software is likely to be significantly less than the time you learn to become a proficient typist. What's more, you will end up producing typed copy much faster. Would an investment like that be reasonable to consider?"

"You are leading me towards something," I said. "What is the catch?"

"A little bit of courage, some persistence, a little problem solving, and the breaking of some habitual routines you may have. If you have not already guessed, I am talking about voice dictation directly to a computer. The technology is now ready for exploitation."

"Voice dictation always sounds too good to be true," I said. "I am conscious of two problems. The first is that I will have too many misinterpreted words. The second is that the office is not a particularly good place to do voice dictation. I work in a semi-open plan office environment."

"But this is where some of the persistence comes in," said the professor. "You can train the computer to recognize your voice, very quickly. About half an hour will get you started once you are set up and your accuracy will automatically improve to a level where it does not concern you. As regards your office, if you have a laptop, you have mobility. If you do not have a laptop, I would suggest that you persuade your organisation to get you one on the basis that you will be able to do more work on the move, or even study at home. You may be able to make a case on the basis of trying out voice recognition software as a productivity aid."

"I have a laptop," I said.

"Then you can take it with you to meeting rooms to do any special notes, minutes or long pieces of text. If you can hook up to your local server, you may be able to do your e-mails in a meeting room. Nothing is impossible in business, you just need to do some problem-solving, take courage and be persistent. Do you, or any of your staff, have to type many figures into a computer?"

"Yes," I said.

"Much easier to dictate them in, and check them," he said. "Be determined to do better and you will find the opportunities!"

"OK," I said, "but what happens if the software goes wrong. Software is full of bugs, and it can be very frustrating if you are trying to get something done, and you cannot do it."

"Not really a problem," he said. "You dictate into your normal word processing software. You save what you dictate to your hard disk, or s on a regular basis. If the software goes wrong, you simply resort to you. way of working. It does not happen much these days, as technology and experience of many users have improved dictation systems. The risk is very low. Do you think there is anything that would stop you from getting started on this next week?"

"I would like to investigate it," I said. "Where would I find this dictation software?"

"Most specialist computer shops would have it, so your first step is to go to a computer shop or Office equipment store" said the professor. "As time is getting on, let's go back to the acronyms. I would like to offer you two – 'Technology Improves Management Efficiency', and 'Training Improves Management Effectiveness.' You may like to quote these at your boss, from time to time, and see whether you can swing her around to support any initiatives you suggest. I would also like to suggest that you find a different third acronym. An acronym that can act as a lever to gaining you and your department time. Your own suggestion is very inventive, although a little conceptual – management engineering is an interesting concept!

"Are you not going to help me with that?" I asked.

"No. That is down to you. The more you work at it, the better the expression you will find and the more you will value it. That really brings us to the end of this session. I hope, John, that you have felt a little challenged today. I know that I cannot solve all the issues you may have, but I would say to you that if you give up attempting to improve, you'll end up being less efficient, and less productive than you could be. The world does need highly productive people to show the way. And talking of showing the way, I have a tutorial to give, so I will have to show you the way back down to reception and wish you well. If you are going straight back to London, I would suggest that you review what we talked about, and make an action list and allocate some time in your diary to take the first two steps of any action. It usually needs more than one to start breaking a habit! I also look forward to any report that you might make of the meetings you have with my fellow professors."

I picked up my bag as the professor put his jacket back on. We both then headed back to reception. I did say to the professor, as we made our way back to reception, that given his area of expertise, I suspected we might have been talking about systems theory.

"We could have done that," he said. "You will find there are textbooks on the subject, and some of them are more about systems than the reality of what you can do personally to manage time. My aim today has been to suggest that you consider breaking up a system – a system that involves good and bad time habits. You need to keep the good and break out of the bad, so you end up with a continuously reviewed collection of very productive habits. By the way, I do like playing around with new things in systems engineering, which means that I'm always breaking habits. This is why I am so interested in the subject. Why don't you let me know how you get on with reviewing your teams time management habits?"

I agreed. His last statement was quite clever. He was forcing me to consider what I would be doing, so I could write something back to him. Writing to people to thank them for their time, and acknowledging what they might have done for me, is something I do well. It seems to work well in business for fostering relationships, and well fostered relationships usually foster more business. I'm always surprised that more people don't do this. Perhaps they have not had the time!

I thanked the professor very much. He had made me think, and that was making me feel a bit uncomfortable about what I currently did, but maybe that was a good thing.

We made our way back down to reception, where he left me to organise a taxi.

On my journey back to London I considered a question that Mary had left with me. She wondered whether she might be able to learn indirectly from what the professors say to me. She had simply asked me to review what I have learnt, straight after each meeting, so I could pass that on to her.

So what have I learnt? In summary, I have some small picture stuff and some big picture stuff. The big picture was about the role of training, and technology, and the fact that we manage time through a series of habits. The small picture was about improving my office software skills, and at least finding out what I didn't know about what it could do. I also have some productivity benefits to consider in relation to voice dictation.

By the time I got to London, I still had not worked out a satisfactory third acronym for TIME. I did find, just as it happened whilst I was waiting for the professor, that I got into a groove of thinking and it was not long before I became stuck. I then had to get an inspiration from somewhere else to get me into a better groove. This simple activity seems to have such a powerful message. Simply put, it means you get stuck into a groove unless you actively seek out other possibilities. This could be true of many things. I thought I would ask other people for their inspirational ideas for the acronym. The professor was keen that I should actively seek improvements!

I resolved, however, that I would spend half an hour outside my normal work time to review the potential of my word processor and spreadsheet programs and I would also investigate voice dictation software.

I felt I ought to capture my personal resolutions and other actions on an action list and add to it any actions that might come from meeting with any of the other professors.

So with Professor Tinker, my personal action list was:-

	Action List	Timscale
1	List the processes I use from the most simple to the most complex.	1-4 weeks
2	Seek to standardise the simplest.	1-2 months
3	Seek to simplify the most complex.	1-2 months
4	Consider publishing FAQ to provide answers and reduce confusion.	1-3 months
5	Review my personal understanding of office technology.	Immediate
6	Review technology usage with my team	1-4 weeks
7	Identify my time habits and organisational time habits	Continuous

8	Review and improve the training under my control.	1-3 Months
9	Seek new ways of doing what I do through networks	Continuous
10	Suggest managers get together to discuss training / technology	Opportunistic
11	Investigate Voice Dictation	1-4 weeks
12	Find the third acronym	Immediate

Whilst reviewing the list, I also started thinking about what my time management habits were. I also thought about some of the time habits we have in the company, particularly in regard to meetings.

Each manager conducts his, or her, meetings in their own style. There is no common approach, nor protocols about how meetings are conducted. It occurred to me that there are organisational habits in managing time, as well as personal habits. This may be a subject to discuss with one of the other professors.

In some ways, I was thinking, as I got arrived back in London, Professor Tinker's philosophy is stronger than any techniques he gave me. Sure, it is useful to list the work I do from the most complex to the simplest, to create FAQ lists, and learn how to use technology properly. The philosophy is much more about being determined to seek out highly productive habits and discard old ones!

Readers Note:

A major challenge is to find a useful third acronym that is a lever for gaining time. John will return to this task in future chapters. Can you beat him to discovering the lever?

You will have now come across a strange mug. A Mezzo mug. It represents an activity. You may have worked out what it is about. If not, you can cheat by looking it up on the internet or build up clues when you meet the other professors. There is an activity here that links the professors. There is a further clue in the next chapter.

In the next chapter, and it only happens on this occasion, you will immediately know the location of the professor, but not the institution he represents. Can you identify the most likely prospect?

The professor's advice in the next chapter can be life changing - be warned!

Chapter 5
Branding Conversations
'Perceptual Magic.'

On arriving back in London Victoria station, I walked to the London Underground. My destination was South Kensington. It was near here that I was to meet Dick Taylor. He is the marketing guru that my boss had identified from the list of professors. He was not going to meet me at the University, but at his consulting rooms near South Kensington.

South Kensington is an interesting place. You can visit the Natural History Museum, the Science Museum, and the Victoria and Albert Museum, by taking a long pedestrian tunnel from the tube station. Beyond the museums is the Albert Hall and Hyde Park. Sandwiched between the museums and the Albert Hall, there is a world-famous university, and many specialist institutions and colleges. This area to the north of South Kensington is the home of some of the top specialists and scientists in the UK.

Dick Taylor was associated with one of these institutions. He had originally attended Cambridge University, but most of his career had been based in London. He did not start off in marketing, but had formed an interest at an early stage. His specialist subject was product and organisational branding. He had an innate ability to formulate practical commercial ideas that were almost always successful. He was well respected. I had come across an article in my research that suggested his fees could be several thousand pounds a day.

It was a surprise to me that he would make time to see me. He must be giving up a thousand or more to do so. It was also a surprise to me that he was happy to discuss how I managed my time, and share his views on time management, in general.

I was pleased to get out of South Kensington underground station. Don't get me wrong. It is a light and airy station, and is not really under the ground at all. There are even green plants growing on the platform. There are solid wooden benches to sit on, just as you might find in a garden. It is a much nicer station than Gloucester Road, the next station around the circle line, which has rather a haunting feel to it.

The problem with South Kensington is the noise of all the school parties gathering themselves together for roll calls before they set off to the museums.

Leaving the station, and the very busy interchange beside it, I quickly found the professor's offices. The front door was set back from the pavement and you had to walk up a couple of steps. I noticed immediately that the door was completely dark glass with a large engraving of the word "Welcome" etched on it.

I stepped up to the door and announced my arrival through the intercom. A female voice answered and confirmed I was expected. There was a buzz on the door and I walked through closing the door behind me.

"This way, Mr Watson." A lively woman's voice came from a room directly to the left of the hall. As I walked into the room, I was greeted by a well-dressed lady in her thirties.

"I am pleased you are expecting me," I said.

"Professor Taylor is looking forward to meeting you, Mr Watson. My name is Denise. My job is to show you the waiting room and ask you whether you would like a cup of coffee, or tea."

"A cup of tea would be marvellous," I said.

"I will be back in a moment with your tea," said Denise, "Professor Taylor suggested you might like to look at some of the press coverage he has enjoyed with previous visitors. It would give you an idea about how he works . Would you like to take a seat in this room over here? The press coverage is in the display folder on the table."

I followed Denise to the waiting area and sat down. The waiting area was a small room connected to the one where I had met Denise. Denise then went off to make the tea, and I just glanced around my surroundings. There were a number of pictures on the wall just above the back of the seats on the opposite side of the room. These pictures were all about award ceremonies, or conferences. The common feature was a bald, but long bearded man, with large alert eyes. He was smiling on virtually every picture. On some, he was shaking hands with people as if to award them a prize; on others, he was clearly at a rostrum talking to an audience. In the background of the pictures was either the name of a well-known institution, or a well-known company.

I opened the press folder with a sense of curiosity. The first article was about a lady who had been to see the professor for a coaching session. I had just finished the first paragraph of introduction, when Denise came back with the tea. "You will enjoy meeting Professor Taylor," she said, "He is a charming man."

I helped myself to the tea and continued reading the article. The lady concerned had just been promoted to be a director of a large company. She was reflecting on the one thing that had helped her before her promotion – and that was the visit to Professor Taylor!

She described him as a charming man, who put her totally at ease to begin with and then took her through some challenging moments through the rest of the following hour. 'It was a bit of an emotional roller coaster for me,' she explained, 'as he asked some really good questions. At the end of the session, I felt quite exhausted, and it was only after I had left his office, that I realised the power of his questions and the usefulness of a simple tool that he'd given me to try out.' She went on to say that it was not at the meeting, where she felt she got the most benefit. It was in the days that followed the meeting, as she thought about what he had said and as she started to make changes. She felt every executive should meet the professor.

I somehow suspected that the professor might be inviting me to read this to prepare me for something similar. However, I was here on the subject of time management rather than general executive coaching.

"Are you ready?" said Denise. I had only finished half my tea but signalled with a thumbs up.

Denise took me from the waiting room, back into the hall and towards a flight of stairs. We went up the stairs to a turning point, halfway up. Here was a wooden door to the right bearing, in an old English font, the name – Professor Richard Taylor.

Denise went straight into the room. It was on two levels, with a couple of steps in the middle of the room separating the levels. On the lower level where we were, there were two solid three-seater leather sofas facing each other. On the higher level, in one of the corners, was a desk facing outwards. In the other corner of the higher level was a door. There were windows on one side of the room, and pictures along the other side. Denise asked me to take a seat on the window side and said the professor would be along very shortly.

I made myself comfortable on the sofa and looked across to the pictures. They were rather interesting. There were pictures of optical illusions, including the very famous one of the young lady and the old woman. Look at the picture with one mindset, and you will see the old woman. Change your mindset, and look for the young lady and you will see her. Some of the other pictures were of Escher's drawings. Further up the wall, towards the desk, I could see there were some hologram pictures, but I was too far away to be able to work out the objects portrayed.

As I was staring at the pictures, Professor Taylor made an entrance from the far corner of the room. What an entrance! He moved across the floor very quickly, with a broad smile across his face and the following words of welcome "John, I am really pleased to meet you. Richard Holmes has told me what you might be able to do for us, and that could be quite exciting."

By this time he was down the steps in the middle of the room, with his hand outstretched. I started to get to my feet. "No don't get up," he said, coming over to shake my hand, whilst I was sitting down. "Just keep comfortable," he said. After a firm handshake, when I found myself looking up into his smiling face, he half turned and made himself comfortable on the other sofa.

"Did you find us alright?" he asked.

"It was very easy," I said. "I am pleased to say that I know my way around London, and particularly this neck of the woods, so you are not difficult to find. You are only a short walk from the tube station. I would not like to have to park round here though."

"Cars will always be an issue round here," he said. "I am lucky. I come up the Brompton Road every morning, when I can, on a bike of the same name. It is a pleasure to get some exercise before starting. However, we must get down to some work, as we have limited time this afternoon. Now you have come to talk to me about managing time better and you may be pulling together some of my ideas, and those of my colleagues. I think it best that we concentrate on your needs as much as we can to make sure I offer you something relevant to your situation. So let's get started. Here is a question. How important is time management to you?"

"Very important," I said.

"And what do you mean by it being very important," he asked.

"If I could manage my time better, and learn some new techniques, then I could get more done, and that could mean better results."

"Very logical," said the professor. "Have you ever quantified that?"

"Not in so many words, or figures," I replied. "It just seems so logical. If we could do all our work in half the time, then we must be better off."

"Provided you productively use the time you have gained," said the professor with a smile. "One starting point in considering time management is to consider what the extra time would do for you." He paused. "And, of course, what that would do for your organisation. It is interesting to note that some people would seek better time management for an easier life. Others would fill up all the extra time with other activity. You will need to decide what better time management will do for you personally. Does your boss complain about your time management?"

"No," I replied. "She is just interested in better results."

"Naturally," said the professor. "What will producing better results do for you – a minor salary improvement, maybe?"

"I think from my point of view," I said slowly, "better results could help provide a better foundation for my career."

"Right," said the professor. "That is an important statement and I will bear it in mind as we go through. It means that you have to work on several levels. For the first level, I would like to look at another question. How do you know you are *not* managing time well at the moment?"

That was a show stopper. If the question, was 'How did I know that I am managing time well', then I would have pointed to my results. To ask me how I knew that I was not managing time well was something that I had not considered.

"I can see from the look on your face that you are struggling with this question. Let's explore it. I want you to turn the clock back two weeks and tell me, in some detail, what you have been doing, and tell me what worked, and what didn't work."

Over the next fifteen minutes, I talked through some of the activities that I had been up to. The professor took a notebook out of his pocket and made occasional notes. He asked me several questions, as we were talking.

Towards the end of that period, I noticed the professor glance towards a clock, positioned between the windows.

"Let me stop you there," he said. "I am beginning to notice that there are a number of time wasting activities that are taking place in your work. Some of them are very simple. Let me give you a summary of some of those I picked up."

He turned his notebook around and gave it to me. On the page, was a series of points: –

- You can't find things when you want to.
- Mobile phones are going off in your meetings.
- Meetings tend to start late as not everyone arrives on time.
- Some people do not read the papers before they come.
- One of your staff is taking too long to process material.
- You have problems with suppliers getting you what you want, when you want it.

- Some of your staff do not tell other staff what is going on, thereby wasting time.
- Another member of staff takes time to get going in the morning.
- When your boss ticks you off, it takes you sometime to get back down to work.
- Decision makers in other departments are not readily available.
- Incoming telephone messages get lost if they are put on people's desks.
- You have little time to concentrate on writing up notes, and this has to be done in your own time.
- You seem to have an increasing workload.
- If you don't use some of the technology regularly you forget how to use it.

"I am sure if we went on," he commented, "we would find lots of other things. I suspect this is the tip of an iceberg. There are some common themes, e.g. about meetings and responses, but there are lots of other things which seem to be holding either you, or your team up, and wasting time in doing so. We have spent just under the the first half of this meeting talking about this, and these points were easy to extract. They all came from you, so therefore you must know them as problems. Another question. If you know you have these problems, why are you not doing anything about them?"

"OK," I said, sitting up a bit straighter, and perhaps more defensively, "I accept that some of them are in my control, but a lot are not."

The professor looked me in the eye. "Because you do not think they are in your control, you do nothing about them. Have you raised the subject of meetings with the Chair of the meetings? For each of your problems, there is a solution, or a way to approach the solution. I am going to set you a task. Over the next month, I want you to list down on the left-hand side of a piece of paper, or several pieces of paper, all the events that are similar to the above and that waste your time. Categorise them and redo the list. Then, on the right hand side of the paper, note down actions to start resolving the problems. I will give you a technique at the end of our time together that might set the scene for a quicker resolution. Have I your commitment to make the list?"

"OK, I will do that," I said. This seemed to be a better approach to one advocated on the time management course I had attended. On that course, they advocated writing down everything I did, noting when I did it and for how long. Here, I only had to note the problems.

"Let's think about things at a different level, and about your career for a moment," said the professor, "At present, it seems that you consider yourself stretched. There is danger, as you take on more work, you will become overstretched, and therefore less effective, and less organised. What is your boss going to think about you, if that is what she notices?"

"Well, she will know that I am overstretched, as I would have told her," I responded.

"Telling her is useful," said the professor, "but do you want her to see you falling behind."

"No. I guess I will have to quantify what I do, so she can determine what to do about it."

"That is also useful," continued the professor. "However, it is worth doing that from a position of strength. Before I go further with this, how does your staff feel about the amount of work your team has to do?"

"They feel driven by it," I ventured.

"OK. Let's start to break this pattern. How would a good time manager come across to his boss, and his colleagues?"

"They would come across as organised and knowing what they were doing," I said.

"So, if that is to be you, what would you have to do, to have them believe that you are organised and knowing what you were doing?"

"Uh, I would be ready for every meeting, and fully prepared. I would be up to speed with recent events and have some views about our current position, our capability, and the ways we can move forward."

"And what would they notice on your desk?"

"They would see only the things that I am working on."

"And they could also see," said the professor, "in the vicinity of your desk, and perhaps on a wall, a quote about time management somewhere, a wall chart used for planning, and perhaps just a few things in your in tray. If you have a notice board, you could arrange it tidily, with a few graphs indicating progress, and perhaps some checklists. You could visually arrange your workspace to give the impression that you were organised, whether or not you are totally in control. Is there anything to stop you doing any of this?"

"Not really," I said.

"And what would your staff and your boss hear you regularly talk about?" he asked.

"I am not sure I understand the question," I responded.

"How would your boss and your team know that you are interested in good time management?"

"Ah. I get it now. If I talked about the importance of time, they would understand that using time wisely is important to me, and they might adjust their behaviour, so that I know it is important to them as well."

"I think you are latching on now," said the professor. "If you do not speak about the importance of saving time, or doing things to save time, or even valuing time, then it is just going to be one of a number of things that are in the background noise. My guess is that you would not be able to give me an accurate figure for the cost of an hour of your time, or of a standard meeting that is held at your workplace. Would that be right?" I nodded. "Do not go overboard with these figures, but have such information up your sleeve for when it is appropriate to use it. Are you aware of the concept of opportunity cost?"

"You mean that whilst I am doing one thing," I replied, "I cannot do something else and there may be a cost to not doing that something else."

"That's right," said the professor. "You cannot relive the same time. Time is irreplaceable. The real cost of wasting time, is not just the cost of the wasted time, but the opportunity cost as well. This is another argument to save up your sleeve. Don't overplay these arguments, keep them up your sleeve until you really need them. And don't, whatever you do, use the tactic of frequently looking at your watch in a meeting. You may think you are sending a message that the meeting is wasting time. However, your message could be interpreted that you do not value the other people at the meeting. If the meeting is wasting time, go and talk to the Chairperson afterwards. They may even be grateful for some feedback."

The professor looked at me in silence for a few seconds. He looked into my eyes, stroked his beard and continued. "Now, let's go back to the idea of being seen to be organised. If you were seen as organised, and you went to your boss to ask for more resources, are they more likely to believe you need them if you are perceived as organised rather than if you were perceived as disorganised, or unable to cope?"

"I get the point, I replied. "At least, I think I do. You are suggesting that I take on the persona of someone who is organised. In doing so, I will naturally become seen as someone who is organised. I can then talk to my team and other people with more credibility about time and organisation. I sense you are also suggesting that by acting, as if I am organised, being organised becomes a self fulfilling prophecy."

"Pretty good," said the professor. "You are learning two important points. The first is that perceptions are important. The second is that, by altering the way you act, you give yourself some scope to influence others. What you then have is a basis for boosting your career. I would suggest that next Monday, as one of the first things you do, you have a look at your desk and ask yourself what messages it radiates about your abilities to manage time and be organised. You might also find it of value this week to find some quotes about Time. Not only would you then be able to quote them appropriately to show how you value time, but you may also find a quote you like that you can put up on a wall near your desk. Such an action will tell people that using time productively is important."

The professor paused and stroked his bearded chin again, as if in thought. "Lastly, let me mention to you the five adjective technique. It is very simple. If your boss, or your team had to describe you using five adjectives, which five adjectives would you like them to use? You may like to find out what they think later, but you should first establish those that you think are right for enhancing your career. You can work out how you can get those messages across from the way you organise your desk, from the way you conduct meetings, and the way you talk to people in your workplace. Then you can use these adjectives as a basis of comparing what people actually do think. That could lead to you changing what you do until people begin to think what you want them to think. This same technique, incidentally, can be used for your team as well. What five adjectives should other teams in your workplace use about your team? And I could go on to say that this works at an organisational level. You meet with customers, what five adjectives would you like them to notice? I have to say that there should be some consistency and compatibility between the organisation, your team and you, but that is another subject!"

"Gosh!" I exclaimed. "I have never thought about this at all. I can fully understand what you're saying and would like to give more thought to it. I have not told you what my desk actually looks like, but although I'm not clear on the five adjectives yet, my desk will look a little different by Monday evening next week."

"Your staff will notice that too," said the professor," ...and they will know that you have been influenced by your activities this week. That will help their understanding. There are better times to make changes than other times. It is always helpful to have an understandable event that causes the change. Other examples of an understandable event include announcing to your staff that you are reading a good book that is causing you to reassess some aspects of what you do. The reason for the change in approach becomes the book. It is an easy reason for your staff to understand. To introduce things, without reason, can create suspicion. So enjoy your opportunity, and take it, starting this coming Monday."

There was a knock on the door of the entrance that I had come in. It opened slightly and Denise popped her head around the door. The professor acknowledged her and said, "Two minutes."

He leant forward. "There is one final thing," he said. "Can I look at the list of those of my ex-colleagues that you will be meeting." I took a list from the folder in my airline shoulder bag and gave it to him.

He quickly looked at the list. "There is one other person I think you should meet," he said. He got up off the sofa, walked up the couple of steps in the middle of the room, and went to the desk. Standing by a PC, he bent down to operate a key board and I could hear the keys rattling, as they would for a fast touch typist. "I am just writing to Professor Holmes," he went on. "I have asked him if he could arrange for you to meet Jane..." He looked down, as if to check what he was writing, "...and her son," he said slowly. Then with a flourish, he banged a key, as if to send the message. He then came back towards me, down the steps to wave me a cheery, and I have to say a charming "Goodbye", with a two handed handshake of my single hand. "Remember one thing," he said, "Your first loyalty is to yourself."

Denise came in at that point, as if on cue, and I walked out of the room with her, with a short wave back to the professor.

"Did you get on OK?" said Denise, as we got to the bottom of the stairs.

"I am a bit shell-shocked," I said. "Time whizzed by. He made some good points, and very quickly."

"That is not unusual," she said, shaking my hands by the reception. "Those points will grow stronger as you think about what he asked you. He always says to me that people are responsible for evolving themselves to what they want to be. The few people he sees on a personal basis, always come back to tell him how they have done. They either secure a promotion or a career change, but best of all, they seem noticeably happier. Hope you have an enjoyable journey, both right now, and into the future."

"Thank you," I said and walked out into the street not too sure about what I should think about first.

I turned back to South Kensington. It was approaching rush hour and was getting busier. As I approached the station, the sun broke through the clouds onto the red brick building that is South Kensington underground station. It looks so incongruous. South Kensington is a collection of grand properties, mostly in white. This incongruity of the station should lead to its preservation as an oddity!

I stopped on the other side of the road to the station. Since I would be disappearing into the underground very soon, I decided to give Mary a ring.

When I got through, I suggested that we could meet, if she was free, in a different place that night – The Reef restaurant..

"What has brought this on?" she asked.

"I am just seeking to break a regular habit," I replied.

"I see you have learnt something," she said. "You will have to explain what it is when we meet. I will make the booking as it is probably easier that I do it. If you don't hear from me, I will see you at a restaurant at 7.30 pm"

I said goodbye to Mary and made my way home. On the way back I added the following to my action list:-

	Action List	Time scale
1	List all the ways my time gets wasted and work out an action for them.	Ongoing
2	Work through the perception exercise.	1-3 days
3	Reorganise my workspace so it radiates the messages I want.	1-3 days
4	Work out the value of my time.	1-3 days
5	Work out the cost of regular activities such as meetings.	1-2 weeks
6	Talk about the importance of time with people at work.	Immediate
7	Find some time quotes	1-4 weeks
8	Review this experience frequently.	Continuous

Later that evening, I made my way to the Reef restaurant. The Reef was by a boatyard, setback from the river. It was not an expensive place, and the food was straightforward. It had very pleasant surroundings, and Mary and I could walk there from our respective houses.

"This is a surprise," said Mary, as she spotted me waiting for her at the bar.

"As long as you see it as a good surprise that is all that matters!" said I.

"Indeed it is," she said, "It also provides you a good opportunity to give me a blow by blow account of what happened to you today, whilst it is fresh in your mind. Something must have happened today for you to decide to come here."

And that is what I did over most of the meal. I got her to do the acronym test with TIME. She was intrigued by this and the challenge to find a third version. Her trap of thinking was to start with the word 'time' followed by the word 'is'. Her initial favourite was 'Time is money earned', followed by 'Time is money evaporating'." I gave her my one about management engineering. We both played with the concept of management engineering for a short while.

Suddenly, Mary said, "I have thought of a much more personal acronym, which has nothing to do with time. The first two words are ' This' and 'is' and the clue is that the expression is related to telephones. My second clue is that I can use this expression as a form of introduction. You already know enough to work out the final two words. "

"Is it 'Telephones interrupt my efforts'," I suggested, with a flash of silliness.

"That does not start with 'This'," she said laughing, "and I would not say that about your telephone calls – just so you know. It is not a bad expression though. You may want to look at how you handle telephones at work, if you can remember the expression."

"Good point," I said. "and so is the question of how you can quickly remember something, when you have not got a pencil and paper to hand. I got caught out the other day trying to remember details of an event on the local community notice board. By the time I got home, I had forgotten the details."

"You mean you had forgotten to use your mobile to send a message to yourself," said Mary, laughing even louder.

"Come on," I said. "My mobile is not that cheap. It has got a few facilities. It is just that I forgot I could use it. "

"You really are giving a good example of someone who has technology that they don't know how to use," Mary said still laughing.

It was a few more laughs, a glass of wine, and the end of the first course, before we could return to my story.

"I will give you a serious acronym to think about," said Mary, "but I don't personally like it. It is a reasonably well known expression. Here it is. 'Time is my enemy.'"

"That sounds spot on," I said. "Why don't you like it?"

"To me, it creates a sense of anxiety, almost as if you will never complete what you are aiming to do. I would not like to consider it in terms of growing older either. I much prefer the philosophy of simply being who you are."

"I had not thought about it like that," I said. "I had thought much more about the context of too much to do and one should not stand still."

"Sometimes, it is important to stand still and relax, and take stock," said Mary. "I would like to see time as a friend and a teacher. Time equals experience. Perhaps the acronym should read ' this is my experience'? Let's move on. Tell me more about what you learnt today, in case I can help you with anything else."

I told how about Roland Tinker's challenge to learn more about the potential of office software and to get involved in voice dictation.

"That's interesting," she said. "Why don't we do that together. It always seems to me that if two people work on something, it is much more fun, and it is often easier to get over any blocks to accomplishment. How about spending some time on the office software next Sunday evening. I will get some lists off the Internet about what it can do, and then we can both check whether we understand whether we can do it. We could then have a go with voice dictation on another weekend."

"Done," I said. Here was an action I could report on to Roland Tinker.

Mary was much more reflective, when it came to my description of my afternoon meeting. Her comment, as we were finishing coffee and waiting for the waitress to organise the bill, was that we all seem to run on autopilot for an awful lot of what we do. It is so easy to miss how somebody else might perceive our actions.

She looked me in the eye, and leaning forward slightly, asked, "I know Dick Taylor was more interested in work perceptions, but using his test, how would you describe me?"

That caught me by surprise. After a quick look up to see whether the waitress was coming, I ventured "beautiful", with a smile. What else could I say?

"Careful!" she said.

"That too," I said.

"Beauty is in the eye of the beholder," she said, "both of us have had some wine this evening with our meal. How else would you describe me?"

"Sensible," I said. I actually believed this to be absolutely accurate about Mary.

She hesitated. "I cannot make much sense of that, at this moment," she said, "However, I believe it *sensible* that we pack up now, and you have an early night, as you have to travel a fair way tomorrow. Are you packed?"

"Toothbrush is at the ready," I said, knowing it was anything but ready. "You are right. I do have to pack and prepare, and it is *sensible* that we go now. There I told you – you are sensible. I will ask you what five adjectives, you would use to describe me on another occasion!"

Mary just looked at me and changed the subject. "You know I said to you," she said, "that I had thought of another acronym for T I M E. Well, I have thought of yet another connection between the word 'TIME' and where we've been tonight. You probably need something to think about on the train tomorrow, and now you have one puzzle to solve from this morning and two puzzles to solve from me tonight. Time to say goodnight, I think."

We departed!

Readers notes:

Note the five adjective technique. It can be very powerful. Will your desk ever look the same?

Did you notice Professor Taylor mentioned an activity that also came up in the visit to Professor Tinker? It is easily missed. There is also an activity connection coming up in the next chapter.

Keep seeking a good acronym for TIME. John is still some way away from finding Professor Tinker's third lever for time management.

Remember the restaurant. It is connected to another restaurant later. Mary's last challenge also connects to the same point.

Remember also the nature of Professor Taylor's reference to Jane, a person whom John should meet in the future.

Will you be able to work out the university city in the next chapter? You will hear of a professor's command centre and a symbaloo.

Chapter 6
Event Management
'Precision Planning'

Tuesday was another early morning start. I was heading west this time, together with my airline shoulder bag complete with a toothbrush and a change of clothing. I was going to a beautiful city and one that I had visited before. The famous recreation ground was a particular area of interest to my favourite sports team who play away matches here.

Once again, I was on the train and I was pleased that I had been able to make the connections to get to the station on time. It had been a struggle and I vowed that I simply must allow more time to get to where I am going!

Unlike some of my companions on the train, I was not interested in the contents of the day's newspapers. What was occupying my thoughts was something that Professor Taylor had said the previous day. I was applying his methods to what I had said about Mary.

I had referred to Mary as "sensible". If I wanted to radiate a perception of being sensible, what would I do? Mary often puts an event into a bigger picture. She also takes a different view to me, from time to time, and then works out a first action to take, depending on how I react to that different view. She seems to have a talent at doing this.

I suppose I could always ask myself in any situation, what is the bigger picture, and what is the opposite viewpoint. I suspect, though, I will still make silly mistakes. Maybe that is what sensible means to me – a way of avoiding silly mistakes.

My thoughts drifted back to my work situation. The managers never get together on the basis of informally coaching each other to avoid silly mistakes. We always tend to be in coordination mode, or trying to sort out a specific problem. Nor do we have any independent coaches, or mentors, at work. The HR department always gives the impression that it is delighted to talk to us if we go to them, but it does not have the experience that would actually help. My suspicion is that this is also true of life coaches. My fear is that they help you work out what you want to do, and maybe give you a push, but they cannot tell you in a business context whether that is sensible or not, nor would they necessarily know the business, or management techniques, or legislation to steer you well. Proper business coaches are probably the ones to talk to since they will be more aware of what is available in a business context, and they can probably save me time on the practical things.

Yet having had that thought, here am I visiting a number of professors who only have indirect knowledge of what it is like to be a manager, although I'm sure they have held some responsibilities, as they have progressed up the academic ladder. They also have particular expertise on offer. Maybe the best coaches are those who have undertaken responsibility, and can offer some expertise.

I think it would be useful to have a long term business coach though. He or she could help me in my career, save me a lot of time avoiding silly mistakes, show me short cuts and offer guidance for difficult situations. I don't see anyone at work being able to do this. Perhaps I should contact my professional institution, to see whether they have any mentors. Another action to add to my list!

This morning's appointment is with Anton Soljer. From my brief research on the Internet, I discovered that not only is he a professor, but he is an adventurer, a consultant to oil companies, a charity fund raiser, an author of fiction, a school governor and he has an interest in electric bicycles! On the Internet, there was a long list of research papers that he had published. There does not seem much room in his life to do all his other academic duties! I hope it is not going to be a case that university life is so lax that you can fill your life with lots of other things.

The other interesting thing about Professor Soljer was that his academic discipline of geophysics had no connection to management. I could understand some connection between Professor Tinker studying systems engineering and having an interest in aspects of management, but it was very difficult to make the connection between Professor Soljer's discipline and management.

The train slowed down and crossed a river immediately before arriving at the station. I alighted from the train and decided to check times on the departures board nearby. In the meantime, my train continued its journey and left the station.

Looking across the station, you have the impression of space. There was a major gap between the platforms and only two sets of track between them. It was almost as if another track had existed in the past, and had now disappeared.

I had been advised that the easiest way to get to the University was by bus. So I found my way to the University bus stop. The bus service is very regular and it was not long before I was travelling on my way back across the river and up the hill to the University.

The School of Geology, where the geophysics department was based, is a five storey building towards the top of a hill. Finding it was no difficulty. I announced myself to the administrative offices on the ground floor, and they contacted Professor Soljer's' assistant to let her know that I had arrived. I was asked to wait in a nearby chair, and was able to observe the current generation of students drifting in, and out, with various queries.

After a few minutes, I noticed out of the corner of my eye, a much smarter student. At least this was my initial impression as she came towards me.

"John Watson?" she asked. I nodded. "Would you like to come this way? Professor Soljer will see you upstairs in his command centre."

"A command centre," I said "That sounds a bit unusual for a university."

"It is what everyone calls it," said the well dressed young woman. "The professor has raised a lot of money for the Department, so they have given him his own special office. He is not there all the time, but when he is, he uses it to the full."

She took me up to the fourth floor and a corner of the building. She asked me just to hang on while she checked the professor was ready. She then knocked on a door, walked in ahead of me and said to the professor, "John Watson is here. Shall I send him in?"

"Yes, please do," said a very clear and firm voice. She ushered me into the room, and made her own exit, as soon as I had passed her.

Professor Soljer, a grey-haired clean-shaven man, about six foot tall, and wearing a collar and tie, gave an immediate first impression of someone in authority. He walked out from behind three large PC screens on his desk at the end of the room. In front of his desk was a round table. He invited me to join him around it.

"Welcome to the command centre," he said. "This is where I organise my work, do some of it, and meet visitors."

"I am impressed with the three PC screens that I can see on your desk," I said. "I have seen software engineers work on two, but I have never seen anyone work on three. Is this part of the way you organise what you have to do?"

"Yes," he said. "It makes life easier.. I would normally have just two screens. If I am doing any petrophysics, a type of geophysics, two screens are really useful. I really need the third screen to keep myself organised, when I am doing other work. When I am doing organisational work, I do it primarily on the screen that is straight in front of me. I do use voice dictation and that helps me to quickly do reports, or I can use it to send e-mails. On my right hand screen, I have my diary open on the top half of the screen, and any relevant diaries of other people, or events, are open on the bottom part. On the left hand screen, is both the internal intranet and a symbaloo."

"What is a symbaloo?" I asked.

"Imagine a six by ten matrix of buttons, each with a link to a website that you use frequently. It is a very simple way to access information. If you go to the website www.symbaloo.com, you can see how it works and you can currently get a copy free for personal use. It is a very convenient time saver!"

"Do you work completely electronically?" I asked.

"Not entirely," he smiled. "In my top drawer, I keep some wire bound documents that I have printed off. These are mostly about the data I need for my job here at the University. These include details of students and their progress, budget papers, telephone lists, emergency information and a whole host of other things that I can instantly refer to. You will notice that I also have a filing cabinet within reach of my arm. Most things I can access by simply swinging around, or moving my chair."

He got up and invited me to sit in the chair behind his desk. Not only was it true that I could reach most things easily by simply swivelling in the chair. I could also swivel to read some low level lists he had placed on a low level noticeboard behind him.

"What all this means," said the professor, "is that if I am working on something, I can very quickly have all the information in front of me, and not have to go backwards and forwards into various other computer files, or Internet locations, or physical places. Layout of workspaces, particularly in offices, is often overlooked. The time taken in dealing with inefficient arrangements can add up significantly over the weeks, months, and years. Have you ever thought about your office in this way?"

I had to admit that I hadn't. "I just have a standard office in a semi-open environment," I said. "Everyone has something similar where I work."

"It may be worth reviewing that," said the professor. "Think about what you do at your desk. Work out a value of the direct interactions you may have with your staff in the environment. Then decide whether a better arrangement would be beneficial to you. Standard office arrangements can be very inefficient. If you're forced to accept a certain arrangement, at the very least, you should be able to point out how efficient, or inefficient, it is. Now where was I?"

"You were describing your screens before that." I said. "I noticed that you mentioned e-mails as one of the screens you might have open."

"It is only open for a short while," said the professor. "I have three distinct times for looking at e-mails. I look at them first thing in the morning to check whether there is any emergency e.g. someone is sick.

The next time is straight after lunch. Finally, I look at them just before I go home. It is the second last activity I do, before leaving. I suppose that begs the question what is the last activity. My last activity is to write out what I'm going to be doing the next morning. It should not involve getting out any papers because they would have already been prepared earlier. Is this conversation useful to you? Why don't you tell me what you would specifically like to achieve in the next forty five minutes? Let's go back to the round table to discuss it"

We returned to the round table and made ourselves comfortable.

"I suspect you know from Professor Holmes," I said, " that my aim is to capture different views and techniques on time management, and then coordinate those views in order to distribute them through the business channels I know. My aim includes reviewing my personal approach to time management, and using that as a basis for evaluating what I learn. So far, and from just meeting two other professors yesterday, I have learnt that I have a lot to learn. I guess the $64,000 question, professor, that I want to know is how do you manage to do all that I read you do? It seems an enormous amount."

"I am sure my secrets are worth more than $64,000," said the professor with a laugh, "but if there is one word that mostly sums up all that I do, I guess that word would be "routines". I create them, let people know about them, and then work with them. When I mention this to anybody else, they say that they suspect this is very boring. I don't look at it that way. I see them as a quick way to get onto more interesting work and a way to accomplish all that I have to do."

"What sort of routines are we talking about?" I asked.

"Let us start with the easy ones," he said. "Every year, there will be some defined events that will take place during the year. So the routines we are about to discuss, are all about events. For example, I suspect you will be involved in health and safety meetings, staff appraisals, coaching sessions, budget reviews, planning sequences, customer reviews, staff briefings, etc. There is probably quite a long list. So the first step is either to work out when you're going to carry out those events, and persuade others, where appropriate, to set the dates for those events. I think, for most people, the main events go into the diary every year, but a lot of other events do not go into the diary until someone decides to organise the event much nearer to the time. That is when a lot of time is wasted. Diaries do not match, and there could be much messing around in spite of electronic diaries to get the right people together. Does any of this sound familiar?"

I nodded. "It certainly does," I said.

"I probably go further than most people in pinning down future dates," said the professor. "I also make some virtual dates and reminders for those things that are not possible to go directly in the diary, but I am sure will happen. Then importantly, once I have the events in my diary, I make time allowances for what I call event management. If you are organising a meeting, you need to prepare for it, by agreeing, and sending out agendas. You also need to write up notes, or take actions afterwards. You need to get some time in your diary for those activities as well. Even if it is not your meeting, you should allow, in your diary, time to read any papers, or take any actions as a result of the meeting. Does this make sense?"

"It is good sense," I said, "but does this not mean you overplan?"

"You will soon be able to judge how much planning is needed," said the professor. "In your next few meetings, work out who has not given much thought to the meeting. More than likely they will take time in the meeting to catch up. Better managers are not like that. They are on top of the situation and all I am doing is practising a routine that helps me stay on top of situations."

"I wish all our managers practised that routine" I said. "It would make our meetings much more productive."

"You can be an exemplar," said the professor, "and it will increase your influence. Some managers will notice what you do and learn from you. Are you ready for the next point?"

"Yes," I said. "Are we still talking about event management?"

"In a way," said the professor. "This is more about how you might sequence events. You need to work out, and follow a daily, weekly, or monthly rhythm. This will not only help you plan things properly, but it helps your colleagues know what you are likely to be doing.

"For instance, I have a definite set of routines in the morning when I am here. Having an opening set of routines first thing in the morning is important, because it is normally the only time of day when you can actually practise the routine with some certainty. I will tell you what I do, but it may not be what anybody else would choose to do, and it's up to any individual to decide what is best for them."

"I normally arrive at work at 8:15 am and come up to the command centre and look at my emails and schedule. My staff and my colleagues know that they have to let me know before 8:30 am whether there is a problem for the day or not. Also in my emails, there may be some bookings for telephone or meeting slots of ten minutes each between at 9:00 am and 9:40 am On the assumption there are no problems at 8.30am, I use the next half hour to prepare for the day. I have an understanding with everyone concerned, that I will not be disturbed until nine o'clock and my time between 9am and 9.40am has to be booked in advance and it is only for short discussions."

"Why stop at 9.40 am," I asked.

"It allows me to get to wherever else I need to be in good time for a start time of 10am," said the professor. "This break avoids the usual chaos caused by back to back meetings, and allows for a small overrun, although everyone knows that I don't allow my morning meetings to overrun! Anyone who has back to back meetings almost inevitably wastes somebody else's time waiting for them to finish a meeting. I am then into the events of the day. I still endeavour to have routines as much as I can for the rest of the day and make sure everyone knows about them. For instance, I only look at e-mails at certain times of the day. I also make a habit of going to the staff common room in the morning, so people know they can find me there, if they need me. Those times in the common room have a dual purpose. Not only can we deal with business of the day informally, but we can also talk about other work-related matters. It is also a way of me picking up activities in other departments, which could have a bearing on any plans that I am making."

"You also mentioned weekly rhythms," I said.

"As far as a weekly rhythm goes," said the professor, "I have brief meetings with key staff at approximately the same time every week, and I always make sure that if I'm going somewhere, it is normally a Tuesday, or Thursday, when I have little in the way of teaching commitments. My monthly rhythm consists of budget reviews, coaching sessions and a few other things, all of which are placed in the diary, as far ahead as possible."

"Business is nothing like that," I said, "Customers phone, suppliers phone, colleagues come round for advice, the boss wants something urgently. It is all chop and change."

"And you allow that to be the case," said the professor. "Ask yourself, how important it is for the customer to speak to you at that moment. You can make one of your staff the recipient of external telephone calls. They will no doubt be covering you this week. As long as the recipient of the call fixes a time to get back to the customer, which they agree with the customer, then that may be sufficient. It depends on your business. For suppliers, there is no reason why there should not be a window for taking their calls, or making calls to them. You may just have to educate them. You could also have a policy on cold callers, such as the first contact must always be in writing, and you will phone them if you are interested. There is always something you can do to segment your time."

"And what about the boss?" I asked. "Mine often wants things at short notice."

"If they do not know what you're doing, of course they are going to mess it up for you. The best bet is to build them into your set routines, and look in to see if they have anything for you at least twice a day. You can also tell them that you are trying to improve your productivity, by concentrating hard on certain things, at certain times. They would then be aware of what you are doing, and the consequences of disturbing you. So far, we have simply talked about building up timeslots. I hope you can accept the principle and I wonder if you can see a further advantage to this that we have not yet discussed."

"I can understand," I said, "that timeslots are likely to allow one to concentrate on similar activities and it is more productive to keep interruptions down. I can also see sense in planning time before a meeting, as this allows you to manage your part in the meetings better. Those are both advantages. Is it one of those you mean?"

"No, although both of those are good points. This advantage is to do with change. If you have to make a change to arrangements, and you have planned your daily and event activities well, you can see immediately the consequences of a change. It is very easy to agree to something, if you seem to have an empty diary. That agreement may not take into account the time that was mentally allocated to doing other things that you have simply forgotten about. In addition, disorganising events can strike at any moment, and suddenly you have too much to do, in a way that is out of control. If you can first know the consequences of a change, you can better manage your situation."

"How do you make all this work?" I asked "It would seem that a simple distraction would ruin your day."

"I am always careful," said the professor, "to make it clear, when I start talking to somebody, how long they have got, before I have got to do something else. I may have some advantages compared to people in business," he went on, "in that I do have to do work outside the command centre, and I can also choose to go to other locations to complete some of my work. I wouldn't necessarily do marking in the command centre as the environment is full of distractions to do with organisational matters. If I want to concentrate on the marking, I go to a "hot desk" and work there. I guess the equivalent, in a business setting, would be a meeting room. You would simply be having a meeting with yourself, and by being in a meeting room, it might suggest to others that they should not disturb you, unless it is important."

"Does this not give the impression you are unapproachable?" I asked, remembering something of what Professor Taylor had said to me about managing perceptions.

"There is always a balance," said the professor, "between being infinitely available, and getting work done. You have to strike a balance appropriate to the circumstances. The best thing to do is always make sure that people can approach you in a different way other than face-to-face, particularly if they cannot meet you when you are available for face-to-face meetings. Hence e-mails, the morning appointment and the visit to the common room. I have also arranged that when I am out, another member of staff can be approached to deal with any of the issues that are my responsibility. I have endeavoured to communicate this to all my colleagues, so they know there is always another channel. It is on my checklist of the key people that I meet every week that I update them on current issues, so they can answer questions, if I was ill, etc. It seems to me that managers from business always want to be infinitely approachable. Their role suggests that they cannot be, and they need to accept that point and make arrangements that are clear to all relevant parties. To me, this is part of the responsibility of being a manager. It is important that the manager remembers that it is the team that needs to be approachable as a whole, not just the manager."

I decided I might be a little cheeky. "Isn't it the case, Professor, that in your situation you can be a little bit more distant from your team, than in business? Quick team access to me would seem pretty important in my situation."

"Maybe," said the professor. "The roles are different, and mine is probably more like that of your boss. However, I come back to the point that you are here today, so someone must be taking decisions. It suggests that whilst you think your staff need quick access to you, it may not be universally true, and it would seem, from what you appear to be telling me, that you could exercise more control on your time than perhaps you do at the moment."

It seemed to me that the professor was being assertive in reply to my cheeky suggestion about delegation. He was right in what he was saying. I was not too sure how to reply to his point. I hesitated, which probably meant that I could have some more control on my time if I followed his logic. I'm sure he noticed I was struggling with what he had just said.

"Let's go on," continued the professor. "We are about halfway through the time available to us. So far we have discussed some controls on your diary time. What I would like to move on to now is an extension of the idea of daily, weekly and monthly rhythms. Have you heard of the expression 'agenda calendar'?"

"No," I replied. "I feel like I should have done though."

"It is an useful idea that particularly applies to regular meetings," he said. "Let's take health and safety meetings, as an example. Just say that you have six health and safety meetings a year. What would you discuss?" He looked at me for a response.

"I guess, we would review accidents, near misses, and any relevant event that has happened since the last meeting."

"I believe every one of your six meetings would review accidents," said the professor. "This is an example of something that would occur every meeting. A regular item on your agenda. During the year, you would probably review other items, e.g. campaigns, fire practices, the state of risk assessments, special audits, plans, signage, etc. You probably would not review these at every meeting, only at special meetings in certain months of the year. An agenda calendar for a year will layout when these items would be discussed. As they are discussed regularly every year, the agenda calendar forms a checklist of what regular items to discuss when. In a very simple form, it could look like this table." He showed me a diagram that he had quickly drawn on a blank sheet of paper.

	Jan	Mar	May	July	Sept	Nov
Once a year	Campaigns	Audits	Fire Practice	Risk Assessments	Signage	Plans
Every meeting	Accidents	Accidents	Accidents	Accidents	Accidents	Accidents

"A real agenda calendar would have many more items upon it. However, I hope this illustrates the basic idea. If all the committee members had a copy of this, they would know exactly what is coming up when, and it can also be published to the rest of the staff too. This basic idea can be extended into a form of planning. Just say, that you were not going to review something this year but were going to review it next year. In fact, it may be the case that you reviewed this particular thing every two years. If we stick to health and safety, you may wish to 1) review the health and safety policy every three years, 2) the members on the committee every two years, 3) practices on various aspects of safety at two and four year intervals, etc.

Your plan could look like this diagram." He turned around another piece of paper that he had been quickly drawing upon.

	Year 1	Year 2	Year 3	Year 4
Policy 1	X			X
Policy 2	X		X	
Practice 1		X		X
Practice 2			X	
Practice 3		X		

"The benefit of this," he continued, "is that you, and everybody else, knows when things are going to be discussed. In addition, if you get everything on the list that you need to review, you will ensure that you won't forget things in the future. Are there any meetings you have that could use a similar process?"

"Supplier reviews is an obvious one for us," I said. "We have a policy to review these every three years, or in some cases, two years. Sometimes we have to scratch our heads to remind ourselves when we started a contract. For annual contracts, I have to admit that we have missed the review date on the odd occasion. In practice, suppliers usually want price increases, so they are not backward at coming forward. However, they do tend to do it at the last moment. This is probably to ensure that we have not had time to consider any alternative supplier, so it could be an advantage for us to schedule time to review their service well beforehand.

You will probably find more examples when you come to think about your departmental policy and practices," said the professor. "All of these should be reviewed on a regular basis. You can plan when you are next going to review something. You do not do a review every time someone has a bright idea. You review all the bright ideas about the same subject together at the due time. Urgent matters may have to be reviewed beforehand, but if there is no urgency, they can wait until the next review. Again everyone knows when that will be, and you don't waste time continuously discussing odd things in isolation."

The professor paused. He lent back in the chair, moved his hand across his head and then came forward again. "When I go to visit some local companies," he went on, with some signs of frustration in his voice, "they seem to be always changing things. Instead, if they planned to review likely items to be changed, they can at least take the time to consider changes in the context of the bigger picture. They could then work out the likely consequences of a change they are about to make. I have seen several examples of emotive and reactive changes that solve a small presenting problem immediately, but this has led to significant consequences for time wasting, and inefficiency, elsewhere and later on."

"I know companies like that," I said. "There is usually a driving force to get something done for an immediate issue. Sometimes though, you cannot avoid the need to drop everything!"

"There will be times when immediacy is necessary," said the professor. "However, simple planning and updating can avoid many issues. Apart from items likely to be changed, it is possible to schedule items for review that need to be kept updated e.g. legislative processes, risk assessments. Reviews keep things up to date, rather than letting the key practices descend into chaos. Some people may thrive on chaos, but if it is avoidable, then it should be avoided. I think that is enough of me sounding off on my soapbox on this particular subject. There is one other area about meetings that is important. Are you OK to continue?"

"Fine," I said. "Is this about the conduct of meetings?"

"No. although that is also an important area. This is about the role of the regular meeting. If purposes of meetings, or terms of reference are not set, then a meeting can waste considerable time determining whether any particular subject is a subject for them, or not. I thoroughly recommend that for any meeting you conduct on a regular basis, you set out in writing the purpose of that meeting. In this way you can determine whether it actually meets that purpose in practice."

"I suspect that, if I did that," I said, "no one would remember to bring those terms of reference to the meeting and the discussion about the scope of the meeting would still continue. In our company, some people tend to forget to bring all the relevant papers to meetings."

"This next tip may then help you," said the professor. "I use something I refer to as an 'Operating Manual'. This is a ring binder that I create for every meeting that happens regularly. The main binder has a number of key sections. I will write them down for you."

He quickly wrote down a number of bullet points as below and passed them over.

The file contains:-

- the agenda of the meeting about to happen
- copies of the last three minutes
- the terms of reference of the meeting
- the major policies that are appropriate
- the agenda calendar and any plans and budget resources
- any key data
- relevant papers for the meeting itself - spread over no more than 5 sections, so you can find the relevant papers quickly.

"In this way, I have all the information I need in one folder," said the professor. "As information comes through, I print it off, and put it in the folder, destroying out of date information, as I go."

"That might be a useful habit," I said. "Do you have any thoughts about the stacking of thinner ring binders? I find it very difficult to keep them upright, when I put them in a cupboard."

"That is a regular problem," said the professor, "and I have no ideal solution. The best bet is to keep your eyes on stationery suppliers for their ideas and solutions. I have seen plastic boxes which have five different vertical partitions allowing you to put one file into each of the spaces between partitions. For cupboards you can buy specially fitted partitions to separate folders. You can also use a series of book ends or separate the ring binders between other items which are more stackable. This is what I have done. Anyway, we are digressing from another important subject which links to agenda calendars. Are you OK to move on?"

"Yes," I said slowly. "I have just realised that such an operating manual for a regular meeting is a very useful delegation or training tool and it does create a perception of being organised as well actually being organised! I like that. I am happy to move on now."

"An agenda calendar is a form of checklist," said the professor. "I am a great believer in checklists. I tend to have checklists for most regular activities. This includes going to meetings, conferences, visiting industrial sites, long car journeys. If a checklist is possible, I tend to make one. Some people say that memory is paler than the faintest ink. I believe that is right, and this is where checklists play their part. If it wasn't for my checklists, then I would have forgotten many things, and worried myself unduly. Ignore the making of checklists at your peril. Is there anything that you would like to ask before we finish?"

"Are you not vulnerable to your command centre breaking down, or being away from it for long time?" I asked.

"Good question," he said, "What is on the command centre about how I organise my activities is also on my laptop, and I regularly synchronise the two. The command centre allows me to see several documents at once. It just takes me longer on the laptop. I also do some synchronisation between the laptop and my smart phone. My smart phone tends to be with me at all times, particularly, if I am away. It has the capacity to take notes, or remind me with memory joggers, and even receive e-mails. I have used a PDA (personal digital assistant) in the past. They can be very good, and you can download plenty of applications, e.g. list management software. Now, you can get smart phones with the same sort of applications. You might like to consider one of those. When they get as good as my laptop, I will ditch my laptop. Any final questions?"

"How do you manage all your activities outside work?" I asked.

"I decided many years ago," replied the professor, "that, if planning worked for business, it would work for things outside business. So I tend to use exactly the same habits. I think there is a danger in life, that if we treat home as somewhere to sit and relax, then that is all we do. I would like to think that I do what a number of businessmen don't do. They may have a well-planned week but they fail to plan for the weekend.

He looked at me with a smile. "I usually do have a reasonably active weekend, and some of my activity is based on checklists, and routine. My first tip for you, on housework, is to plan a short time with your partner so you both do housework at the same time. My second tip is to have a house work list of what you will achieve, on any particular weekend, in an average month for both you and your partner, and then swap roles the following month. It shares responsibility. I'm afraid that is it as far as our time together will allow, as I now have a tutorial to go to. Let me take you down to reception. I gather you're going to another local university this afternoon?"

"That's right," I said. "It has been very useful to hear your views Professor. Thank you." I picked up my bag and we both returned to reception.

On the way, he asked me how I was travelling. When I told him that it was by train, he asked me whether I use the train or Underground to get to work. I told him I live three miles away from work and mostly used the car.

"Three miles is a good distance for a bike," he commented. "Let me tell you a secret. Get an electric bike. You can do the journey and arrive without a sweat. There are some very modern designs around, which are pretty good at disguising the battery and motor." He then went on to point out that the journey to my next university can be easily done on half a battery charge.

We arrived at reception. He shook my hand, wished me good luck ...and I made my departure back towards a bus stop to get me back to the station.

As I made my way down to the station, I felt that the meeting could easily have gone on for longer. It would be have been nice to see some examples, but I guessed that all of these will be related to the actual work he had to do.

As I reflected on what I had learnt, it did occur to me that I was not as well planned as I could be. Putting aside times before and after meetings was a sensible thing to do and would save a lot of last minute stress. He was also right that I could use my staff more in taking calls to give me more time to concentrate.

Having agenda calendars would be a good thing for my team, particularly as one member was always seeking to change things. She could be told when we are going to review her particular points, rather than creating a frustrating few minutes at a meeting arguing about whether we were going to do it at that moment, or not.

Checklists also made good sense. Whenever I'm about to go somewhere, I get focused on the journey and assume I have things, which it later turns out I have forgotten. I will start some of those as soon as I can. We have a plastic laminator at work. I will get some of the checklists laminated so they can be used time and again. As a first step, I will make sure there is a checklist for my overnight stays!

So my actions look like this:-

	Action List	Time scale
1	Get in touch with my professional institute about a suitable mentor.	1-2 weeks
2	Work out my annual events and plan them / get others to plan.	1-4 weeks
3	Define review dates for major policies and processes.	1-4 weeks
4	Define my rhythms.	1-2 weeks
5	Practice event management for the above 3 items.	Ongoing
6	Develop agenda calendars for regular meetings.	1-2 months
7	Try out an operating manual for two meetings.	1-2 months
8	Review my workspace for optimum access to what I need.	1 week
9	Get a special notebook for recording checklists	Immediate
10	Identify routines both at work and at home.	Immediate
11	Put a checklist my shoulder bag for overnight items.	Immediate
12	Take an interest in Smartphone capability.	1-3 month
13	Get a bigger computer screen.	1-2 months

As for the command centre, I do not think I need three screens. However, having a bigger screen would help me have two documents open at the same time, in a way that I can more easily refer between the two. I need to get this suggestion into my boss, in a way that she will accept it!

Readers notes:

Did you notice the continuing activity that the earlier professors have referred to? Did you also noted the reference to the recreation ground which is a further small clue about John's favourite sport?

If you worked out the city for Professor Soljer, then you may already know the next city. Can you appreciate why there is a short boat ride in prospect? There is something strange about the railway station platforms too. It's all in the next chapter. If you get stuck on the puzzles, you can cheat by using an internet search engine.

Once he has met the next professor, John moves onto an intriguing pub. Note carefully how the landlord says what he says!

Chapter 7

Measures for Success

Visually Mighty!

It was just a short train journey to see the next professor. So much so that I just enjoyed looking out the window and watching the countryside go by, without a thought about time management.

On arriving at the station, I grabbed a bite to eat and then set off for my appointment with Professor Roger Sayler, who was based at the business school. I was not clear on whether he had a specialist subject, although I had seen reference to a paper he had written on supply chain effectiveness.

I had been advised by Mary to try the water ferry. It was apparently very near the station and it would take you across the floating harbour, where you can connect to the road that takes you up a hill to the University. It did not take me long to find it. It is about three minutes from the station and you just follow the white ferry signs. Fortunately, there was a ferry due to go, otherwise I would have had to give up the idea.

It was a pleasant thing to do. It was also easy to know where the university was, when you get off the ferry. The gothic university tower is easily spotted.

Professor Sayler's department was also very easy to find, as was the administrative office on the ground floor. It was a bit noisy there, with lots of undergraduates hanging around waiting for lectures to start. The administrative office contacted the professor and one of the staff took me straight up to meet him.

His office was on the fifth floor. When we got to his door, which was half open, we heard him making his goodbyes to someone else. I could just see part of his office, mainly his desk area. I could not help but notice that they were a number of framed graphs on the wall around his desk, and in every case the graph was going upwards.

I was a little early, so did not mind waiting a moment or two. Very shortly, a student came out and I was taken in, and introduced to the Professor Sayler. Beckoning me to take a chair, in front of his desk, Roger Sayler took an adjacent chair, so we were both the same side of his desk. As he sat down, he enquired of my journey, and whether I had found his department OK. When he saw me nodding, he asked me about my first impressions on entering the building.

"The noise," I said, "and also the efficiency of being whisked straight up here to meet you."

"Thank you," he said. "Any other impressions?"

"Only the graphs on your wall behind you. In these challenging times, it is nice to see graphs going upwards."

"Ah, yes," said the professor. "I am very pleased with what those represent. A local company has adopted an approach that I recommended to them, and over the course of the last eighteen months, they have gone from strength to strength. Perhaps I will tell you more about that later. In the meantime, I would like to come to some agreement with you about how to get the best out of the next hour, for both of us. My purpose, as indicated by Richard Holmes, is to give you some of my views on time management. It would be nice to be able to give you something relevant to what you do, and that would be my ideal starting point – to learn what you do. What would be on your agenda?"

"I am here to learn," I said, "and to determine whether what I learn can be useful to relay down through other business networks. Hopefully, I can learn to become more efficient and effective at what I do. Perhaps the starting point is for me to explain what I do, and then we can go from there."

"Yes. Agreed," said the professor, "but before we do that there is one other thing to have in mind about what you should become. You talked about being more efficient and effective and there are dangers here. The more efficient you become, the more you will want to improve the efficiency still further. What could be wrong with that you may well ask?"

I nodded.

"The danger is that, if the market changes, and you need to change the efficient processes, you are more reluctant to do so the more efficient you are. There was a professor in Canada, Paul Mott, who pointed out that we don't just need processes that become efficient, we also need processes that can adapt those processes to the market or a new way of doing things. So, coming back to your expression of becoming more efficient and effective, my recommendation is that you consider becoming more efficient, effective, and adaptive. It may seem an academic point right at this very moment, but I think you'll find it a real point as we go through this afternoon.

"That is a good point," I said. "I need to be good at running things, but also good at changing what I run."

"Exactly," said the professor. "Let me give you a trivial example of reluctance to change from an efficient process. A company I know gained a quality accreditation, and was very pleased with itself for the quality of the documentation and training that it had developed to accompany its major processes. It was also proud of the efficiency by which it operated. The market changed, which meant that the processes also had to be changed quite radically. The two key managers involved were not at all keen. Their fear was that this meant they had to change all the documentation, the way they did training, the number of 'non conformances' would increase, and that could all lead to them losing their quality accreditation. That would have been an unlikely scenario as the accreditation body would have accommodated the change, but the feelings of the managers were of reluctance. They had invested so much effort in what they had already achieved and were so proud of that achievement. This was **not** a very inspiring mindset to make the changes required.

"So you are also saying that a detached but adaptive mindset is important," I said.

"A professional management mindset is the ideal" said the professor. "Always remember that, if we can efficiently change what we do efficiently, then we can save time and keep productivity where it should be. So, with that as a starting point before the starting point, let me now ask you what you do."

I spent the next ten minutes running through what my team did, and what I personally did.

"How does your boss know you do a good job?" asked the professor.

"Things get done and neither my boss, nor my customers complain about what the team does," I said.

"So your success is measured more by getting stuff done, without creating any fuss. If there is any fuss, your boss would interpret this as meaning you are doing a poor job?" he summarised and then looked at me with a smile.

I nodded. "Maybe that is a bit of an over simplification, but it does have several grains of truth in my context."

The professor went on, "When I ask managers and executives that question, I normally get one or more of the following replies:- sufficient work gets done, internal and external customers seem happy, the team seems to work without undue disruption and complaint, there are indications that something is improving. If this is the case, your boss can then be reasonably happy. She can rely on you to do what is asked, without having to bother with any undue difficulty. Even though the boss does not feel they have to get involved, it does not mean that those managers are well organised, or in control, or developing their people to their highest level, or that all processes are being improved, or indeed the manager's area can cope with the normal sort of disruptions. Bosses tend to assume that all these things are happening OK, because there is no major fuss that reaches their ears. As a consequence, many managers just work as best they can with the practices they know, and they would probably be a little defensive if anyone wanted to audit them on their ability to properly manage. The picture that I am painting is that managers often tend to work in ad hoc ways, and this can be very time inefficient. Does that happen at your place?"

"To a certain extent," I replied, "we don't have any common

management approach or management development so we tend to cope as best we can."

"Coping as best you can is a potential sign for wasted time," said the professor. "If you want to find out what really wastes time in an organisation, I can tell you. It is poor processes, or poor management practices. Let me give you some examples of poor management practices. If a team member is uncertain about what they should be doing, it is either down to poor planning, training, or communication. If a meeting wastes time on a distraction, it is down to poor chairmanship and an absence of good organisational meeting protocols. If someone cannot find what work somebody else has done, it is down to poor control practices. Does any of this make sense?"

"So what you are saying," I said, "is that I can save far more time for myself, and my team by concentrating on my management practices. I would challenge you however on the generalisation about poor management practices. It implies all time wasting is down to poor management and the only exception could be a poorly designed process a manager is forced to operate. Surely this is not always the case. What about the poor employee?"

"Good question," said the professor. "Ask who recruited the poor employee, who trained them, who motivated them, who set the standards, who made them aware of a performance requirements and issues. You may conclude that there is some managerial input in some of these decisions."

"OK," I said. "I will think of another counter example shortly."

"Before you do," said the professor, "there is an exercise you might like to try later on. If you think of all the things that frustrate you, or waste your time, there is a good chance you can put the cause down to a lack of something, or too much of something. Let me give you some examples. Causes of time wasting could be a lack of communication, lack of attention, lack of confidence, or lack of competence. If you want examples of too much of something, they could be too much demand, too much bureaucracy, too much complexity. Do you get the idea?"

I nodded. "I could add a lack of tact, a lack of money, a lack of understanding, and on the other side of the equation, too many e-mails, too many interruptions, too much legislation, too many rules."

"And you, or your staff if you ask them, can probably add quite a number more to what we have already identified," said the professor. "One of the most important is a lack of respect between people. It is a real killer of productivity. It is especially true for leaders. If leaders do not respect the people they lead, and engage in blame or backstabbing, especially when the staff in question are not around, it is an abuse of power, which will ultimately develop into a high waste of time as people give up going out of their way to support such a person."

"I acknowledge that," I said. "I have seen the problems if the staff lose faith in their leader."

"It is easily done," said the professor, "Now going back to my earlier comments, I would expect you to easily make a list of twenty things where there is likely to be too little of something, and a slightly lesser number where there is too much of something. Then comes the interesting bit. Against each item on the list, identify the management routine, or management skill, that would have avoided the time wasting situation. Each item on your list will give rise to something that a manager can do to have avoided or controlled the situation."

"The manager wouldn't need to implement them all," I said. "It depends on the risk of the problem."

"Quite so," said the professor. "You balance the routine that managers need to take against the risks of the problem occurring. My point is that if you don't identify the routines you cannot make the balance against the risks. If a risk is to become reality you could be wasting a lot of time that you don't need to. I believe this further make the case that good management routines are also good routines for ensuring everything works smoothly and saves time."

"It sounds to me that managers can't win," I said. "In my case, I don't think I can be all that bad, as I do not have too many problems from my team. I must be doing something right, in spite of not having done such an exercise."

"You may be doing lots of things right," said the professor, "that's what we really should look at. So let me ask you this question. 'How do you know you are managing, and leading, well?'"

This seemed like a similar question to what he had originally asked me, although it had to be answered from my perspective rather than my boss' perspective. I sought to clarify a bit further what he meant. "By manage and lead, do you mean how I plan, organise, control, and monitor the work, and make sure everyone knows what is required and is energised to do it?"

"That is a good start," said the professor. "Why not develop those themes."

I started to tell him some of the things I did to plan work. I also mentioned staff appraisals and a few similar things, but I was conscious that I was giving a very unstructured reply, and I was not doing very well on the question of controlling work, as opposed to controlling the cost of resources.

The professor listened at first and then held up his hand. "Let me stop you there," he said with a smile. "I don't think you've had that question before. If someone came round to audit your management capability, they may get the impression that you are not yet ready for a promotion! I think it is worth doing some work on this. What actual measures are used in your work?"

"Well, we have some money measures such as costs, and some activity measures, such as the number of items we have successfully configured and delivered. There are also some overall customer satisfaction measures, and, as we have direct contact with the customer, those measures are reflective of some of our activity. In addition there are some quality governed processes, so I'm used to the concept of non conformances." I looked at the professor, "Are these the sorts of things you mean?"

"Interesting," said the professor. "There is nothing there that really tells me how well you are really managing, although non conformances may give me a clue. The things that you have mentioned are mostly about results. They don't necessarily tell me how efficient you are at managing your team to produce those results. My impression is that you have not changed your processes that much over the years, and extra work tends to be done in extra time. What I'd like to do is to create, with you, a list of the common things you manage, and then we will set up a scoring system to see how well you do. This process might be useful to you after this meeting, as you develop what we do into a measure about how efficient and effective you are at what you do. So as a manager, let's list out the processes and things you manage. You have mentioned one or two already, so let's put these up on a whiteboard and add to them."

The professor stood up and went to the whiteboard, near the door. We then spent fifteen minutes writing a series of items on the whiteboard. The professor was mostly writing what I put forward. If I seemed to run out of things, he prompted me to consider other areas of management. We then grouped the topics under headings as below:-

	Topic	Examples
1	Communications	Upwards, downwards, sideways, outwards, inwards
2	Managing Co-ordination	Meetings, actions, internal perceptions, consultation
3	Managing Customers	Proposals, expectations, T&Cs, perceptions, feedback
4	Managing Difficulty	Disciplinaries, grievances, equal opportunities, bullying etc.
5	Managing Externally	Community activity, school visits, peer meetings, other visits
6	Managing Finances	Budget reporting, reallocations, predictions, expenses
7	Managing Information	Physical filing, electronic filing, data security, archiving.
8	Managing Innovation	Problem identification, reviews, issues
9	Managing other risks	Hiccup lists, disasters, emergency cover

10	Managing Performance	Objectives, coaching, performance appraisal, motivation
11	Managing Planning	One year plans, milestones, objectives, reporting
12	Managing Projects	Project definitions, responsibility, plans, monitoring, predictions
13	Managing Quality	Process documentation, standards, non-conformances
14	Managing Resources	Time, energy, extra staff,
15	Managing Safety	Safety plans, risks, standards, training, health, housekeeping
16	Managing Security	Area security, security of assets, intellectual property
17	Managing Staff	Roles, job descriptions, recruitment, training, culture
18	Managing Suppliers	Performance, costs, delivery, , reviews
19	Managing the Future	Vision for my section, statement of purpose, monitoring trends
20	Managing Time	Diary controls, working time, holidays, absence
21	Managing Waste	Energy conservation, environmental disposal, recycling
22	Managing Work	Allocation, output planning, work flow, processes, delivery

Once we had done that the professor kept prompting for more, and items kept on coming e.g. Managing Strategy, Managing Legislation, Managing Knowledge and as the professor pointed out some of the above headings could be broken down further. After a while, the professor counted the number of items. There were over seventy.

"This is quite a list," said the professor, "and there are probably a lot more things we could add. We could beneficially put some of the headings together such as managing the future and planning, or managing staff and managing difficulties, but the list makes a key point. Managers are sometimes surprised by how much they have to manage. They rely often on existing well known routines, and help from perhaps a central function. Yet, at the end of the day, they are accountable for dealing with the many items above, *in addition* to their normal operational activity."

"I have a joint responsibility on some of the above," I said, "Someone else is in charge of the routine e.g. performance appraisals. I just have to carry it out."

"That may be so," said the professor, "but there is a lot you have to manage in carrying it out. It is very easy to get the process and outcomes of performance appraisals wrong. However, you make a good point in that your responsibility for a certain function may only go up to a certain level. The next stage in developing what we have done on the whiteboard is to define what we would expect to be happening if someone was doing well in any of these subjects in the context of their organisation. This definition may vary between organisations, precisely for the point you have made. What comes out from our discussion may not be universally applicable."

"Let's take three items from the lists," continued the professor "you have mentioned performance appraisals. How about adding budget monitoring and safety risk assessments."

"OK," I said.

"What we need is some success criteria for each of these three," said the professor. "What do you think would be appropriate?"

The professor asked me to write down any items I wanted from the whiteboard and then he cleared an area so we could work on success criteria. After ten minutes, we arrived at the following: --

Item Managed	Success Criteria
Performance Appraisals	Staff are notified well in advance of dates and content. Evidence of preparation exists. All parties report that the appraisal was professionally done. Agreed actions are actioned by agreed dates and any paperwork is sent to where it should be by the deadline.
Budget Monitoring	The Manager can demonstrate bottom up budgeting and has well ordered paperwork showing budget compilation. The manager can quote the budget position at the end of every month, any significant accruals, and give a reasonable projection for the outcome at the end of the period.
Safety Assessments	All required risk assessments have been completed. They are readily available for inspection. There is a record of staff awareness and training. There are processes practised for ensuring that assessments are still valid.

"That seems reasonable," I said, "I suspect that my organisation would tweak it a bit. Now we have done this, I can fully understand that if someone left doing their appraisals to the last moment, then their time would be disrupted just before the deadline. This will cause them to lose some respect from their staff, and they might not do themselves any good from a central department viewpoint. However, there are some other management areas where I am unsure what the success criteria could be. Some of the relationship areas, for instance, and perhaps my management activity on equal opportunities. How can I deal with these?"

"You must see your boss, or your HR Department," said the professor, "and get them to define what they believe are success criteria for you. I believe that you are seeing Professor Richmond tomorrow, and he may be able to give you some help in determining how to work out what is expected of you in a relationship. The next step is for you to complete success criteria against each of the other things we have already identified in the list of what you manage. The actual process of doing it will make you think about what your management responsibilities really are. This is a project for you to take away."

"Does all of this really matter?" I asked the professor. "Most managers muddle through somehow."

"That is the point," said the professor, "They muddle through, and, in the muddling through, some of them make classic errors that either waste an enormous amount of time, or lose staff motivation. If you know what is expected of you, as a manager, you are more likely to deliver it. Once you have the proper routines in place, you will be saving yourself considerable time and, I would add, considerable stress. What I want to do now is to score each of the three items we identified by how well they are being managed. The score is to be based on evidence. This is an important point. If there is no evidence of any management, the score must be zero. At the other end of the scale, if you are managing an activity at an excellent level, I would expect that you will have the evidence of good delivery, with all of the procedures formalised, and a quality routine in place that enables you to get feedback and generate even better results in the future. To achieve this level three, or more, cycles of this activity should have taken place, so it is certain that excellence is being maintained. I usually score this level four points."

"What about the scores in between," I asked.

"I would define these as follows," said the professor. He proceeded to write out definitions on the whiteboard as follows: –

Score	Criteria for scoring
0	No evidence of any management, or meeting of the success criteria.

1	An ad hoc approach is taken when something happens, in a reactive way, or something existed in the past but there is little formalisation, planning, or other management activity in the present.
2	There is some management and process formalisation and 50% of any description is delivered. There is evidence of an emerging and systematic approach.
3	There is good formalisation with most procedures well known and well understood with a minimum of 75% delivery.
4	Has been carried out well for at least three cycles at a level of 100% delivery with good feedback. There is a quality regime for the process which enables sustainable processes and improvements to continue.

At this point, I looked at my watch as I was concerned that we were going to run out of time. The professor saw me. "Don't worry," he said. "I have allowed a little extra time to cover this sort of subject. It can make a terrific difference when you get down to it. Now how do you think you scored on the items we have done?"

"A mixture of two or three," I said, "I am not always good at making sure things happen from one year to the next. I tend to get paperwork done dead on the deadline. If you had asked me about some of the other items that we brainstormed earlier, I believe I will be offering you a range of scores from zero to four."

"For those items that score four, you probably do not need to take any further action," said the professor. "For those items that score zero or one, it is likely that you need to give them some priority. The simplest way to prioritise them is to give them a letter from A to D, with A being high priority and D meaning that it does not need any attention. B would mean that the item needed some priority and C would mean that it was a low priority item, but still needs some attention. Let's say that you said performance appraisals was a priority B, then we could construct a table like this." He drew the following table on the whiteboard.

Item	Criteria	Score 0-4	Next step	Priority A-D
Performance Appraisals	Staff are notified well in advance of dates and content. The appraisal is seen to be well done and agreed actions are actioned by agreed dates and any paperwork is sent to where it should be by the deadline.	3		B
Budget Monitoring	The Manager can demonstrate bottom up budgeting and has well ordered paperwork showing budget compilation. The manager can quote the budget position at the end of every month, any significant accruals, and give a projection of what the outcome will be at the end of the period.	2		
Safety Assessment	All risk assessments have been completed that should have been. They are readily available for inspection. There is a record of staff awareness and training. There are processes for ensuring that assessments are still valid.	3		

"Notice I have included a column headed 'Next step'. This is to prompt you to think about what you must do to improve your score. What this exercise will tell you," continued the professor, "is whether there are management practices that you could do better. However, there are a couple of other benefits this scoring activity could give you as well. If you have several items in this table, what could you do with the scores?"

"I could add them up," I said, and then with a flash of insight, I recognised I could do more than that. "I could then divide them by the total score possible, and that would give me a percentage figure for how well I am managing. So, for the performance appraisal item above, I scored three out of a possible four. That's 75%. If I took the three items, I would have a total of eight. I would need to divide this by twelve, which is the highest score possible and then multiply by a hundred get a percentage. In this case I would have 67%. If I had fifty items about my management, then I could get an overall figure of how I am doing. Wow!"

"You will find that such an arrangement works well in Microsoft Excel," said the professor. "It will also give you a way of showing your manager how good you are, and what you plan to do. You will have to use this approach in the correct way, otherwise they may feel threatened by you being far better at managing than they are."

The professor looked at me with a wide grin. "Always ask their opinion," he continued, "about how you can do better in defining your success criteria, and working your way to higher scores. Also bear in mind, that when you come to prioritise any particular item, you are conscious of how much time it will take to develop the item, and how much time you will save. You should choose some quick wins first, almost regardless of priority. Firstly, it will make you feel better as your score is going up, and secondly, it will give you more time to improve the rest."

"There will be some items," I said slowly, "where I may not know what to do even though I know what the success criteria mean."

"Good point," said the professor. "The first thing you should do is to ask around the other managers at work to find out what they do. If somebody is already doing something well, find out how they do it, and copy that. If no one is doing anything you can copy, you could always attend some external seminars and talk to the people there about what they would do. It may not be the subject of a seminar, but I'm sure other managers would help you, if you asked them informally, either beforehand or after.

"Thanks," I said. "I can sense this approach will focus me on what needs to be improved and a push in the direction of improving it."

"Exactly," said the professor, "Let me give you one other tip. Once you have set up your measure, you can produce a graph your monthly score. It is important that you put this somewhere where the team can see it. It will involve them in the process. After you have explained what you are trying to achieve, they are likely to work with you to achieve it. Notice that this approach also works well when you have detailed processes. You ask yourself what would be the signs of a detailed process working well and this will give you your success criteria."

I pointed to the set of graphs on the wall beside the professor's desk. "Is that what those are about?" I asked.

"Yes," said the professor. "These were produced by another business executive for his department. He not only looked at the question of whether he was managing well, he also looked at whether particular processes in his department were being done well. He had four major processes and he was able to identify approximately thirty success criteria for two of them and fifty for the other two. He then set about improving them over the course of a year. Those graphs are the results." The professor went over to the pictures and took one off the wall and brought it over to show me the detail. "Notice that there are some months when he was not able to work on improving the processes. That explains the occasional straight line amongst the gradually rising trend. You will notice that he got up to about 70% for all of the processes. That is a good figure. It means that most processes are in good order and he is probably working efficiently in using these processes."

"I wonder what would happen if he got to 100%," I said.

"You may be interested to know," replied the professor, "that, as a result of this work, he got promoted to the position of an improvement consultant within his multinational. He now produces measures with other departments and coaches them to increase their performance. It just goes to show that if you can focus on what needs to be done, and demonstrate your improvements, it is likely to get you noticed in a good way. Not only that, you would be able to improve the use of your own time, and your department's time as you would be improving things that mattered. This could happen to you, perhaps!"

"Thank you, Professor," I said. "I am not sure my score for what I manage is going to be terribly high but I will have a go at producing a measure."

"That's good," said the professor, "I will hold you to that. Write to me in three months time and let me know how you get on."

"Is there a published set of measures like this?" I asked.

"Not yet," he replied, with a smile. "There are certainly common sets of management competencies, but there are quite a lot of variations in what managers actually do. For the time being, I am advocating that interested managers work up their own set of measures. Soon it may be possible to produce something for wider circulation. We will have to leave the subject there, I'm afraid , as our time is up. I will now take you down to reception".

We then engaged in small talk as we went back to reception. It turned out that the professor was considering purchasing a folding bike, with a high gear ratio, to get him up the nearby hill, so he could commute to work. As we got down to the ground floor, the professor commented, "By the way, I have suggested to Professor Holmes that you meet someone else he knows, Jane..." Just then, a student rushed by us both, in rather a rude way. I missed the next bit of his sentence, but I heard him say 'son' and I knew Professor Taylor had given Professor Holmes the same message.

"Thank you," I said.

On arrival at reception, I wished the professor goodbye. He gave me one parting message. "Do not waste any time looking for platform 14, when you get to the station. Get advice if anyone tells you to go there."

I was not too sure of the relevance of this remark. I was leaving a little bit later than planned, so I did not query it.

On departing the university building, I made my way quickly down the hill to the train station. I went the whole way by foot, rather than wait for a ferry. If I was quick enough I would just catch a train going in my direction.

The train left punctually at the due time, heading north, and not, I might add, from platform 14. I had noticed on finding the train that the platform numbering was a bit odd.

On the train, I thought through the list of items that I managed to copy down from the whiteboard. I added several extra items to the list, mostly of an operational nature.

I came to the conclusion that the way you manage broadly fell into three different categories. You could manage badly through incompetence, or laziness. You could manage just about well enough and muddle through, provided your results were OK. Lastly, you could take a proactive approach to managing what you do and begin to manage well. This needed an initial effort, but the return will be a smooth operation. If Professor Sayler is right, and I feel he just may be, I could now work towards a better managed operation that should lead to better control, better results, less stress, and, of course, better use of time.

I got out my action list and added to it as follows:-

	Action List	Time scale
1	Find out how my boss knows I am doing a good job.	1-4 weeks
2	Find out what really pleases or upsets my boss.	1-4 weeks
3	Make a lack of / too much of list and work out avoidance routines.	1-2 months
4	Build a list of all the processes and practices I manage.	1-4 weeks
5	Work out success criteria for all the practices / processes managed.	1-2 months
6	Consult where appropriate on what the success criteria should be.	1-2 months
7	Build up a measure of what I do and measure my performance.	1-3 months
8	Put a plan together to improve my performance.	2-5 months
9	Consider putting individual process measures into a similar format	2-5 months
10	Talk to managers who seem to do well about how they do it.	1-2 months
11	Take advantage of external networks in a focussed way.	Ongoing

The other thing I did, was to get out my laptop and start putting in the structure for a measure on Microsoft Excel. I decided that I'd break management into different categories such as: – managing the future, managing relationships, managing activities, managing resources, managing information and knowledge and put one on each different worksheet within an overall spreadsheet file. I then formed a consolidation table that could pull all the results together. In this way, I could give myself a percentage on the individual categories as well as an overall percentage score. As I did it, I wondered whether in two or three months, I can get to a score that might be higher than my boss. I wondered what she would make of that!

I arrived at my destination station on the outskirts of a major city. A short taxi ride took me to an Inn called 'The Hunter', which was near the top of a reasonably high hill. The light was fading as I arrived, and I noticed that the pub sign, which contained a picture of a hunter, had a light at the top, and then three small lights halfway down the sign, arranged in a short diagonal straight line about 30° to the horizontal.

I told the landlord that I had noticed this, as he showed me up to my bedroom. They are LEDs which line up with possible holes in the Hunters belt he told me. I was not concentrating very hard, and it was only after he had gone downstairs again, that I realised he had told me what the lights were, not why they were there.

I had my supper downstairs in the bar. I asked the landlord whether he had ever experienced looking out of the windows from upstairs and seeing layers of mist in the valleys below.

"Yes," he replied, "There is much less pollution out here compared to the city. You've probably worked out that we are mostly facing away from the city, so we get less light pollution as well. On a good night, you can see M42 from here." At that moment he was called over to another person at the bar. I thought I understood what he meant, by his comment. I was to learn at the end of the week that I was wrong.

As it was getting late, I went upstairs to phone Mary to let her know how I got on. I told her that Professor Soljer was hot on diary routines and checklists, and such an approach would take a lot of discipline. I also said that I felt that Professor Sayler had a good idea about improving management performance, but it would take time to implement it.

"Some of them seem to be giving you some work to do," she

commented, "and some of that work you will have to do on top of your normal work next week. You will have a real challenge when you go back to work about what to do first. You better start planning now. I hope you're making some good notes about what they have all been saying."

"As regards Professor Soljer, he does, by all accounts, succeed in achieving a lot and now you know how he does it. Didn't Professor Sayler say that if someone does something well, you should seek to copy it? You could try out Professor Soljer's approach. Once you're practising it, you may appreciate its value even more and that may convince you that the discipline is worthwhile."

She was right, of course. I guess Professor Soljer had a different way of working to me, and it could be copied.

"Who are you seeing tomorrow?" asked Mary.

"Professor David Richmond is my first professor," I said. "He works in an engineering department"

"That's interesting, if not a bit strange," said Mary. "There is a strange pattern that seems to connect these professors. I won't distract you now just in case I am wrong. I look forward to hearing more tomorrow."

I was left with a mystery. Mary also commented that it would be handy if there was an easy acronym or expression which would bring the key points of each of the professors I had met to life. I replied that I would let my subconscious work on that overnight!

In the meantime, I fleshed out some notes on what the professors had said and pressed ahead with Professor Sayler's measure. I was beginning to feel that I could improve its structure. The interesting thing was that the process of defining standards for managing well was forcing me to think a lot about what I was doing. As a result, I have several ideas on what to do better.

Readers notes:

Mary is beginning to notice a pattern; a more significant pattern than the activity theme you have come across so far.

Did you notice the activity theme was still there with Professor Soljer? The same activity is in the next chapter but more subtly expressed. Will you spot it?

Have you a theory about the pub sign? Can you spot a relationship between this pub and the previous ones John has visited? Why could John's assumption that the landlord was talking about the M42 be incorrect? There are some more clues ahead!

Notice that there is another reference to Jane. Could Jane be the tenth professor? You will have to read further to find out.

You also have a challenge to identify the next city. As a clue, you may find a matador in the city centre!

Chapter 8

Purposefully Engaging

'The SCOPE Test.'

It was a beautiful morning. From the Inn, where I had stayed the night before, I had taken a taxi down to the nearest train station, and from there took a train to the city centre. A lot of the area around the main station had recently been redeveloped. The name of the station had become appropriate once again!

The university was in the south-west part of the city. So, I boarded a local train to get to the nearest station to the university campus. It was a straightforward journey, with many glimpses of a canal that ran in parallel with the rail tracks. This part of the canal system had always been scenic. The canal system is connected to a basin a couple of miles to the North which had recently been completely redeveloped. Canals seem back in fashion!

On arrival at my station, I had a short walk, across a main road, to get into the campus itself. The department I was seeking was on the corner of the campus, and it seemed to have no connection at all with the subject of time management. It was an engineering department and it was there that I had agreed to meet Professor David Richmond. The professor's primary field of interest was micro-engineering, again nothing to do with time management!

Arriving in the department, I headed for the administrative office to tell them about my appointment.

As I started talking to the girl there, a tall middle-aged man, in a sports jacket and tie, initially just standing nearby, walked over to me. "I think you're looking for me," he said. "I am Professor Richmond, John. I am expecting you and am looking forward to our meeting."

We shook hands. The professor continued, "We have about an hour together, so let's find a room and get started. There are a series of tutorial rooms on the first floor and we will use one of those."

As we went up the stairs, I said to him that I thought it interesting that a professor of micro-engineering had an interest in time management.

"I think we all have an interest in time management," he said, "In engineering, we stress to the students that they should not only be clear on the specification of any work they do, but also the function of any object they are designing. Any lack of clarity can involve a tremendous waste of time and cost. Clarity of purpose is really important."

We moved into the tutorial room, which was fitted with a large whiteboard. The professor organised a cup of coffee for me, and we both sat down in a relaxed way across a desk. The professor's first action was to take a copy of Professor Holmes's letter from his jacket pocket.

"It would seem from Richard Holmes's letter that we may have two purposes today," he said. The first is to enable you to understand my views on time management, and the second is to enable you to better practise the management of time in your own circumstances. The overall result of those two activities is to help you evaluate whether what you are learning is useful enough to distribute through some business networks you know. Is that's about right?"

The professor had good eye contact and just lifted his eyebrows as he finished the sentence. I nodded with a smile.

"To get us going, why don't you tell me something about your circumstances," the professor suggested.

I explained to him that I worked in a small department that involved configuring customer's equipment after they had placed an order but before they had taken delivery of our products. I gave him an outline of how we were organised and the pressures, year on year, for more productivity. I also said that I was often under time pressure to meet deadlines.

After about five minutes, the professor changed his posture noticeably and said, "Let me come in here, John. I would like to take the conversation back to the customer. Tell me again, in one sentence, about your relationship to the customer."

"Essentially," I said, "I get the equipment working for the customer so as to meet their order."

"Hmm," said the professor. "From the way you have described your work, it sounds to me like you visit the customer to get agreement to the work you will do. You then return to your company, do another job of work, implement it all, and that's it. So what is important about all of that?"

"It means that the customer will have a working machine, and will therefore pay us," I said.

"Hmm," the professor said again. "Let's try this from a different angle. What is it you enable the customer to do?"

"I enable the customer," I said slowly, "to get a machine that works."

"So far, so good," said the professor. "You enable the customer to get something, but what is it you actually enable the customer *to do*? That is what I am interested in.

"To use our equipment for their particular purposes," I said.

"So, your team enables the company's customers to best use your products. We have so far talked about the customer getting something and now we are talking about the customer using something. What do customers do all this activity for?"

"To produce better designs," I said. The professor looked at me as if he was expecting me to say something else. His conversational manner had been politely assertive rather than aggressive.

"So, where I have got to is this," said the professor, after a delay. "Your team enables the company customers to produce better designs, by configuring the equipment and training the users. Now, what is the purpose of all that activity from your point of view?"

"They will pay us," I said.

"And…?" asked the professor.

"Er," I hesitated, and then with a quick flash of inspiration," …and they will recommend us as a company." Suddenly I felt relieved This must be what he was seeking.

"That sounds fine," said the professor. "If they are going to recommend you, it is most likely that they will be paying you." His voice had changed to being slightly softer. "Recommending you seems to be a higher level of attainment, and a very necessary one in a competitive marketplace. So my final summary of what your team does is as follows. Your team enables the company's customers to produce better designs, by configuring equipment, and training users, in a way that gives rise to a strong recommendation for your company. Does that sound right to you?"

"Yes, it does. It sounds such a simple statement and so obvious, but I have not thought about it in those terms before. It seems more of a mission statement for me."

"I am never too sure about mission statements," said the professor. "In practice there seems to be a number of different ways to construct a mission statement. I'm convinced some of them have absorbed considerable management time, and I am equally convinced some of them have no real value. What I am interested in is what organisations enable their customers to do. That seems to be where the focus should be. If you can get your customers to recommend you for what you enable them to do, then that should bring in more customers, or higher satisfaction levels, or whatever."

"I am beginning to sense that this is about saving time in a more strategic way," I said.

"Maybe," said the professor. "I see it as being purposeful. If you are clear on your purpose, then you will be more effective and save time. Conversely, if you do activities that do not align with your purpose then you are wasting time."

"Just remind me of the process you used to get me to this point?" I asked.

"I simply asked you to define the expression 'my team enables my customers to do something' in a meaningful way" said the professor. "We tweaked it a bit to ensure that it was very clear what you enabled your customers to do, and added something about the way you did it, so the customer would recommend you."

"Does this approach work for other managers, who might not have activities directly with the customer, and does it also work for organisations?" I asked.

"You have two questions there," said the professor. "The basic principle does work for both. Organisations might need some extra help to properly define their customers, and make sure they're doing all that is necessary to conform to the statement they create. Service organisations can do it just as easily as production organisations. For Managers in different functions, I can confirm that operational departments, can usually do it just as well as central departments. My experience is that central departments are less customer focused and more confused about their role, so there is often a great benefit for them to have a go at writing such a statement."

"How will any manager, or department head know they have got it right?" I asked.

"There are a few tests you can apply," said the professor. "If you cannot easily state the sentence in one breath, it is far too long. That test is called the breath test. There is also the ***SCOPE*** test. This does what it says it does and it challenges the scope of the expression. SCOPE is an acronym. Have you a notebook? You may like to write this down." I nodded.

"As a brief summary," said the professor, "***S stands for Simple***. The expression should be simple in nature. If you have a sentence which says *'you enable your customers to do this and that and something else'*, you are either in multiple businesses, or your sentence isn't simple enough, or there is a higher purpose to your work that you have yet to find. ***C stands for customer.*** You do not serve all the customers in the world, so you need to define who they are. In your case, it is very easy. These are customers that your sales people have found and they are a defined group. If you are in a central department you tend to believe that everyone is your customer. In reality, you will have a primary customer, and your activities with the other customers support the work you do with your primary customer. *O stands for ownership*. The challenge here is whether your team, and not some other team, are responsible for doing everything in the statement that has been produced. *P stands for positively expressed.* You enable your customers to do things, not to get things, or just to be happy. It is what you enable them to do that counts. *E stands for easy to understand.* If there is ambiguity in your statement, then there will be confusion, and confusion wastes time. Does all of this make sense?" asked the professor.

"Yes, it does," I said. "I'm really beginning to warm to this idea. You could apply it to just about anything. Take my local garage. They just do routine servicing, although they do sell cars as well. When I collect my car, I get told 'Here it is, Mr. Watson. There are no problems. Your paperwork is in the car. That will be £…' They do not consider going the extra mile to get my recommendation."

"They could," said the professor, "do all sorts of things from giving you more detail on your car, to recommending what to monitor, and checking whether it was easy for you to deliver your car, to offering you a discount voucher to return, or to recommend someone else. They clearly are not determined to get your recommendation and that should be their primary purpose."

"The more I think about it," I said, "the more organisations I can think of that are not customer centric. There are a lot of lost opportunities out there!"

"And probably some very loose notions of purpose in those organisations," said the professor, "…and don't forget, this also could apply to departments within organisations too."

"I would like to learn some more about this at some time," I said.

"Bear in mind," said the professor, "that what you have achieved this morning is a reasonably robust statement. It does not mean that the statement is either right, or wrong. That is a management judgement. What we need to do now is use the statement to help us save time."

"You mean apart from saving time acquiring customers and getting everyone on the same wavelength?" I said with a smile.

"If you have a purpose," continued the professor, smiling as he did so, "there may be things in your organisation that hold you back from achieving that purpose. These 'holdbacks' can be expensive time killers or profit takers. We need to focus on these 'holdbacks' to see if we can do something about them."

"That's interesting," I said. "Do you mean bottlenecks, rather than holdbacks? Releasing bottlenecks is the classic time saver in production."

"It is a pity that other departments in organisations are not trained in the same way ," said the professor. "However, releasing bottlenecks is only part of the answer. Ultimately, we need to deal with blockages, wasted effort, existing 'time sinks' and future time wasters. I would like to offer you a simple approach and test it out on the statement we have developed about your customers."

He went over to the whiteboard and wrote.

1. You enable your customers to define the best configuration that works for them

2. You enable your team to produce that configuration in conjunction with others.

3. You enable your customers to learn how to use that configuration in practice.

"I have written these points based on what you told me earlier," he said. "If you do all of those things well, would that strongly contribute to achieving your overall department purpose?" I nodded.

The professor returned to his seat, turned it to face the whiteboard, and sat down. "All of your current activities in your department should be contributing to those three purposes and the way you carry them out. The logic is that those three contribute to your overall purpose. Therefore most of your activity should contribute to those three. If something doesn't contribute, then it is likely to be a wasteful activity. Don't forget each activity also must contribute in a way that gets a recommendation form your customer. Are you with me so far?"

"Yes, absolutely," I said.

"So," said the professor, "we can test each and all of your activities to see if they contribute. If I was to do that now, I would ask you to write down each of your activities and ask you about the purpose of each activity to make sure that link was solid."

"I seem to waste a lot of time on filling out forms for tax purposes," I said, chuckling as I did so, "as well as doing things for more senior management. Those items do not seem to directly contribute to what I exist to do. I would like to classify those as wasteful activities, but I will not be able to."

"Those items are not in your control," said the professor more soberly, "I should have made that point clear earlier. You are responsible for what is in your control. You can always challenge the purpose of what someone else needs things for, but if they are in control of it, you will have to live with their response. Let's go back to the purposes on the board. For each of the three, we are going to turn the statements into a question."

He got up and walked over to the whiteboard and changed the statements to read as follows: -

1. How can we better enable our customers to define the best configuration that works for them?

2. How can we better produce the defined configuration in conjunction with others?

3. How can we better enable our customers to learn how to use that configuration in practice?

"What I have done is simply add in front of the statement the words 'How can we better...' This turns your statements into challenging questions. Your role as a manager is to find answers to these. You don't have to do it all yourself. You can involve your team. Putting the statements into question form often helps with set up a good brainstorming session. There is one overall thing I would continue to stress though. Whatever ideas you have, they should contribute to the customer recommending you."

"This is like having a question and then testing the answer," I said.

"Precisely," said the professor. "The most important thing you need to achieve is a recommendation from your customer. Shall we do some work on one of the challenges so we can find some areas for time saving."

"OK," I said.

"Let's take the second challenge," said the professor. "This would seem to involve a number of people and that usually indicates there is potential for time-saving. Co-ordination always costs money in the form of time, and this is not usually well controlled."

He cleared an area of the whiteboard and rewrote the second challenge.

How can we better produce the defined configuration in conjunction with others?

He then turned to me, pointing to the question. "Notice that the question contains the expression 'better produce'. Do you know how well you are doing this at the moment?"

"Roughly," I said. "I have no detailed measures, but I know that on average we can do this in three to four days."

"I think you have some further challenges about measurement," said the professor. "It means that we may not know how good the solutions are going to be. The SCOPE test demands that the statement is easy to understand in concrete terms, so we would really want both a better measurement and a better definition of 'others' but we will act with approximations so you get the basic idea. Time to ask you another question. What are the major issues involved in doing the activity in the statement well?"

"There is a issue with workload planning," I said. "There is also a possible problem with the speed at which we work, and there are delays in getting stuff from other departments."

"Fine," said the professor. "We will use those three problems. We are going to put each of those problems into a similar form of question as we have above." He pointed to the whiteboard again, and then started writing underneath the last question, the following sentences: --

1. *How can we better plan the workload?*

2. *How can we increase the speed at which the team works?*

3. *How can we influence other departments to speed up their service to us?*

"Notice that we have not enough definition to satisfy the SCOPE test, so I am taking a short cut today to illustrate the method. The SCOPE test would challenge who is responsible for these challenges and whether their meaning is clear. For instance does the responsibility for number one belong to you, or your team. To move us on without getting into too much detail, let me apply another check on what we have written. If we assume that we can better plan the workload, will that help us better produce a defined configuration?"

"Yes, it would," I said. "I can understand that we may have to define what we mean by 'better produce', but these statements do, at least, mean we can produce what we do slightly quicker."

"And would the same be true for increasing our speed of working, and influencing other departments to speed up their service?"

"Yes," I said. "I also like the way you have written the last question. We cannot make other departments do things, we can only influence them to do what we want. That influence is in our control. If we had written that last statement as 'How can other departments speed up their service to us?', then we are trying to solve a problem which does not belong to us. I am now beginning to understand the need for the SCOPE test. You have used it here to illustrate what part of the problem we own. I guess it would also help us define what we have just done more precisely and and give more meaning to words like *better*."

"That's exactly right," said the professor. "Problems that are well defined are usually easier to solve. A major learning point for organisations is to have a common way of defining problems. Here, we have used a particular approach to turn a problem into a challenging question for people to solve. Whilst we are talking about solving things, let me share with you a solution to your last challenge that somebody else discovered. They also had problems with other departments. In the end they decided to make the due date very clear for when they wanted to receive what they needed, and measured on each occasion how late the response was. This was then displayed in that department alongside their other departmental measures. It had the desired effect. Deliveries improved. It was probably going a step too far, and simply going to the other department's head with the measure might have been good enough. Depending on the circumstances and culture, even letting the other department know that something is being measured might have had a positive effect. There may be other solutions that would work for you in your situation. However, you will notice that, as we have defined the real nature of the problems, I am starting to offer you solutions. This is one of the benefits of this approach. Turning problems into questions leads people to think of appropriate solutions."

"Those are good ideas," I said. "I am going to let it be known that we will be measuring when work come back to us."

"Let's go back to your three statements," said the professor. Given what we have just done, I suggest we examine your second challenge

How can we increase the speed at which the team works?

"It struck me from what you have already said that there may be an element of planning that will contribute, but there may also be a number of other issues. Can you give me an idea of what they may be?"

"Part of the problem," I said, "is that I have to live with the company's flexitime arrangement which applies to all the non professionals. It means that outside the core time, I am not too sure who will be around, and for how long. I also have a member of staff who is a little slow, and another who is a bit inflexible."

"It would seem that you have a dilemma here," said the professor, "From what you have said, the challenges that spin-off the one we've just considered are: –

1. *How can I ensure my staff are here when I need them?*

2. *How can I influence or help my slow person to speed up?*

3. How can I increase another's willingness to help out with other work?

"You will notice the question starts with 'How can I'. I have changed responsibility for these challenges to you alone. You will probably need to talk to your HR Department, and the individuals concerned, in order to resolve these questions. I would say the dilemma is whether you take the problem as your problem, or whether you give the team the higher challenge of delivering faster to see if they can work out the underlying problems and solutions for themselves. I think that is the route I would take. At the very least, the team would become more aware that there is a problem here that needs resolving and the slower person can appreciate they have a major role to play in the solution. I believe that discussing it with HR in advance might be a good idea. You could then be more certain of your ground if you had to take action. What do you think?"

"I think you are really helping me face up to my problems," I said, "I am also going to follow your suggestion on this last issue. This has been a really good way to get down to the nitty-gritty. Just take me through the steps again, so I can apply it in other areas. It seems what you did first is work out my overall purpose and then the core activities I do to achieve them. I then had to put them into the form of a question. What happened next?"

"Having worked with you to define the main activities, we turned them into a challenging question, I then simply asked you what were the issues in responding to the question. When we find an issue we simply turn it into another question and examine the issues involved in responding to that. We keep on going until we can find a question that we can deal with." said the professor. "Issues can be bottlenecks, or holdbacks, or 'time sinks' in disguise. If you can resolve an issue, then work should flow more easily and, in theory there should be more time available to complete all the other work.

"I am impressed," I said. "Bringing out the issues is a good way to face up to problems and achieve our purpose better. I like the fact that once you had identified the major issues, you broke them down into further smaller challenges we could address. That seems a powerful part of the process.

"You are beginning to understand the full process," said the professor. "You can form a map of the challenges you break down from other challenges. It means you can work right down to the core of a problem. Have you noticed this process could be used at a team meeting? I have been using it with you as an individual. It is quite possible to use it with teams if you have a good facilitator, a whiteboard, ...and an eraser! There are many other potential applications here. The process helps teams achieve clarity of purpose, and the team can delegate ownership of smaller challenge questions to individual members of the team."

"It is beginning to blow my mind," I said. "However, let me take you back a step. There is one question I would like to ask you," I said, "Could I have started from a question which simply said 'How can I save time?'"

"Not really," said the professor. "That question is very ambiguous. It would fail the SCOPE test as not easy to understand. You would have to be more specific. For instance, you could have a question that read 'How can I save time in dealing with e-mails?' That is much more focused and that's what you need to be. I think there is one other thing you should know about, before we draw to a close," he added.

"There's more!" I said.

"Yes, quite a lot, but I'm going to get you to do the work. You will remember that we started from an expression about what your team enabled your customers to do. As some organisations will tell you, everyone you deal with is a customer. Some people may not be your primary customer, but they may help you serve your primary customer. These secondary customers include the other departments you work with, any external stakeholders or regulators, and any suppliers. There are also two other categories of customer that are very important to you personally. Your staff are customers of you, and your boss is a customer of you. I therefore have two other questions for you to work on, so you can find answers that fit your circumstances. And these are '*What do you enable your boss to do?*' and '*What do you enable your staff to do?*' There is more than one answer to each of those questions. So the best way to approach them is to construct a form like this."

The professor sketched out a table on the whiteboard.

What do I enable my boss to do?	How do I know I am doing it well?
Answer 1	
Answer 2	
Answer 3	
Etc.	

"You can use a similar tabulation for the second question. I should tell you that I would expect you to come up with a least twenty answers. Do you understand the second column?"

"To do something well, I have to take an action," I said. "I guess that I need to identify what actions I should be taking, and then doing them. If I do them to the standard that has been set, then I know I am doing something well."

"Maybe," said the professor. "What you have identified is one third of the story. If you are enabling somebody else to do something, you only have real success if they can do it. You would also want to do it in a way that they appreciate. The bottom line is that you will have to ask them about whether you have helped them, whether that help worked, and what they thought of the experience. You must be careful of presumptions as well. You may believe that your role is to enable your boss to do certain things, but is that what they want? You need to be certain. This would involve a discussion. It could also be the case that you have missed something out that you should be doing, which is another good reason for a discussion. Have I given you enough to make some progress?"

"I think so," I said, "You have certainly given me some inspiring ideas, and practical techniques. I still think I might need more help as I work them through."

"Have a go and see how far you get," said the professor. "If you have a mentor, why not go through the process with them. Alternatively, if you want to learn more, you can come back and see me again. Your starting point, though, is to review, and then extend these ideas as far as you can. Personal energy put into thinking these ideas through will help you appreciate the technique, and will undoubtedly help you form other questions for a further meeting."

"I think you've got enough to take things forward for now. You should be able to identify your time consuming issues. You have had a lot to take in and I think we are coming to a natural close. Lets make our way back to reception."

I gathered my notes, put them in a folder in my airline shoulder bag and we made our way back to reception. I thanked him very much for showing me such brilliant ideas in such a short space of time. I indicated that I would like to talk to him again sometime.

We said goodbye in the reception area and I made my way to the door. As I was heading to the door, I noticed a blown up picture of a set of bicycle gears. Interesting, I thought.

I had a mixture of feelings as I walked to the local station. I was excited as I had acquired a mission and a major technique. The professor had directly helped me face up to a couple of challenges and given me some direction on how to improve how I deal with my boss, and my staff. All of this was inspirational. My slight worry was that it would take some practice to master the technique.

Mary could probably help me. I decided that I would ask her for help with the boss and subordinate relationship exercise. Between us we could make a list of possible things we enabled our respective bosses to do and then I would could use that as a starting point for a discussion with my boss.

I took the local train back to the mainline station. I then connected to my next train, which was heading North. I decided that I ought to improve my notes from the last session, so I could properly brief Mary later that day. 'How can I brief her in the best possible way,' I thought. And then I thought, what does that mean? The SCOPE test would seem to have some value. So I changed my approach to 'What could I enable Mary to do with my briefing?'

Mary wanted to learn what I was learning. I therefore had two aims. By enabling Mary to understand Professor Richmond's process, she will be able to give me her thoughts. So what might the issues be in enabling Mary to understand Professor Richmond's process?

I would have to communicate the process in a clear and logical order, so my challenge became 'How can I communicate to Mary what I have learnt clearly and logically?' I would have to give Mary the context so she could understand the professor's comments. So my challenge became 'How could I demonstrate the process in a context understood by Mary?' I also had to get over a wide set of applications without overloading her. So was the challenge 'How could I enable Mary to appreciate all the possibilities of this process?' Then I used the check that Professor Richmond used. If I could do each of these well would that enable Mary to understand Professor Richmond's process. Clearly yes!

Usually, I would just have unconsciously described the events as they happened and my interpretation of those events. This process was making me think about Mary as a recipient of my briefing. That is quite a useful process. True, you do not need it for trivial matters, but if you are doing something of a more important nature for someone else, it would seem to have a strong value. If you can enable your customer, in all senses of the word, to say they understand something well, you can reduce confusion, save your future time, and probably save them time as well!

This is interesting. I decided I would work on this later. It was more important to do my action list and make some notes on this journey before I got to the next city.

My action list now includes:-.

	Action List	Time scale
1	Practice defining customer oriented missions for other contexts.	Ongoing
2	Review my major activities contributing to my mission.	0-1 week
3	Form an extended issues list.	0-1 week
4	Turn each issue into a proper challenge using the SCOPE test.	0-1 week
5	Seek solutions to the challenge in a way that involves the team.	Ongoing
6	Make a list of departmental activities and check they can be related to my mission.	1-2 months
7	Adopt the challenge approach in meetings.	As appropriate
8	Get feedback when I enable somebody to do something.	As appropriate
9	Work out and agree what I enable my boss to do.	1-4 weeks
10	Work out what I enable my staff to do and consult them.	1-2 months

Readers notes:

Did you notice the indirect reference to the underlying activity theme?

Are you keeping track of the academic expertise of each professor?

Are you ready for another intriguing pub? There is one in the next chapter? First you have to work out the city where the action happens with the next professor. Think of a barber, banker, fireman and some pouring rain?

Chapter 9

Choices to Change

'Swanning Around.'

There was very little time to get to the next university. I literally had to keep my fingers crossed that the train would not be late and I would be able to get quickly from the station to the University. My arrival time was particularly important as Professor Jean Perman had indicated that we should allow an hour and a half for the meeting.

The train slowed through a cutting just before reaching the station. So there was time to get well-prepared for a quick exit. Thankfully the train arrived on time.

The station itself was like a smaller version of St Pancras in London. It had one unusual feature. There were two statues within the station. Some would say that these were statues of two comedians. One was certainly a comedian, who was instantly recognizable. The other is a local politician who was by all accounts quite a character.

I had arrived at a city of culture, with an imaginatively named airport. The city is famous for two tunnels. Strangely, it is also picking up an increasing reputation for its association with the sea. It was becoming a stopping point for cruise ships and is expecting the number of visits to significantly increase over the next few years. The city was also home to the a command centre in the Battle of the Atlantic in the Second World War. Across the estuary from this city is another city where the last U-boat sunk in the war now resides. This has only been recovered recently and there is a real story in how it was transported to its new resting place, which is shorter than the length of the U-boat. This meant that the U-boat had to be cut into sections and how this was done is a story in its own right.

The Time Advantage

How do I know all of this? It just happens that I know someone who does know all of this!

On this occasion, I would not be able to explore the city. The university was not far away and the directions to it were clear in my journey details. I started walking briskly, and after a short while the reddish University tower appeared as a landmark to head towards.

Professor Perman has an interesting background. She is a nuclear physicist. Her interest in time management arose when she was teaching students. She was concerned that her students should be able to handle organisational life as well as being good scientists. Her first steps were to consult the School of Management and introduce a series of modules on project management, project finance, report writing, and presentation skills. She then took an interest in what technical managers actually did in organisations. This involved her in a series of investigations with the School for Management. Along the way, she discovered that some managers made far better use of their time than others and that many of them could do better if they were prepared to change existing ways of working. This led her to devise a coaching strategy which was then improved through a number of further projects at the School for Management. Some of this work she fed back into her student modules. She is still, first and foremost, a nuclear physicist, although she now has a strong capability to help managers achieve more. I was looking forward to meeting her. She was meeting me at the School of Management, which had a large number of students.

When I arrived the ground floor near the administrative office was pretty crowded with students coming and going. The administrative office told me to go straight up to the fourth floor and they pointed me in the direction of the lift. I eventually made my way, unaccompanied up to the correct floor. I expected to step out of the lift to be met by someone. So I stepped out, looked in both directions, and my heart sank. There was no one there!

A door opened further up the corridor. A woman's head popped round the door. "Hello, have you come to see Professor Perman?"

"Yes," I said, very much relieved.

"This way, please," said the woman, as she vanished inside.

I walked to the door, and into a fairly small room, with plenty of daylight. It contained a table and four chairs.

"Hello, I am Sylvie. I am Professor Perman's assistant," said the woman, "She will be meeting you in a few minutes. Would you like some coffee?"

I nodded. "Black, please, with no sugar."

Sylvie poured the coffee and put it on the table. "The professor would like you to do something before you meet with her," she said. She passed me three sheets of paper. "Don't worry – it is just some basic forms to prepare you for your meeting. Professor Perman will be along in a few minutes." Sylvie then left the room.

I sat down and looked at the three sheets of paper. All were similar in layout. I studied the top document, which contained questions about time preferences.

(See following diagram)

Subject:-- *Time Preferences*
No   Part A – Questions
1   *What sort of work do you like doing?*
2   *What sort of work don't you like doing?*
3   *What sort of work do you do most efficiently?*
4   *What sort of work do you do inefficiently?*
5   *What sort of work do you find easy?*
6   *What sort of work do you find difficult?*
7   *What sort of work makes you feel uncomfortable?*
8   *When is the best time for you to have meetings or to concentrate?*
Q1   What do your responses above tell you about your approach?
Q2   Is there any scope for improvement?
Part B – Follow through
Your *First* Resolution
First Step to success
Second step to success
The Pain of no change
The Benefits if you succeed
Your Personal Reward
Your *Second* Resolution
First Step to success
Second step to success
The Pain of no change
The Benefits if you succeed
Your Personal Reward

I formed some answers to my mind, but was not too sure what to do with them. Part B on the form looked interesting, but I was not sure how to use it. As I was thinking about this, Professor Jean Perman entered. She was a tall assured lady, with a longish face and short greying hair. I got up to shake her hand.

"Good afternoon John," she said, with a smile as she shook my hand, "Did you have a good journey?"

"Yes," I said, "The train took the strain and I walked up from the station."

"The weather should remain dry if you are thinking of walking back. It has been a bit wet around these parts recently. I got soaked on my bicycle the other day. Now, I hope you can stay with us for at least the next hour and a half. I believe I can interest you in a number of points about how to manage time better."

She sat down opposite me. "Time management, as you will know, embraces a large number of different issues. There are micro techniques and macro techniques. Micro techniques could be about how to take messages. Macro techniques can be about systems for the effective use of resources in the longer term. There are a wide range of techniques about which cover such items as planning, meetings, decision making, dealing with information, and importantly, dealing with relationships. However, these are all about techniques. They are not about the person carrying out the technique and it's the person that I am interested in. How someone thinks about their job, or elements within it, or even themselves, can have a distinct impact on their ability to manage time efficiently. What I have developed, as a secondary interest to what I do at the university, is a series of coaching forms that can help managers identify issues related to how they manage time. This includes not only time at work, but also time that is sacrificed for work from an individuals own time."

The professor pointed to the papers that Sylvie had handed to me. "I have ten of these forms altogether, but that is far too many to do in one session. What I propose to do is run through three of them and draw out, not only some personal issues for you to think about, but also to show you a process for bringing about change. This process you can use for other things apart from time management." She looked at me. "Are you OK with this approach to the afternoon?"

I smiled. "Let's go for it"

"First of all," she said, "let me explain the structure of the forms that we will be running through. They are pretty similar. Each one is designed to aid a discussion about different feelings, and thoughts you might have on the way you currently manage your time. I would stress the phrase 'aid a discussion', as I am not seeking detailed answers to the questions only broad ways of discovering what could be done better. If we find there is a need to do something better, then we can use the second part of the form."

"That second part looks interesting," I said. "I was surprised that you ask people to think of a second success step in completing the form. You also use the word 'pain' in relation to allowing the present situation to continue, which feels a bit extreme. I did like the word 'reward' though. Is there anything else you can tell me about the process here, before we begin?"

"There are certainly some reasons for using those expressions," said the professor. "I ask people to think of a second success step, as it forces them to think through what they are going to do. Experience suggests that people find it very easy to agree with something, and then not do very much about it. By thinking about the step beyond the first step, it somehow makes it easier to take the first step. We also use the pain and pleasure motivation factors. If you can think of the pain that any inefficiency causes you, then you are likely to be motivated to do something different to ease the pain. If you get a personal reward, as well as the company getting a benefit, then it is easier to move towards a different way of doing things. Breaking habits is not very easy. Think of this process as a way of forming good reasons to move away from one way of doing things, towards another way.

"I notice there is room on the form for a second resolution," I said. "Are there normally two resolutions?"

The professor smiled. "The number will vary between one and four when you first run through the questions. We don't want to focus on any more than that as it will dilute the resolutions you have already made. The reason why there are two on the form is to prompt you think about whether there is one or not. It avoids the issue of feeling you have completed the section, just by finding one resolution to put into practice. OK, shall we discuss your time preferences now? Would you like to tell me what you think of the questions on the first sheet?"

"I guess my first interest is in the structure of the questions," I said, looking at the form. "There seem to be three pairs, 'like' versus 'don't like', 'efficient' versus 'inefficient', 'easy' versus 'difficult', plus a couple of oddities. Can you tell me why you ask these questions?"

"It is really to get you talking, and help you analyse what you do," she said. "If you can find a pattern in why you like things, and why you don't like things, you may find a better way of handling them. If it turns out you like certain things, there is a danger that you will do more of them at the expense of those you don't like. This might lead you to think about segmenting how you spend your time in a stricter way, or doing the things you don't like first, so you can then spend more time on the things you do like. The efficiency question is quite interesting. As an example, you may be very good with your maths, or typing, and you can get through that sort of work very quickly. If the opposite is true, there may be some training on typing, or the need to give somebody else the maths, or set up a spreadsheet, that might help you. The work that is too easy might lead you to make errors with it. Work that is difficult might be put off. Any work that feels uncomfortable is almost certain to be put off!

"What about the last question about when I do things?" I asked.

"The question of when you do things is interesting in its own right," replied the professor. "Your body clock may have something to do with it. You may be a morning person, or an evening person. Your staff morning people, or evening people. Generally speaking, people feel they can do more challenging tasks in the morning, and more repetitive tasks in the afternoon. Does that apply to you? Does it apply to your staff? Should you think about when you do certain work together? Those are some of the issues that could come up. Do the questions now make more sense?"

"Very much," I said. "I understand now that they are the general structure which will bring out some key points for discussion. I would like to do this review of the questions for the other two forms. I find that once I understand something, then I am very happy to work with it, even on my own."

"We will do what time permits," said the professor. "Normally, in the time we have, we will go through two sheets and I would ask you to take away the rest and come back at another time. In your case, we are not going to be able to do that, so what you have suggested is very sensible. We will do the first sheet in detail though to find at least one resolution, so you can appreciate what the follow through process can do. We might skip looking for a second resolution, if we are to talk about finding at least one resolution for the other two sheets. So, thinking about your context, and perhaps thinking about what you were doing a fortnight ago, take me through a week telling me what some of your thoughts might be around the questions we have on the Time Preferences document."

I did just that. It did take a little time. There were some things that I identified, where she commented that there might be other solutions. She did offer a few alternative solutions for me to consider, but mostly she asked me to note areas for discussion with my staff, or other managers. I had to admit that it was proving quite a useful exercise. At some stages, I did not feel comfortable admitting that I was not very good at something, but as the professor was independent, I felt I could do that, and I also felt I could ask for help.

After about twenty minutes, we seemed to come to a natural conclusion on the first page. The professor summarised some of the things that had come out. There were some minor things which were very easy to action. There were some things where I had expressed an interest in more knowledge, such as body time clocks, and I agreed to read up on them separately. She encouraged me to look at voice dictation seriously, as it did seem I was both inefficient, and bored, by having to do a chunk of typing. We also hit upon what to me was a major problem, although it was not that difficult for everyone else, or perhaps anyone else!

"The fact that you do not like doing your monthly expenses, is a very strong point that has come out of this," said the professor, "Look at the questions at the end of part A. What is the message that radiates out, about your inability to get these done on time?"

Expenses were a bugbear for me. I used to lose the odd receipt, and that would hold me up. I would fully acknowledge that a lot of people do them smoothly, but they might have a bugbear with some other trivial matter. In my case, there always seemed to be something more important to do, so I got that done first. I would slip a few days from the due date and then it didn't seem to matter if I slipped another day. It did matter though when I had to go to the boss to ask her to sign very late expenses – some of which perhaps should have been declared in the accounts for the previous period. I used to feel guilty about it, but that feeling used to lead to putting them off further or not claiming what I was entitled to. It sounds pathetic, but it is an issue.

"The message must be that I'm not well organised," I said in a quiet voice.

"I think there is also message to yourself that you regard your work as more important than you are. You may serve others, but you will be less able to do that if you do not look after yourself. You could also be destroying any promotion prospects, where you can use your talents to make a better contribution to the company. You would want to make a better contribution, wouldn't you?"

I didn't like this forced question, but I had to agree with it. "Yes," I said, somewhat meekly.

"So what are your options?" asked the professor.

"To carry on as I am, or make a change," I said.

"And thinking of how you might make the change, what are your options then?"

"I suppose I could schedule some time," I said.

"That does not sound very resolute," she said. "When is the ideal time to do your expenses?"

"The end of every week is the logical time."

"If this is an option, you could schedule ten minutes first thing on a Friday morning every week, to keep your expenses up to date. If you miss it one week, for a good reason, you know you have the time schedule set for the next week. Maybe you believe you would find it more efficient to do all your expenses in one go, but it isn't working. This is an important point. It does not matter if it works for anyone else. It does not work for you and that means that you will need to approach the task in a different way. What we have discussed is simply an alternative approach."

"It's not a bad one," I commented. "It is much better than giving my expenses to somebody else to complete on my behalf. That would just seem to be exploiting them. I would not be happy with that. It would also distract them from the other things I want them to do. I accept it is better than scheduling in just one block of time at the end of the month, which I probably would not do anyway. Yes, I could do them once a week on a Friday morning as my first activity!"

"I think we have a resolution from you," said the professor, "to do your expenses every week, first thing on a Friday morning. Is that right?"

"Yes. I put that in the resolution box on the form, do I?"

"Absolutely. Now what are the first two steps you have to take to achieve success?"

"Well, the first is to put a recurring entry in my diary. The second step would be to get an expense's folder set up, that I could easily get out of my desk every Friday morning. If I marked it "Friday first thing – expenses" on the folder, seeing that would remind me what I have to do."

"If you didn't do both those things, what would be the pain you will experience."

"I think it would be the usual pain that I have already discussed," I said.

"Let's find a way of making the pain, more painful," she said, "If I put a note in my diary to give you a ring in three weeks time, would you want the embarrassment of telling me you have not done anything about it?"

"I think you have found your pain point," I said.

"So what is the benefit of making this change?"

"My boss will not notice that I am disorganised. I do not have the fear of accounts ticking me off for missing the last pay period. The company gets to know its books are in order. I get paid my expenses quicker."

"Some of those points are pretty negative," she replied. "For instance, you say your boss will not notice, and you may no longer have the fear of talking to your accounts department. Let's turn those negatives into something positive. If you make a change, would not your boss notice that positively? If she misses the fact that the expenses are now in on time, you can tell her how you feel having adopted a new way of doing expenses, and then ask her whether it is working out better from her perspective. Your accounts department will save some time if they don't have to chase you, won't they? And you will personally note that by succeeding in doing your expenses you have made a positive change and broken a bad habit."

"Yes. You are right," I said. "Putting everything into the positive is much more motivational."

"And if you get this new habit going, how are you going to reward yourself?" asked the professor.

"I guess it has to be something special," I said. "Perhaps something I would not ordinarily buy, or do. I think I might get a fridge magnet. At the very least, it will be a constant reminder that I achieved a change of habit and, if it was a funny one, it might give me some amusement as well. I could afford that as I will now have claimed all my expenses."

"Excellent," she said. "You can now complete part B for the first set of questions and we can move on to the second set of questions. I am going to skip searching with you to find whether there is a second resolution, but I would like you to review the document afterwards and see whether a second resolution occurs to you."

The professor then asked me to look at the form on Time Boundaries. I scanned it to remind myself of the questions.

"I promised to let you know some of the reasoning behind the questions," said the professor.

Subject:-- *Work Time Boundaries*	
No	**Part A - Questions**
1	*What time do you get to work in the morning and why that time?*
2	*What time to leave in the evening and why that time?*
3	*What do you do over lunch with regard to work?*
4	*What happens when you go out of the office for a few days?*
5	*What happens before you go on holiday?*
6	*When is your prime time for thinking about work?*
7	*What happens when your staff go on holiday?*
8	*What other events at work impact on your own time?*
Q1	What do your responses above tell you about your approach?
Q2	Is there any scope for improvement?
Part B – Follow through	
Your *First* Resolution	
First Step to success	
Second step to success	
The Pain of no change	
The Benefits if you succeed	
Your Personal Reward	
Your *Second* Resolution	
First Step to success	
Second step to success	
The Pain of no change	
The Benefits if you succeed	
Your Personal Reward	

"The basic assumption is that work and personal activities should be reasonably well separated. If work invades your personal time, you get very limited personal time. If personal time invades work, you are likely to fail to perform. The trick of course is to strike a good balance. More junior staff can often do this with ease. For managers and professionals, it is much more challenging. The questions are designed to gather some facts, and ask you about your motivation. If what you do seems out of balance, then it is your motivation we discuss. So let me now hear your views about time boundaries."

This turned out to be another lengthy discussion. There was a distinct pattern about when I went to work, and when I left work. There was also a lot of stress in the week before going on holiday, when I felt I had to deliver a number of things, delegate other things, and generally plan for my absence. It was these items that the professor picked up on at the end of discussion.

"So to summarise," said the professor. "You go into work early, before most of your staff arrive, so you can get organised for the day and monitor their arrival time. You leave later than most of your staff, as you like talking to some of your peer group in the evening, and it is quiet enough for you to concentrate on a few things as well. The end result is that you work far longer hours than your staff at both ends of the day. We also established that there was little incentive for you to go home earlier, as you currently live on your own. As a separate point, we established that your last week before you went on a holiday could be extremely stressful, as was the first week you came back from holiday. What does all this tell you?"

"That I have chosen a lifestyle that is very work oriented and I must do something better before going on holiday," I ventured.

"I hear a resolution," said the professor, "to do something about your holidays and we will work with that in a moment. I am a little concerned that you are burning the candle at both ends. I think it is perfectly understandable that you would want to get in early to sort out the day. I can appreciate that the end of the day is quieter and you may like talking to some of your peer group. My challenge would be that you could schedule quiet time work during the day and you could decide to have a chat with your peer group at lunchtime, rather than continuing to work through lunch, which is what you appear to do. My general feeling is that you should go home a little earlier, and have a routine to do at home before relaxing into the evening. What do you make of that?"

"I am not organised for that," I said. "I fear that some work would not get done, and I would be caught out, in some way or other. I am also not sure what my colleagues would think if I was to suddenly make a dramatic change."

"I know one thing about you that might be relevant," said the professor. "You want to be better at time management. If you were to go home earlier, would that not be a sign that you were better at time management? Could you not use some of the time you gain to go out to a movie, an evening class, or some other activity, that you do not currently do?"

"I suppose so," I said. "I have not really thought about it. I think going out every night would not be what I would want to do."

"From the tone of your voice, I suspect there is something holding you back here," said the professor. "Our time together does not allow us to explore this further, but maybe you can commit to a simpler step. How about going home earlier on two occasions a week, with one of those occasions being the Friday? How does that sound?"

"I think that would work," I said, more positively. I realised I did not want to ruin the relationship that I had with some of my colleagues. If I made the two days that I would go home earlier regular days, so they knew when I was around and, if I was to show that I was able to do this because a more effective working practices, that would seem to be a good thing. The professor could see I was thinking it through. I looked at her. "Done!" I said positively.

"We now have to work the magic with two resolutions," said the professor. "I'm going to let you work on your holiday resolution by yourself, but I will give you this tip. You should plan as if you are going away for a longer period, starting the week before you actually go away. By the Friday of that earlier week, you should have a complete plan in place for the next few weeks. This would include arrangements for somebody to deal with items whilst you are away. You may not be able to make use of that, but it is an option and there are probably others you could consider.

Consider your options, resolve to do one of them, and then complete the form. I will ask whether you got the form completed, in three weeks time! For now, I would like to concentrate on your working time. Resolutions should always be specific. Tell me what time you leave now, and what time you will leave in the future."

I chose 6 pm. as a new leaving time. This can be between half an hour, to an hour earlier than I would normally leave.

"So, what are your options for putting your new resolution into practice?" asked the professor.

"I don't think there are many options. It seems quite straightforward to do," I said. "I simply need to make people aware that I am going at that time. So I guess this is the first step to success. I then need to make sure that I do go. I suspect the second step to success is to set a reminder, perhaps on my mobile phone for a quarter of an hour before my leave time. That gives me time to clear up, and beat the target."

"Excellent," said the professor. "What is the pain of continuing as you are if you do not make this change?"

"The pain will be that I will have to admit that I cannot make a simple change stick, and you will no doubt ask me how I'm getting on in three weeks time!"

"And I will," said the professor. "That was fine. And now, what is the benefit of making the change?"

"I can demonstrate that I am managing my time better. I can still talk to my colleagues on other days of the week at the later times. I get more time on the Friday evening, and, possibly, one other evening during the week."

"How are you going to use that extra time?" asked the professor. "This will not work unless we can make the gain more attractive for you."

"I could get my shopping done on Friday, rather than on the weekend, particularly DIY and gardening bits and pieces. That would mean I will actually do some of these odd jobs, rather than leave it to a haphazard arrangement, as at present. I guess, I could use the other evening, when I save an hour, to do the planning for this."

"It might also be useful to consider an evening course as well," said the professor. "Do something totally different from work. Perhaps a physical activity?" She looked at me with a smile. "Now, how are you going to reward yourself for achieving this change?"

"If I accomplish something, say, the completion of an odd job, I can look at it, and remember, with a sense of satisfaction, that I accomplished it during extra time I created for myself. I think that will be sufficient reward for me."

"I think you have enough now to complete Part B for that resolution. You have gone through a couple of very personal experiences so far. Other people may have different issues. The main thing to recognise is you are going through a process of identifying them and committing to actions that should conquer them. Are you getting the idea of how this process works?"

"I think so," I said. "We used the questions, in a general way, to discover whether there are any issues of concern. If there are, and if it is worth improving the situation, we seek to form a very specific resolution. We consider the options for putting it into practice, and then follow through the questions on the form."

"Excellent," she said. "We use that approach for all the sheets I have on time management. If you can, you should discuss the questions on these sheets with somebody else. They will firstly, help you explore the subject thoroughly and secondly, if you make a resolution, they will seek to help you achieve it, and remind you of it from time to time. If you do it by yourself, you will have to be very strong willed. Are you happy to now move on to the third form which is about Time Attitudes?"

"Yes, that's fine," I said, "Is this about habits again?" I smiled.

"To a certain extent," she said. "It is more about the motivation that drives the habit. Some motivations lead to time destructive habits."

Subject:-- *Time Attitudes*	

No	Part A - Questions
1	*What time do you normally arrive for other people's meetings?*
2	*What time do you arrive for your own meetings?*
3	*How much time do you allow for travel problems?*
4	*How do you value the alternatives to travelling to meet someone?*
5	*What tasks do you treat as having particularly high importance?*
6	*What are you like with deadlines?*
7	*How easy is it for you to get started on your major tasks?*
8	*How would you rate out of a hundred your preparation for events?*
Q1	What do your responses above tell you about your approach?
Q2	Is there any scope for improvement?

Part B – Follow through
Your *First* Resolution
First Step to success
Second step to success
The Pain of no change
The Benefits if you succeed
Your Personal Reward

Your *Second* Resolution
First Step to success
Second step to success
The Pain of no change
The Benefits if you succeed
Your Personal Reward

"Let's look at the first question," said the professor "When do you normally arrive for your company meetings?"

"Normally, I arrive dead on time," I replied.

"So if someone catches you on the way, you could be late?"

"Not by much, only two or three minutes. I would simply say to the person who caught me that I will see them later."

"So, that person may be disappointed they have not been able to tell you the nature of the problem as you are pressing to get to the meeting. What's more, the chairman of the meeting might be upset that you are late."

"Company meetings do not normally start on time," I said. "Not everyone turns up on time. Even when they do, some will have forgotten papers, others will not have read them. It usually takes a few minutes for a meeting to get going after we have got together. If I am a moment or two late, then it does not usually matter."

"There is clearly a corporate problem here," said the professor, "as well as a motivation in you to arrive at the meeting, at the point that you do. The corporate problem can be addressed by costing the wasted time and perhaps bringing pressure to bear on a number of meeting chairpersons. The subject is the meat and drink of many time management books, so I do not intend to repeat it all today, when information is readily available externally. What I want to concentrate on is your motivation for arriving just in time. Why do you do that?"

"I am normally working on something else right up to the moment that I have to go," I said. "This allows me to maximise my productivity. It is not only my motivation, but also my responsibility." I felt I was challenging the professor here and I wondered what she would say.

"You choose to arrive dead on time, or perhaps a fraction late," she said. "I suspect that the impression given to others is that you are busy, if not a bit rushed off your feet. Arriving dead on time, means to you, I suspect, that you want to be seen to be busy. If you are to be a leader, and someone who is good at time management, what other impressions can be important to give to the participants in a meeting."

"I guess, it is important to be seen to be taking the meeting seriously and to be seen to be on top of the subject that is about to be discussed," I replied. "This would mean I need to be seen to be prepared."

"Do you attend these meetings at work, so you can influence the outcome of the meeting," asked the professor.

"Generally speaking, yes," I said, "although some meetings are purely one-way information traffic."

"Is it useful to talk to some of the others, before a meeting starts, on what is important to them, about a subject that is important to you? This will allow you to influence everyone in the right way from your point of view?"

"Well, yes,"

"Do I hear a resolution coming?" asked the professor.

"Yes," I said. "My resolution is to read the papers and be at the meeting five minutes early fully prepared, so I can ask the early arrivals what they think. I'm not too sure that would make the meeting start any earlier."

"Maybe not," said the professor, "but you can be an exemplar for how meetings should be conducted for any meetings that you organise. If there are no corporate protocols, you could ask your boss whether any are being developed, as you want to develop your own. Your boss may not have even thought about the subject, but if they are any good, they may think it a good idea that some corporate protocols are set. They may raise this at a higher level. You can also, with tact, raise the question at the appropriate meetings. If no one says anything, then everything is going to continue just as it is. So you now have a resolution. Can you finish off the rest of the process for me?"

"My first step is to put some time in my diary for preparing for the meeting. Funnily enough that is exactly what Professor Soljer does. My second step is to decide, before I attend a meeting, who I want to influence. The pain of continuing, as I have been, is that I will know I am not doing myself any favours. It is more of a 'guilt' pain. The benefit is that I'll have more impact in meetings, which may help my career. How am I doing?"

"Pretty well," said the professor. "You're getting to know the process now. The company will also benefit from your better contributions to meetings. We have one resolution already. I wonder if there is a second one of a similar nature. Tell me about those times when you have to get to external meetings. How have you treated those in the past?"

"I tend to allow the average time of the journey, so I more or less arrive when expected. If I find myself running a little late, I can usually make a few minutes up on the journey. It is very unusual for me to be the first person there, if the meeting involves other people from other companies. It is more usual for me to be one of the last. I'm beginning to think now that this is not sending the right signals."

"I suspect that on the times you are late," said the professor, "you are also giving yourself unnecessary stress and creating higher risks. It may not put you in a good mood to start the meeting. You also miss the opportunity of obtaining market intelligence, or benchmarking on matters not to do with the meeting. Is there another resolution here?"

"Yes," I said, "From henceforth, I resolve to add quarter of an hour to all my regular journey times. My fist step to success is telling my staff the reason for an earlier departure. The second about setting a reminder to go early. The pain of continuing as I'm doing at the moment is the stress involved, the potential for an accident and the lost opportunity to talk to others. The benefit is the opportunity to do some benchmarking. The company will gain as we will have more market intelligence, or knowledge of business and management processes."

"You have made a resolution come alive," said the professor, "although remember to be specific about your actions steps. For instance if you plan to do something, you should set a date for when you will have accomplished it."

I nodded in understanding.

"Now, next question, what tasks do you treat as having particularly high importance?" she asked.

"Anything from a customer, or my boss. Those things tend to get done immediately."

"Regardless of their priority," asked the professor.

"Regardless of their priority," I repeated in a resigned voice.

"Customers are important," said the professor, "but not everything they want is a priority. A good tip is to agree with them when they would be happy to receive whatever it is. As long as you have an agreement, which you can deliver upon with certainty, that may give you a better way to proceed."

"And bosses?" I asked.

"Bosses are important too. Managers tell me that bosses ask for things without actually saying why they want them. Sometimes it could be a priority, sometimes not." I nodded. "You can always ask your boss, if you feel that their task would be very disruptive to do immediately, whether you can fit it into a specific time slot after another specific event, or activity. The boss can tell you whether their request is more important or not. So much depends on the relationship you have with your boss as to how you discuss things. It is certain that if you drop everything for any request, then you will not be as time efficient as you could be. This may sound like common sense, but for many common sense is not common practice. I could ask you to do the process again right now on this direct subject of priorities. However, I think it will be more beneficial if you were to review the process on your journey away from here. It will help cement the learning you have achieved in the last couple of hours"

I looked at my watch. Time had flown by. She had given me more of her time than planned. I guess a lot of time was spent on the earlier discussions on time preferences. It had been a long session.

"We ought to draw this meeting to a close now," said the professor. "Have you got any questions for me, before I take you back to the lift?"

"We seem to have spent a lot of time on three documents," I said. "I suspect I would have more resolutions if we had spent even more time on those three. However, you did say that these are part of a set of documents. What are the other documents all about?"

"Discussing these issues does take time," said the professor. "The benefit comes from putting in place the resolutions you identify. You have several resolutions now and they will give you a decent payback. As for the other documents, they cover issues such as Time Aids, Time Pressures, Time Overflows, Time Controls, Time Sharing, Time Direction, Time Routines. There is a little overlap between some of them, but they all have a part to play in improving time management.

"I wouldn't mind having a set like that," I said. "Would you be happy to let me have one?"

"I will do a deal with you," said the professor. "You will have enough to do on your first couple of weeks back to work, and you have still got your resolutions from this meeting to achieve. When you can convince me that you have achieved them, and after you have reflected on what you've learnt today, you still believe that these documents can help you, then I will make a set available to you."

"Thanks," I said.

"Time to go," said the professor, and she proceeded to stand up.

I got up rather stiffly, put the papers in my airline shoulder bag, and moved with the professor to the lift. We shook hands. As she did so, she said, "You have been examining what you should be doing within the context of your job this afternoon. I think there is someone else that you ought to meet, apart from the usual crowd."

"You don't happen to mean Jane and her son," I said speculatively.

She hesitated, as if she had not heard me correctly. "Yes," she said.

"Two of the other professors have mentioned Jane, and I believe they have contacted Richard Holmes," I said.

"I will let Richard know that I support that," she said.

The lift arrived at our floor. I turned and entered, and, as the doors closed, I waved goodbye to Jean Perman.

I walked briskly back to the station as I needed to take a train to get me most of the way to another Northern university. This was a day of significant travelling!

Choices to Change

The train journey took just over an hour, once I had boarded. I was feeling fairly shattered. I mentally reviewed the process that I had learnt from Professor Perman and decided what I wanted to do about interruptions to my work, together with the steps of pain and pleasure.

I had almost forgotten Professor Richmond's work. I got out my notes and added to the forms that he had shown me about enabling my boss and staff to do things. One thing I wrote down under the heading for my boss was that I enabled her to be aware of my work capacity at any moment.

Then I thought about Mary's question. What have I learnt from this afternoon? The positive learning was that I had a checklist of questions that could focus anyone into talking about how they use certain elements of their time, and I had a process for working out what to do about any resolutions made.

As I thought about this, I remembered that Jean Perman had talked about this being a process with wider applications. I understood that now. For any decision made about anything, whether by an individual, or by a group, then the process could help with implementation. It was also a change mechanism in its own right. In a sense, I have gained two major pieces of learning during the afternoon. One was about time management and the other about implementation processes.

I got out my action list. What I was going to put on it personally applied to me and would not apply to everyone. That was the essence of Professor Perman's approach. She concentrated on the person. My personal action list turned out as below:-

	Action List	Time scale
1	Complete the exercise on holiday preparation.	1-3 weeks
2	Work on my expenses resolution.	1-3 weeks
3	Work on my going home earlier on two days.	0-2 weeks
4	Work on my meetings attendance resolution and notify staff.	Immediate
5	Review whether there are any further resolutions.	0-2 weeks

6	Completely memorise the resolution change process.	Immediate
7	Apply to all appropriate decisions.	Ongoing
8	Persuade Professor Perman to give me the extra sheets.	3-4 weeks

When the train arrived at my station, I took a taxi an Inn called the Swan, which was about five miles outside the city that I was due to visit the next day. It was just before 7.30 pm

The landlord was a chatty man. I learnt that the Inn had recently changed its name from the Northern Cross to the Swan, that business was flat, and that there was one other person staying at the Inn apart from me.

I settled into my room, and called Mary. I gave her a briefing on what had occurred and what I thought I had learnt from both Professor Richmond and Professor Perman.

"I like Professor Richmond's idea of forming questions," said Mary. "Those sort of questions are very powerful in getting attention and involvement. It tends to prove that the word is mightier than the sword."

"Don't you mean that the pen is mightier than the sword?" I said.

"I stand corrected," said Mary. "No I don't. The word came first. Don't you remember from the Bible." She adopted a slow and deep toned voice. "In the beginning was the Word, and the Word....."

"Was shortly followed by a question mark," I interjected.

"Well, that explains years of religious scepticism," said Mary returning to her normal voice. "You did start this journey looking for answers."

"The answers are coming," I said. I told her that every professor had given me work to do. If my original objective was to find techniques to save me time, I was in fact finding techniques that needed an investment in time before I would get a payback. This might take a long time.

"Considering it as an investment is not a bad idea," said Mary. "You are having to invest in breaking habits. Think how you will be when you already have some of the good habits that you are learning. You may not have to learn those particular ones again. They could serve you for your entire career. I think what you're learning John, would seem to be very valuable. And from what you have told me so far, each professor has given you something special. I would say that Professor Richmond has giving you a fantastic way to be more purposeful, to deal with issues and engage people. Professor Taylor has given you a way to set and radiate your values. Professor Soljer has given you a way to plan, even if you don't use all of what he said. Professor Tinker has told you how to leverage some of the tools you need. Professor Sayler has given you a way to monitor what you do in a way that you can demonstrate where you are and raise your game. That's all pretty good I would say."

"Well, yes," I said. "You didn't mention Professor Perman and she has undoubtedly added something, although it was mostly about me in particular, apart from her process."

"What she has actually given you as well," said Mary, "is an insight into human nature regarding habits and motivations, and a way of breaking those in order to do something better. Think how you can use the technique to help others. I think she's giving you a very special gift."

Mary had done it again. She had taken a different view, formed a bigger picture, and then asked me to take action in thinking about it in relation to other people.

"John, are you still there?" asked Mary.

"Yes. Sorry I was thinking about what you have just said," I replied. "I guess I'm feeling a little tired."

"You have had a double session with Jean Perman this afternoon," said Mary, "and it is likely that you are feeling tired because you are learning so much. The fact that you are learning so much, would seem a clear indication that you have a lot of potential to improve upon what you do. Why not give yourself a rest this evening and let your subconscious organise itself for you?"

"Good idea," I said.

"Oh. There is one other thing," said Mary, "I believe I can sense an incredible connection between these professors. Who are you seeing tomorrow?

"I think it is a Professor Bergamon and Professor Thieffer."

Mary laughed. "There is a connection between the professors. See if you can work it out before you come back to London."

The telephone call came to an end and I said goodbye to Mary.

Half an hour later, I made my way down to the bar, and ordered a snack and a pint. The chatty landlord introduced me to the other guest, who was also staying just one night.

It turned out that he was a specialist in bio-robotics. This was to do with controlling robotic arms or machinery, using a variety of biological triggers from the body and brain. These included small muscle movements, activity in the brain itself, or changing composition in the air coming out of your lungs. Fascinating stuff!

He was a bit of a boffin, and he kept on quoting Latin names, which I did not understand.

"Steady," I said to him. "I don't know much Latin. Neither do I know very much about what is inside the brain, or the body, apart from the usual things like heart, liver etc."

"OK," he said, and then proceeded to tell me more about the robot instead, again in technical terms. Apparently he was nearing the end of a beta test of some impressive equipment. I got him to explain to me just what a beta test was all about.

"It is a final opportunity to get the errors out of the equipment, before it is commercialised," he said, "You can normally tell whether something has been properly beta tested, or not. Just look at the nature of the errors."

"This would be a bit difficult to do with an art form, wouldn't it?" I commented, in a jokey way.

Somehow, the subject moved on to beautiful paintings and the landlord came and joined us. "What do you think of my new pub sign?" he asked.

I had noticed it on the way in. It was a picture of a big swan, with its rear wings slightly raised, as it swam near a river bank. There was another swan in the background actually on the bank. I commented that I thought it look fine. My colleague said that the Latin for swan was cygnus. I'm not sure why he said that. Possibly just showing off his knowledge.

"But did you see the other side of the sign?" asked the landlord. I had to admit I had not. "Go and have a look," he suggested.

So we went outside and looked up at the sign. There was enough indirect light to make out the pictures. Sure enough, on one side, was a swan on the river with another swan on the bank. We walked round to the other side of the sign, and, lo and behold, there was a picture of a swan on the bank with a swan on the river in the background. It was almost as if the picture had been reversed.

"Two swans and two different angles," I said out loud.

My colleague was on a completely different track. He was trying to think what the plural of swan was in Latin. If the singular was cygnus, was the plural cygni? He then spotted a couple of discrepancies between the two pictures, and pointed them out to me. "It should be a beta version then," he commented. He then scratched his head, and, after a pause, said "Beta Cygni. How appropriate. Now that is beautiful."

I had no idea what he was talking about. At least, not then. My response was to suggest that we went back inside and tell the landlord that we have spotted what he wanted us to spot, and that it was a clever idea, although, personally, I did not think it would do anything for his custom.

Somehow, we got off the subject of robotics and swans, and onto the day's news stories. A couple of pints made these much more interesting!

Readers notes:

Mary is now convinced there is a big connection between the professors. John hasn't spotted it yet. Have you? There are further clues ahead. Have you any theories on how these professors came to know each other?

Have you found the connection between the pubs? An explanation is coming but not just yet.

Have you noticed that the continuing activity theme is still there? Will you spot it in the next chapter?

Note particularly the interchange between Jean Perman and John about Jane.

Are you ready for some fun? You can try one of the next professor's methods at home. She is not based at the university so you may need to do something with the clues given to discover which city she is in. Use the internet if you have no idea or just sit back and enjoy the story as it continues into another set of time management techniques.

Chapter 10
Smiley's Place
'Energy and cats.'

It was Thursday and I started with a slightly thick head. However, a good breakfast with some strong coffee helped to partially clear it. I had an early appointment booked with Professor Anne Bergamon whose area of interest was growing entrepreneurial companies. She had also represented the country in international cycle racing in the past, or so a snapshot of her career on the web had said.

The meeting was not at the University! It was about a mile away from the mainline station on a company's premises.

So it was off in a taxi from the Inn to the local station. Then, a local train to the mainline station. From there, it was another taxi ride to the company.

This was another city that I would not have time to look around. Amongst other things, it has a famous cricket ground. One of my teachers at school came from here. I often remember him quoting 'Beneath the dark arches the river thundered by'. I have no idea where the quote was from. The dark arches were underneath the station. Apart from the river, also underneath the dark arches was a shopping centre which seems to be in decline. This is a surprise in one of the fastest growing cities in the country. If I had the time, I would have gone up to the Civic Hall and looked at the golden owls. A number of people I know raved about them.

I got to the company without any difficulty and I was on time at 9.15 am. Professor Bergamon had indicated she was doing a research project there, and it was where she was spending most of her time.

The company specialised in assembling components to sell on to bigger manufacturers. It was privately owned, and, as I found out later, employed about a hundred people.

The reception was brightly coloured, and the receptionist was bright and breezy too. It also had a professional feel. I was given a health and safety card, properly signed in, asked not to take photographs, or use laser devices, and offered a cup of coffee, which I declined. The receptionist then called Professor Bergamon.

It is always interesting sitting in a company reception. You get to know a lot about a company from the interactions between staff members and the receptionist. It was all very cheerful.

In many places, there seemed to be little thought given to what a visitor would notice, when sitting on the visitor seats. Here, it was noticeable that the company had won some awards recently for quality and innovation. There was also some material on the visitor's table about staff enjoying themselves raising money for charity and about sports successes of staff teams. I had the overall impression that this was a very active company and, probably, a good place to work. It made me think about the reception at my own company. The word 'perceptions' crossed my mind. I had never really thought before about the impact of our own reception on visitors. It occurred to me we could do a lot better.

A lady came through the far door and walked towards the reception desk.

"Thank you, Lucy," she said cheerily to the receptionist, and then looking at me, "You must be John Watson. I am pleased to meet you. Anne Bergamon is my name. We have a room booked on the other side of the building. Let's go and find it!"

She led me through a door, and then into a corridor, which had glass partitions from waist high to the ceiling. Through these I could see an open office on one side and a product assembly area on the other. First impressions count for a lot. Both sides were busy. I had the overall impression that people were moving quickly, and putting energy into their work.

We stopped by a coffee machine. The professor said she was going to have one and asked whether I would like one. This time I said I would. We talked a little about my journey as the coffee was prepared.

"What is it you are actually doing here?" I asked.

"It is a form of employee engagement," she said. "The managing director is keen to increase flexibility and productivity. As work flow is not smooth, in most departments, he wants to create a situation where employees would willingly go and ask other departments for extra help if they needed it, or alternatively, if the employees had spare capacity, they could pro-actively offer to help other departments that might be busier. He also felt that people were not committed to doing the best they can. They were only interested in doing things at a steady pace."

"There seems to be a lot of activity now," I remarked. "What have you done?"

"It is what the staff have done that is impressive," she said. "They were asked what they felt about the company and what would be the characteristics of the place they would like to work in. We gave them some help in bringing out their thoughts and wishes, and also provided some tools and training, to change the culture. Our approach was somewhat novel, but there are good early results. I am interested in how self-perpetuating it can be. We are doing this as consultancy for this company. If it works, I am hoping to put the rigour of some academic approaches together."

By this time, we had moved into a pleasant meeting room with plenty of natural daylight. It had a solid central table, surrounded by eight comfortable chairs. She beckoned me to sit at one end and took an adjacent seat. I could not help but see, as I looked down the table, a large cardboard cartoon smiley, standing vertically on a cupboard, beyond the chair at the far end of the room. Underneath the smiley were two words, which I could not quite read.

The professor noticed my gaze. "The words underneath are 'Match me'," she said. "It is one of the techniques we use to create a bit of fun. Fun has the purpose of breaking down barriers. See if you can match the expression on the smiley."

I tried. It was a virtually impossible grin. I made two attempts, and then started laughing.

"It seems to have worked with you," said the professor. "Imagine doing this with some of your colleagues. The fun element tends to be magnified, especially if there is a camera present. It puts everyone in a good mood and ready to engage in some joint working. If you go around some of the desks and workstations here, you will find a whole range of smileys, which you have to match."

"What about negative smileys?" I asked.

"We asked the staff how we should deal with someone putting up a negative smiley," replied the professor. "We got a clear response that negative smileys should be banned, unless someone needed help. Now, if someone does put a negative smiley by a workstation, everyone goes and asks what they can do to help that person. It has been an interesting way to increase flexibility. I am not sure it would work for every company, but it seems to work here."

"What about a mass protest about management? Everyone could put up a negative smiley." I said, half conscious that I was taking a negative approach to smileys, but I felt that this sort of situation could realistically occur in a cynical workplace.

"I have not seen any yet. It is of course a possibility. The management here have taken the view that they would go round asking everyone their ideas for the first step to getting out of the situation in a way that is practical. We will have to wait and see how that works. Communication, of some form, is probably the only real answer in such a situation. Your question has brought out a more general principle though. The more effort you put into purposeful communications, whether up, down or sideways, the more you are likely to create understanding. The more there is understanding of what needs to be done, the easier it is to get energy applied to it, whether it is meeting a positive or a negative challenge.

"I don't disagree with your logic, professor," I said, "yet most staff complain in most of the organisations I know that communication is poor. Is there a way of getting it right?"

"The first thing I do, with any organisations," said the professor, "is to check the communication practices, as any subsequent work I do in the organisation depends on a good communications approach by the management. I think that there is a possible law of internal communications that says if top management don't feel driven to communicate, then organisational momentum will be low. The next thing I check is what the expectations are of how people should use their time. That sets the base line of our work. Talking of time, let's talk about what you came to find out rather than what we are doing for this organisation. It may be that some of what we have done here will be of use to you, but lets fond out. I understand from Richard Holmes that you are interested in my views on time management, and also you are seeking some particular help for your own situation. Shall I give you a headline on my views and then I can work out, based on what you tell me, whether other things I know may be of use to you?"

"Yes, please carry on," I said.

"There is one word that summarises my general approach," she said. "That word is 'momentum'. What I seek to do is increase organisational momentum. I suspect, from your school days, you will know that momentum is defined as mass multiplied by velocity. In organisational terms, I treat the 'mass' as capability. I define 'velocity' as motivation in the desired direction. Are you OK so far?"

"So far so good," I said, "Organisation momentum is dependent on two components – capability and motivation."

"Not quite," said the professor. "There are three components. Velocity is measured as speed in a given direction. So motivation and capability also have to be exercised in a given direction. The third component is that direction. It is tremendously important for an organisation to be clear on its purpose as that sets the direction. It is also important for staff at every level to be clear on their individual purposes and direction. Without that, energy and time will be wasted."

"So you are interested," I summarised, "in increasing capability and motivation in the right direction. Doesn't that just mean," I added with a smile, "that you put emphasis on training people and give them an occasional teamwork exercise such as the smiley game?"

Thankfully, the professor realised I was joking. "I like a challenging student," she said.

"There are two sorts of training," she went on. "There is training that brings you up to standard competence in a job. This would cover such things as induction, process training, safety training etc. Then there is very specific training to boost capability within the job role. This is about helping employees to learn from what they do today so they could contribute more tomorrow. The specific training might include confidence building, meeting participation, problem solving, process reviewing etc. The training can be generically styled and interlaced with individual coaching. I'm not talking about long-term development here, as in management development. I'm talking about staff development. This is about increasing staff capability, so they can contribute more. It is also about embedding what they do learn into the culture and future activities of the organisation."

"Do you mean you are creating a learning organisation?" I asked.

"Yes. The aim is to create a specific type of learning organisation," replied the professor. "This is not a learning organisation which has 'free for all' external courses. Any external spending on training must be completely related to the greater capability to contribute towards the job."

"I think I have got it," I said. "This is all about learning how to improve one's personal ability to learn on the job, to contribute to the company as a whole, to participate in problem solving and to help embed learning into the organisation."

"Good," said the professor. "Notice that we get productivity payback fairly quickly as we tackle head on such things as how meetings should be run and what common problem solving processes exist. One of my frequent sayings is 'Participation gives you solutions'. Organisations are often inefficient in how they handle participation. The fundamental point here though is learning. Staff need to learn from what they do. Managers need to help them do it and have a responsibility to create a team culture of applied learning." She looked at me firmly. "How would you create a team culture of learning in your own department?"

I paused. There was appraisal process which was related to learning. We are also expected to do coaching. There was no formal emphasis on learning. We never use the term 'contributing more'. We tended to talk about increasing performance. We didn't do very much on soft skills training. My boss thought it was a waste of time. But there was a point here. If you could train staff to more comfortably express themselves, to participate more, to understand and use common problem-solving processes, to improve processes, there was a gain to be made.

"Apart from coaching arrangements, there is nothing I formally do," I replied. "I can understand the value of such training. I had not thought at all about a team culture of learning. What should I be considering?"

"What does a learning culture do?" asked the professor.

"It encourages learning," I said.

"What else?"

"It rewards learning," I suggested, "and creates a climate for learning."

"Can you work out what you, as a manager, should be doing to make this happen?" said the professor. "Think of Professor Taylor."

I paused. The professor kept quiet. She was not going to do the thinking for me. Several seconds ticked by. Cultures are set by managers, I thought, so manager's actions are important. What actions should I then take to be perceived as supportive of learning?

Got it. "I could talk about the importance of learning, and praise those who learn and implement change based on that learning," I said.

"And......," said the professor.

Oh dear! "I'm stuck," I said.

"You have several options," said the professor. "You can talk about how important learning has been to you. You can ask such questions as 'What have we learnt?', 'How can we retain what we have learnt?'. You can draw out from others what they have learnt. You can collect together some learning resources in one place. You can encourage reading by asking about someone's views of a relevant article from a magazine. You can express confidence in other people's ability to learn. There is plenty you can do. It just takes a bit of leadership. All of this appropriately done, can not only increase people's focus on what they are doing, it can also help them to suggest improvements and create learning resources themselves for the organisation. So to summarise where we are. We have been talking about staff capability, and ways to increase it by doing some specific skill training and creating a team culture of learning. This will put up the capability side of the formula for organisational momentum. You are likely to do more, more quickly, if you have people who are more capable. Doing things faster, of course, saves time. OK so far?"

"Understood," I said. "Think not just about your own capability, think about the capability of the team."

"That very nicely leads us to considering raising the energy of individuals and teams," said the professor. "I am still on the theme of momentum and we now need to increase the speed of activity. Where is the starting point for this do you think?"

"I bet the answer is something to do with the manager," I said.

"The manager is responsible for the culture of the team and communications within the culture," said the professor. "The manager is also the leader of the team. How they personally interact with the team will have a major effect on energy levels. In order to create energy, the manager needs to generate some enthusiasm for what needs to occur. This means the manager also has to have personal energy so they can transfer some of that to the team."

"I am not sure that you are going to persuade many managers to be enthusiastic about the paperwork they have to do?" I commented.

"They can be enthusiastic about what it feels like to have completed it, and they can be enthusiastic about what happens next," she said. "I sense, though, that you are not convinced yet. Would that be true?"

"I am convinced that if you can get the staff enthused about doing things, they will work hard at it. I am not totally convinced on how you can achieve this practically. One of the things Professor Taylor said was that you need to make the staff aware that time is important and managers need to think how they can be an exemplar of being organised so the staff know you are serious about using time wisely. That much I understand. I guess, I have not got the bit about how to generate energy. There must be something about motivation here, but I'm not sure what. I am also a bit concerned that as most managers are fairly serious, it is impractical for them to be continuously enthusiastic. Managers often have to do some serious things!"

"Good," said the professor, "This gives us a positive area to discuss, over the next half an hour. Maybe we can find something that might be of value to you. Do not expect that what I'm about to share with you is going to achieve the ultimate enthusiastic switched on manager! Let's go back to basics. You have accepted that when you can get people slightly more enthused, they are more likely to achieve more?" I nodded. "A precondition to achieving more is that the manager can describe, in a very real way, what they want and what they don't want. It would have to be done, in such a way, that there is no doubt that the employees will recognize that they have produced the right thing, in the right way. Where possible, a visual description of the end result should be given. Alongside this description the employee should be given the purpose, and use of, what they are about to deliver, and the importance of that use. Are you OK so far?"

"Yes," I replied, "You have to get over precisely what you want, and the purpose of it, as well as mentioning what you don't want. That is slightly different from how I currently do things. I think I'm fairly precise on what I want but I don't always say why I want it or what not to do. That is a bit of learning that I will take away from here. I suspect this is the direction component of your momentum theme"

"Well recognised," said the professor. "A student of mine developed a routine that may be of value to you. He mentioned what he wanted, why he wanted it, discussed the importance of the work, then mentioned what he didn't want, and lastly came back to mention, in detail, what he wanted again. He felt it important that he mentioned twice what he did want, firstly so it was clear, secondly so someone could think of a question between the first time of mentioning it and the second, and thirdly as what he wanted was the last thing said so people would remember it more clearly. Is that of any value to you?"

"Yes," I replied, "it is another item I could put in my armoury. For some people I could just get them to summarise back to me what I wanted, but for those that don't listen too well the above strategy is a good one."

"Good reply," said the professor, "Let's assume you have done something like that. I am going to share with you some techniques related to how people go about doing tasks. Firstly they have to get started. Then they have to keep moving on what they have to do, and finally they need to feel they will be recognised for what they achieve. Now talking about your own way of doing things, how do you get yourself started, if you have some work to do that you do not find very exciting."

"I have to be honest," I said. "If it was not very exciting, I would tend to put it off until I had to do it. I suppose, a better solution would be to put some time aside for it."

"I have had a number of people say the same," said the professor. "Yet when the scheduled time comes, the reality seems to be that they spend time looking for something else more interesting to do, rather than getting down to the boring job. Time scheduling is not the complete answer."

"Is this about breaking the task into smaller bits," I asked.

"Partly," she said, "That is a very good technique for teams and I will come back to it. This is more about making a start.

"Have you noticed that if you can start something, you can normally continue with it? It is getting started that really matters. Let's apply a technique to something really trivial. I would like you to pretend that you have to complete a report which involves getting a number of files out of a filing cabinet. To complete the report, what is the first thing you do?"

"Get the files from the filing cabinet," I said, thinking this was too easy.

"And what is the first thing you have to do to get the files from the filing cabinet?"

"Open up the filing cabinet."

"And what is the first thing you have to do to open up the filing cabinet?"

"Decide which files I need to go and get?"

"And what is the first thing you have to do, to decide which files to go and get?"

"Open up the uncompleted report."

"And what is the first thing you have to do to open up the uncompleted report."

"Reach forward and pull it to me."

"Can you do that?" said the professor with a smile. "It is easy, isn't it? By working backwards, as we have just done, you get to a very trivial action that is very easy to take. In many cases, it is as simple as moving forward in a chair to get up, or picking up the phone, or checking your inbox. Just by taking a simple action, it propels you to the next action. It is a very simple technique. I use it myself, and so do most of the people I know who have heard about it."

"I am sure that is going to be useful to me as well, both as a team technique and a personal technique," I said. "When lethargy strikes in a team meeting, I can simply break a task down to something that is very easy to do in the here and now. Are there any similar techniques to get a team moving?"

"Yes there are," said the professor, "You will have to decide whether they fit your circumstances. Let me give you a metaphor that might help. This is a variant to the general idea of milestones. Compare a team activity to a train journey. If you take a train journey, you will have a destination in mind. So the first thing to do with your team is to talk about the destination and how important it is. You will also need to explain why you are leaving your existing place to get to this new destination. This brings us back to descriptions of why we want to move away from something, and move towards something else. It may be that a project requires you to leave behind something such as old skills, or old ways of doing things. Leaving things behind may also be important to talk about. Build this in to how you talk about the project you are jointly undertaking."

"This is very similar to asking people to do some work for you as we have previously discussed," I said, "The difference here, is that you are putting more emphasis on what you might leave behind, and you are using words to indicate that you might be on a journey."

"That's right." said the professor. "Your next step is to then outline the

The Time Advantage

stations along the route. The stations represent points at which you know you have achieved a specific outcome. Unlike milestones, you take a moment at a station to consider what you have left behind and to take stock of what you are moving towards. If the journey has required effort, you may want to celebrate at the station before moving on. There is a generic approach to representing stations that can be helpful. It involves creating a horizontal bar chart of the journey. I call this a progress line. It is like a Gantt chart that you would use in project management, but much simpler and designed for a more general mix of staff. What you do is split the journey into ten or twelve different stations. You make the first three stations really easy to achieve, in order to encourage participation. You also make the last two points really easy to achieve so that the work gets properly completed. The hard work is in the middle. However, once you have started the work and got going, then it is easier to continue through the middle of the journey. What it looks like, is something like this." She started drawing on a piece of paper.

Progress	1	2	3	4	5	6	7	8	9	10	11	12

	Station	*Defined in terms of the task*
1	Outcome well defined	
2	Everyone consulted	
3	Plan agreed and documented	
4	Resources acquired	
5	30% complete	
6	50% complete	
7	70% complete	
8	90% complete	
9	100% completed	
10	Customers views sought	
11	Final activities	
12	Records and review complete	

"Notice you can define what the various stations mean. So for instance, 30% could include a number of specific activities that would have been completed. You have probably noticed that this approach also forces you to plan and review what you do. A key point is Station three where you have a documented plan. You should make sure every member of the team brings this outline of the stations to every meeting on the task. Perhaps have a ring binder issued to everyone so they can keep any relevant papers in it. The best bit of this approach for me, is what you do when you have arrived at a station. If everyone in the team has a copy of the progress line, they can shade off the station that has been reached. This simple process can create an enormous amount of team satisfaction, when everyone does the shading together."

"That sounds like a cue for a celebration," I said. "However, in practice I may have several such journeys taking place. How do I deal with that?"

"Progress lines can be pooled together for all the tasks," said the professor. She started drawing on another piece of paper.

Progress	1	2	3	4	5	6	7	8	9	10	11	12
Task 1	▓	▓	▓	▓	▓							
Task 2	▓	▓	▓									
Task 3	▓	▓	▓	▓	▓							
Task 4	▓	▓	▓	▓	▓	▓	▓					

"Just looking at that," I said, "I could write dates for achievement into the unshaded boxes."

"You could do that," said the professor. "Another approach is to simply write the date by which the next station should be reached. This will give more attention to it. You don't always have to put dates in all the unshaded boxes, unless you want to plan your completion date with some precision. Remember we are endeavouring to keep things simple. If you want to run a project management methodology alongside this then that is fine. You can translate achievement back into this format."

"Looking at what you have drawn," I said, "I can see that overall progress is represented by the number of shares that have been shaded. Is it possible to derive a figure that represents how you are doing as a department?"

"Sometimes," said the professor. "You can add up the numbers of stations reached for each journey and divide that figure by the total number of stations possible. If you then multiply this by one hundred, you will have a percentage figure that represents the overall position for all the tasks. The team comes to understand, that to achieve 100%, all the tasks must be moved forward, not just one. There are limitations to this approach. Can you spot what would happen if you included a new task with a new progress line?"

"Ah!" I said. "This introduces more unshaded boxes, so the proportion of shaded boxes goes down and you achieve a lesser percentage. That may then give the impression you are going backwards. I can see the limitation. Is there anyway over this or should I keep all the progress lines separate?"

"There is no easy solution if you are involved with short term tasks," said the professor, "but if you have longer term tasks or annual objectives you can use this approach. Someone I know, grouped tasks by the quarters of the year. So a group of tasks would become known as Q1 tasks, Q2 tasks etc. At the end of every quarter, she would group together all the tasks outstanding from the previous quarter. She used this to calculate an overall percentage figure for the quarter. If a new task came up, it was added to the next quarter's group. If a task was completed, it was taken out of the next quarter's group. This was a way of working that suited her, and her boss with whom she regularly reviewed progress. It may not suit everyone. Would it suit you?"

"I like the idea of being able to quote a percentage level of achievement for my department," I replied. "I also like the idea of keeping things simple and not getting into too much project management methodology. I think it would work for the departments and my own annual objectives. I could use it to show the boss that I had achieved what she wanted me to achieve. She would then have more difficulty disputing my pay rise." I grinned.

"Good luck," said the professor, reflecting my grin. "Now remember what we are discussing. This is a potential motivational tool which gives the team a way to participate together in acknowledging progress. If effort is being put in to achieve the next station or a higher percentage, you should always comment that we are moving forward well. Acknowledge what people have done to reach particular stations, and then look forward to the next station. Make sure you summarise all the steps of the journey you have made up to that point to remind staff that they are achieving good things along the journey. If a particular station has been hard to reach, you could have a team doughnut break, or some similar mini-celebration. Get this right and you achieve motivation and bring more energy to bear on moving forward. This will increase your speed of delivery. It will also save you time in two ways. You will get to the end of your journey quicker, and motivated staff are less time consuming to manage than demotivated staff. Can you sense that we have now covered the three components of organisational momentum. Raise capability, give good direction, create motivation."

"Yes, I can," I said, "but in reality progress is achieved through a few individuals and not the whole team. How do I recognise individual contribution? It is a more general point really, and I know that the normal management mantra is to praise individuals, but I'm not too sure how to do that. Also what do I do about those who do not make a contribution?"

"Let's deal with the non-contributor first." said the professor. "Unfortunately, team leaders are very quick to say that they prefer the non-contributor to be removed. You could, instead, give the non-contributor a chance. Make sure they are aware of what you're moving towards and away from, and why you have to do it. Then tell them what you expect of them in the circumstances. Ask them how you might help them make more of a contribution. Make sure that they have the space to do it e.g. by asking what they think at a meeting, or, what they may like to contribute. If this does not work, then you will have to tell them that you feel they are acting as a passenger, and ask them whether this is what they intend to be. If you want to make the point stronger, tell them it feels like they are a passenger on a tandem, and again do they want to be perceived as that. If that question does not lead you to a solution, then you may have to look at firmer methods through the performance system, or the disciplinary system."

"Just make sure," the professor went on, "you are not personally contributing to the lack of performance. We talked earlier about making things clear, and using metaphors and 'moving' language to move things on. Your language can also have the opposite effect."

"Can you give me an example?" I asked.

"If you said to one of your staff, 'You did a good report, **but** certain parts were not up to standard', your staff member is more likely to remember that you thought certain parts were not up to standard. They would take away a negative. The lesson is to think very carefully about how you might use the word 'but'. People give attention to what follows that word. They tend to forget what went beforehand. A way of dealing with this, would be to replace the word 'but' with the word 'and', then finish off the sentence in a more positive way. So in our example, you could say, 'Overall you did a good report, **and** we can make it better still, by improving a number of key parts.' Obviously it does depend on how good or bad the report really was, and, if it was only slightly away from what you want, then consider this approach.

"I can appreciate that," I said, "When my boss ticks me off, she has a tendency to make it a negative experience. The end result is that I leave her room fed up and I am not able to do anything else until my annoyance has subsided. It seems that there is a genuine message here, that you must tick people off in the right way. However, can we consider the case when someone is genuinely stuck, or perhaps a team is stuck. Have you any tips for what should happen then?"

"There seems to be another secret here," said the professor, "This secret is about using good questions. The whole idea here behind this approach is to keep things moving. So you could involve the staff in such questions as 'How can we move this forward?', 'How can we move around this?', 'How can we keep this moving?', 'How can we influence somebody else to move this forward?' Notice that these questions require joint problem solving on items that will sustain progress. What you're doing here is focusing energy on overcoming obstacles so you can keep moving."

"This seems to have some good parallels with Professor Richmond's approach," I commented. "He uses questions to engage staff in problem solving."

"Yes," replied the professor. "His SCOPE test is very useful for all sorts of problems. I think this is a good example of combining techniques. You will probably find other techniques that you are learning this week, that can be combined synergistically. As time is getting short, I would like to go back to your question about praising staff. Have you come across the CAT acronym for recognising individual work contribution?"

"No," I said.

"In a nutshell", said the professor, "This is what the acronym means." She wrote out the acronym on another piece of paper and turned the paper round so I could see the following:-

C means *congratulate.*

A means *acknowledge.*

T means *thank.*

As I looked at it, she said, "You congratulate people on *completing* a defined piece of work. You acknowledge someone's *ability* to move things forward. You thank someone for their *efforts*. This applies whether someone has achieved the right outcome, or not. If someone has put a distinct effort in, then you should thank them for it. If they put a lot of effort into something that goes wrong, and you do not thank them, they will wonder about doing it again. Does that make sense?"

"Absolutely," I said, "Congratulate on completion; acknowledge ability at any time it is demonstrated; thank for efforts when they are clearly visible. That is terrific. I wish someone had told me that before. If I might take the acronym one stage further. It seems to be a perfect way to get your staff to purr."

"On that note," said the professor, with a grin, "I will take you back to the reception. You have picked up some techniques on generating momentum in an organisation. The more you can increase momentum, the less time it will take to achieve what you want. I am sure that the same approach will help you, in your own work."

I collected my papers together, put them into my shoulder bag, and we left the room. As we were walking back to reception, I asked the professor about the training of staff at this particular company.

"There is slightly different training for the managers and the staff," she said. "The manager programme concentrates on leadership, organising skills, communication skills, momentum techniques, and how to deal with difficulties, and keep things going. The staff programme has a different flavour. We firstly help them adopt strategies to put them in a positive frame of mind. We then offer them strategies to take control of what they are doing, to put aside the past, and to start organising a future for themselves. We help them set a pathway for their success, as well as the organisation's success. Then we give them the strategies on how to get moving, make an impact, build confidence, seek solutions, and keep going. There have also been quite a number of initiatives to support high levels of energy – cycle to work schemes, sponsorship for charitable sporting events aimed at those who have not done sponsored activities before. It is all about investing effort in your staff. Remember, you can increase momentum by putting energy in."

"That is a very good expression on which to finish," I said, "Thank you Professor. I hope I did not give you too much of a rough time."

"It is good to be challenged," said the professor, as we arrived back in reception. "Good luck for the future."

We shook hands. I said goodbye to the professor and turned to the receptionist to organise a taxi back to the station. I did not have long to wait.

As I had my visit early, I got down to the station just after 11am and just caught the train to my next destination. It was not a direct route. There was a need to change trains in Derby which was just over an hour away.

I settled into the seat and reflected on my visit. So what did I learn?

Actually quite a bit! I have learnt about creating learning cultures. This has also made me think about the capabilities and potential contributions of my team. I have learnt a good anti-procrastination technique about how to get myself, or somebody else, moving. I've learnt about how to build a momentum by the way we chart progress, and how to get over obstacles by using questions related to movement. I've learnt not to say 'but'. I felt pleased that I had learnt the CAT acronym. I shall certainly be using it.

The whole idea of movement and momentum seemed to have a value. I could try out the progress chart at work in a small way to see whether it will work for me. One of the best things about it seemed to be this concept of talking about moving, and about trains, and about passengers! I think the expression 'passenger on a tandem' could be a pretty strong message, if I ever needed one!

I was not sure about training staff in the way that the professor suggested. Specific soft skill training will get a thumbs down at work until we had a change of management attitude. However, it did strike me that to train operational managers was an important first step. It will allow all the managers in my company to be on the same wavelength. It all depends on the attitude of the top team. Perhaps my real challenge is "How can I influence the top team to train managers in better ways of working?" I will have to work on that!

Time to get out my action list. In the end I decided to add the following:-

	Action List	Time scale
1	Review team communications with the team.	0-4 weeks
2	Make clear what I expect the team to do in slack / overloaded times.	0-1 week
3	Talk about learning in a practical way as described.	Immediate
4	Recognise learning that will contribute /has contributed to progress.	Immediate
5	Explain why I want something when I ask for it.	Immediate

The Time Advantage

6	Explain what I don't want	Immediate
7	Adopt the Student's approach to instruction when appropriate.	Immediate
8	Adopt and radiate movement type language and the train metaphor	Immediate
9	Adopt the getting started technique	Immediate
10	Enthuse about outcomes more	Immediate
11	Use moving questions to get round obstacles.	Immediate
12	Chart progress across a range of significant tasks	1-2 months
13	Have mini-celebrations when key stations are reached.	1 month
12	Take a firm approach with non contributors.	Immediate
14	Think about my language. Replace 'but' with 'and'.	Immediate
15	Practice the CAT technique.	Immediate

I then sat back in my seat and started to think of the individuals in my team and how they would react if I changed my management style. I also asked myself what I could be enthusiastic about in the company. It had to be more than just finishing a piece of work. It had to be more aligned to the importance of finishing the work to the longer term direction of the company and that also had to have a meaning to my team. This seemed an important point. I had to achieve a greater understanding of what motivates my staff so I could translate success into something meaningful. Having celebrations of work achievement as advocated by the professor was a good idea, yet if I could also translate that into something bigger and more meaningful that should provide an even greater motivation.

As I was preoccupied with my reflections, the time it took to get to Derby seemed to go very quickly!

Readers notes:

You are coming to your last city. You know it will not be too far away from Derby. Some of the other clues in the next chapter may help you identify the right city. It is easy to get it wrong. There is a also a further clue to John's favourite sport coming.

The activity connection was present in the last visit. You can be sure there will be a reference to it again in the next chapter.

Chapter 11
Successful Formulae
'Capturing More.'

I needed to connect to another train at Derby. The connecting train would take approx three quarters of an hour to arrive in Derby, so I grabbed a bite to eat.

After successfully boarding my next train, I began looking forward to my last city. The city was approximately halfway back to London from where I had been this morning. I knew the city reasonably well. I came here regularly to watch my team play. The local stadium had recently been significantly enlarged. This added to the noise and atmosphere in the ground during the match. In principle a good thing but there were always more home supporters to encourage their team than away supporters. The local team was a pretty successful competitor though. I am not too sure it is anything to do with their aggressive animal nickname, which represents a stronger animal than that represented by the city football club!

I arrived at the station on London Road, with plenty of time to spare. My appointment with Professor Cathy Thieffer was in the middle of the afternoon. She was meeting me at the Business School. This gave me the time to have a leisurely stroll to the University.

It was fairly busy outside the station so I decided to cut across to New Walk, which is a pleasant walk that leads into the south side of the shopping area. From here, I walked about half a mile to the west to the Business school.

Although very near a dual carriageway the business school is nicely sheltered near the castle grounds and is a pleasant place to meet, with greenery around most sides.

Professor Thieffer met me on the ground floor within moments of my arrival. She was a similar age, as far as I could tell, to the other professors, although significantly shorter. Her area of expertise was human resource management. Getting closer to time management, I thought.

The professor had an immediate friendly manner. "Good to meet you, John. My office is on the floor above," she said, "Are you OK to use the stairs?"

"Good to meet you Professor," I said. "I have no problem with the stairs."

On arriving at the first floor, she took me to a small office. I was immediately struck by the number of pictures round the walls. There were large groups of people at a conference, small groups of people, who presumably were on a course at the University, and there were a couple of family photographs. This has to be a people person, I thought.

After some polite conversation about my journey she said, "So let's make a start. Give me an overview of your organisation and your department."

I did a little bit more than that.. I told her about the products, the market for them, features of the industry, where our company was positioned in relation to the market, and where my department fitted into the company operations. I was able to include a statement about what my department enabled its external customers to do. I could see her smiling as I did so.

"Now tell me what comes in and what goes out of your department," she said, "and what resources you have to manage. There is a whiteboard over there," she said pointing behind me.

I was well prepared for this question mentally, having done some work on it before even meeting the first professor. So I went over to the whiteboard and started to draw.

I knew exactly what I wanted to draw – a systems diagram.

```
          ┌──────── Feedback ◄────────┐
          │            ▲              │
          ▼            │              │
[Inputs] ──► [    Processes    ] ──► [Outputs]
                       ▲
                       │
                  [Resources]
```

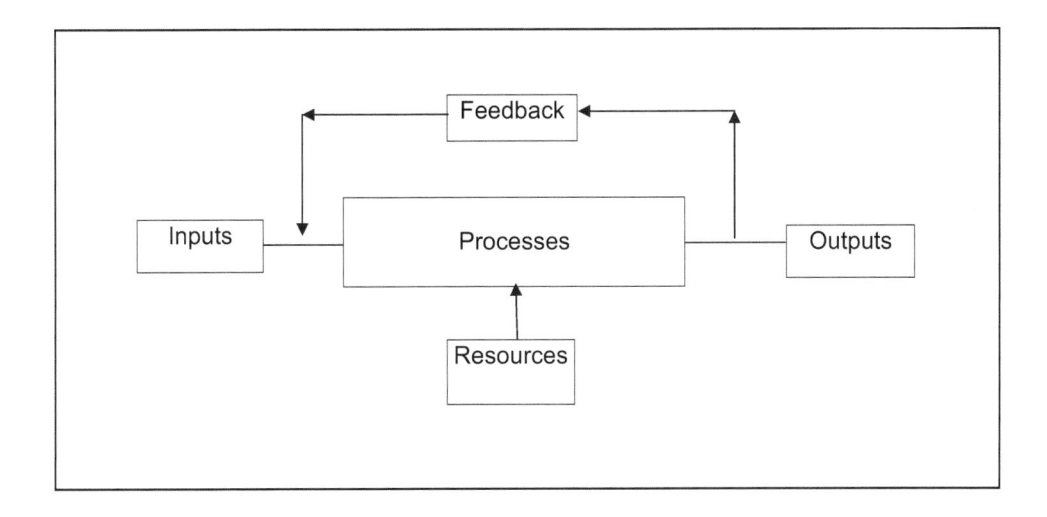

Under each of the headings of the boxes for inputs, outputs and resources, I listed out what I believed them to be. The resources list was pretty straightforward. My list included time, people, money, physical resources, energy etc. I was careful to include perceptions under outputs. The professor prompted me for a few items. She said she was also pleased to see a feedback loop and asked me a bit about it. I had to admit to her that Professor Richmond had given me a few extra ideas, which I had not put into practice. She was quite happy with my explanation, though.

"How much of your own time is spent directly working on the actual work processes?" asked the professor.

"I would say approximately 50%," I replied. "The other 50% I would categorise as planning, coordinating, safe working, corporate needs, legislation adherence that sort of thing."

" OK," said the professor. "You have probably given me enough understanding of the context. Now tell me how you organise yourselves."

I drew an organisational chart, similar to the one that follows.

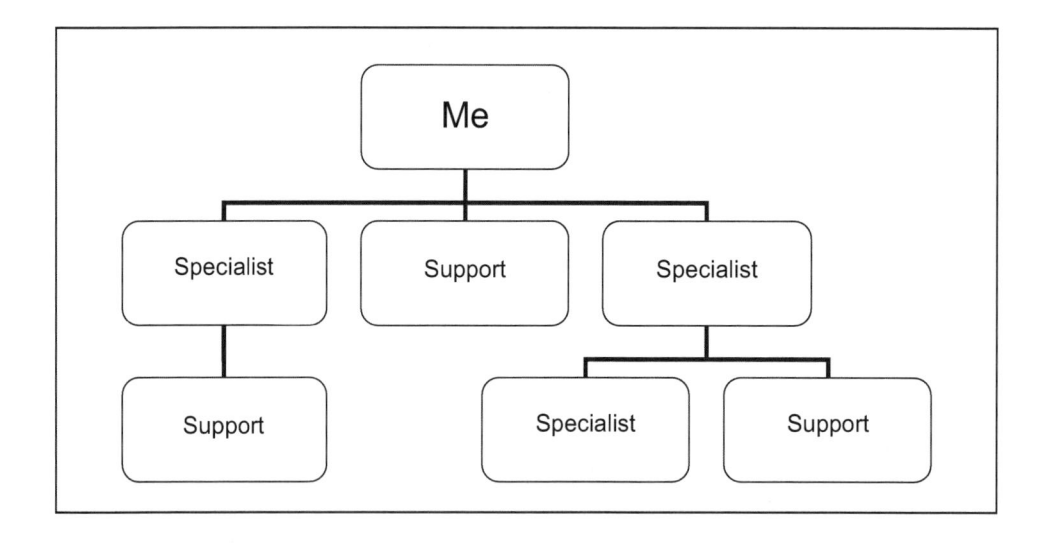

```
        ┌─────────┐
        │   Me    │
        └────┬────┘
   ┌─────────┼─────────┐
┌──┴───┐ ┌───┴───┐ ┌───┴────┐
│Speci-│ │Support│ │Special-│
│alist │ │       │ │ist     │
└──┬───┘ └───────┘ └───┬────┘
   │              ┌────┴────┐
┌──┴────┐    ┌────┴───┐ ┌───┴───┐
│Support│    │Specialist│ │Support│
└───────┘    └──────────┘ └───────┘
```

I discussed what each one of my staff did, as I drew the picture.

"How did this organisation come about?" she asked.

"I don't exactly know," I said, "It existed before I arrived. I have kept it more or less as it is. A couple of the roles are specialist, and would naturally report into me. The specialists tend to be very much into their own specialism.

"That's interesting," said the professor. "Many jobs exist on a historical basis and are often based around the capabilities of those who worked in the job earlier. As the organisation evolves, the job profiles tend to flow around the original structure. The team gets used to working with the structure, and everyone becomes satisfied about incremental performance around existing roles and attitudes. If you try to encourage flexibility, the company's performance and reward system can work against you with its emphasis on individual objectives, individual job descriptions and small pay increases. Sometimes, this situation will only change if there is a need to consider redundancies. However the pressure is on at this time, so the thinking is very much a reaction to events, rather than to creating an ideal structure. Something similar can happen when you promote someone into a department. They will make some minor changes rather than revolutionary ones, as they depend on existing staff maintaining a service.

Think about the following point for a moment. If you have effective people in an ineffective structure, can you have a recipe for time management problems?"

"I am not sure I understand where you are going with this," I said. "I take the point that you could easily have an ineffective structure, and, in my limited experience, this can also arise because you are trying to change job content to keep someone from leaving. However, a structure has value. Within a structure you can make people accountable. Without a structure, no one is accountable, and that would seem a recipe for disaster."

"I am not advocating that you have no structure", said the professor. "Simply that you need to have an appropriate structure to avoid time consuming difficulties. You have hit the 'nail on the head', when you say a structure has a value. Every structure will have a value. My first point is that different structures have different values. It is therefore important to regularly review your operational and organisational structure. My second point is that most managers seem to agree that they would have a lot more productivity, if they could increase flexibility. To increase flexibility, you need a team whose competence is as high as possible, as wide as possible, and you need to create the expectation that individual reward is based on team delivery, as well as individual delivery. You require individuals not only just to do their own job, but also share the work with other team members if it needs doing. This means you need an appropriate structure that can make this happen."

"So what can a manager do to get a better structure that takes these points into account?" I asked.

"One way to appreciate what is possible," said the professor, "is to turn your organisation chart upside down. This puts you at the bottom. It also put your staff at the top. They are then in the front line dealing with work processes. In an ideal world, you would simply be able to allocate staff fluidly along your process flow. If there is a hold-up at one point, you allocate more people resources to speed it up. Now this sounds idealistic, and managers are the first to say that as soon as you have specialists you are back to having job roles. That does not have to be true. The specialist may have to do their individual bit, but there is no reason at all why they cannot be as flexible as the rest."

"I am not sure this would work," I said. "I think everyone would rebel. Specialist staff would regard any encroachment on their activity as interference, or distraction. The other staff would say they are not paid to do everybody else's work. What's more, if someone does not pull their weight, and is inflexible, that is likely to upset the rest of the team."

"It does mean," said the professor, "that the team would have to have some say in how the other members of the team are contributing. A very inflexible member of staff would soon be identified. In a sense, the rest of what you have said is a defence for not considering this approach. It can be uncomfortable to consider something different from the present."

"I am open to new approaches," I said, thinking as I did so, that this might sound defensive too, "but we seem to just about survive as we are. If the wheel isn't broken, why do I need to fix it?"

Ugh! I just realised that I had used the 'but' word, in spite of my learning to use the 'and' word. Habits!

"It is only worth fixing, if you can make a gain," said the professor. "At the moment, you have not convinced me that you have reviewed your structure and *worked out* whether you could do something different, and more productive. As a manager, you have a responsibility to consider how best to achieve your department work. That means reviewing the organisational structure you have."

"OK," I said. "It is not easy to change structures though."

"If there is a better structure that could be worked," said the professor you then have to determine the best time to put it in place. You may decide there is a better structure but now is not the time to implement it for various objective reasons. That is a proper management decision. At the moment, you still need to determine whether there is a better structure. Coming back to the approach of turning your organisation chart upside down, is there anything else you can sense might be a consequence of doing that?"

"The upside-down structure suggests that all my staff do the work. I end up spending my time on planning and coordinating. In days gone by," I said, "most managers might have been able to do this, but in this day and age, most managers are working managers. Besides, I have to do my special bit with the customers."

"What would happen if you were not around? You are not around this week, are you?" asked the professor.

"I have deferred all customer visits to later in the month," I said.

"So if you were not to return to work, who would do them?"

"My boss would not know what to do," I said. "So it would have to be one of the people reporting to me, but they are probably not ready for that. It might be a bit of a mess."

"You have set up your department to be a mess, when you're not around for anything more than the occasional few days," said the professor in mock summary. She had won a point here. I did not know what to say. The professor wanted to say something more though.

"So," said the professor, "is there anything to stop you training your staff now and allowing them to take over some of your customers?"

"I guess not," I replied. "OK. I have talked my way into doing some training. However, training will require more time from me, and use up my staff time as well. The end result is that my department productivity will go down."

"When you make a positive change," said the professor, "you need to make an investment of time. It is no different to dealing with money. You invest for a return. The end result in this case is that you will have a more resilient department and you should gain some time back for yourself. If you can spend more time managing, won't things be better in your department?" She paused, and looked at me, as if to allow the point to sink home.

"Now before we leave this subject," she continued, "why are you doing the work on some of the direct processes?"

"I am probably the most expert, and can do it quicker than the rest," I said meekly. She had won another point!

"I think that makes the case," said the professor, "for you to do some more training. Of course, you will have to have a plan, as you will not be able to do everything at once. Perhaps your first step is to start releasing part of your role, and then you can examine 'cross team' training. As you start on that, you then might look at the reward system, and rewrite the job descriptions."

"I think this will overload my team at busy times," I said. "What do I do if something goes wrong? It strikes me that I will need more resources."

"You can always step back in, and take work back, if there is a peak passing through," said the professor.

"I wonder what my staff will think," I said. "They will see my job get easier, and they will be more pressurised."

"If that is true, you would be able to support them more, as you will have more time to do so," replied the professor. "You will not become less busy, because your role will change. This change of role will allow you to find and implement improvements for your departmental processes, and your customers. If you become a real success, in the interests of creating flexibility across your organisation, you can help other managers do something similar. In the ideal organisation, managers with spare capacity should be able to help other managers who are in difficulty. The interesting thing at manager level is that you can offer advice and show other managers how to make things work. You do not have to do that work for them. So far, we have talked about efficiencies to be gained through reorganisations, but we have not touched the subject of practical skills. We have to consider your competence at making this happen. To make a new structure work, you have to be good at delegation, building a coaching framework and doing coaching, and, of course, empowerment."

"Delegation is straightforward," I said, "I have been on a coaching course. I am not sure what you mean about a coaching framework, although if you describe it, I will probably recognize it. Isn't empowerment the process which forced a lot of managers out of work in the Nineties?"

"Let's take one of those at a time," said the professor. "Delegation is not as straightforward as you think, and many people mess it up. This usually results in frustration all round, and the originator goes back to doing the task themselves. Let me try a question out on you – How do you know you delegate well?"

"Easy," I said. "What I delegate gets done."

"That's an indicator," said the professor, "and one of the most important of the three indicators. What else might matter?"

"Making someone accountable for your delegated task." I ventured.

"That is part of one of the other two," said the professor. "The three major indicators are one, that it works well for you, two that it works well for the person you have delegated to, and three it produces the right result. This means that you know you are doing the right things. It also means that you need to get feedback from the person to whom you delegate. The feedback should not only be about how they felt about the task, but also how they felt about your way of giving them the task. In my mind, it is absolutely essential that you talk to the person to whom you delegate."

"Can you help me?" I asked. "What specifically should I talk to them about, apart from how they feel about my delegation?"

"You can ask them whether they feel you know enough about their workload, whether your instructions are clear, whether you listen enough to understand their views about what to do, whether you understand the consequences for them in giving them this work, whether you readily provide training or coaching, whether you will support them and not blame them, if things don't work out right, whether you are clear on the importance and priority of what you asked them to do. Does that help?"

"Yes," I said, quickly making a note of what she had said. "Is there anything in particular that I should look out for?"

"In terms of the process that has to be carried out," said the professor, "one of the normal failings is that managers don't make other people aware that they have given the task to one of their staff. You should aim to give your member of staff the whole of the task and make others aware that your member of staff is now responsible for the task.

"Now, what about coaching," she said. "What does that mean to you?"

"It is about raising performance against objectives, or helping a member of staff to do things better."

"Is it about telling them what to do?" asked the professor.

"No," I said, somewhat guardedly, thinking this may be a trick question. "On the coaching course, my tutor said that the ownership of the activity has to remain with the member of staff. My role is to suggest options to them, and help them dig themselves out of any hole that they may have fallen into. If we don't do that, coaching becomes a ticking off process."

"Very good," said the professor. "When do you do coaching, and how do you do it?"

"Formally," I said, "we do it three times a year in alignment with a performance process. We set the objectives in January, and then have a coaching session at the end of each of the next three quarters. For each of the sessions, we run through every individual's objectives. In the final quarter, we advise our staff how they have performed and what they will get paid. Within the Department, we do have a monthly meeting and talk about what went right or what went wrong. Informally, I guess the answer is that we should do coaching all the time."

"You should do as much as is needed," said the professor, "I believe you could beneficially review what you do. Your monthly meeting does not sound very inspiring unless someone is performing particularly well. Does your recent meeting with Professor Richmond suggest an approach that could be used?" She paused. I had to quickly remind myself on Professor Richmond's approach. He was interested in the purpose of doing things and forming questions on those things that held you back. He also used the SCOPE test.

"I think so," I said in reply to the professor, half suspecting that she expected me to make a connection. "Just give me a moment." Then something struck me. Under the SCOPE test, questions had to be owned, and they had to be positive. Perhaps this will be it.

"I think I have made the connection," I said slowly, and then speeding up, I went on. "Any issues about performance could be turned into challenges. What I would need to do is make sure the challenge is owned by the staff member and is positively expressed. Once the ownership of the challenge is clear, I can help, or even coach, a member of staff with their challenge."

"You might be able to extend that thought in the context in which you work," said the professor, "not just to performance issues, but also to any future work. Anything that needs to be done can be put in the form of a challenge. Even if it is relatively mundane work, the challenge could be, "How can you get through this faster?"

"Is there anything Professor Soljer might add to this approach?" she continued and then paused again.

"Professor Soljer would have a checklist, and he would have prepared for the coaching meeting." I replied quickly, and then more thoughtfully, I went on. "However, I suspect that he would also have created an agenda, possibly a standard agenda, and he might have a standard way of keeping notes."

"His approach might suggest a standard form," said the professor, "which is completed by the manager, and the employee, for discussion at the meeting. You could imagine the form listing:- issues of the last month, improvements gained, challenges for next month, other points arising. Both parties could write down in advance what they thought was important against the headings and then compare notes. What might Professor Sayler introduce?"

"A measure of some kind," I suggested.

"Undoubtedly," said the professor. "He would have found some way of transferring ownership of the measure to the member of staff. There might be an alternative measure or progress chart that the staff member could use, as advocated by Professor Bergamon. She would also add an additional requirement to come to the meeting with positive energy! Professor Tinker would ask you not to forget training where it is appropriate, and make maximum use of technology, where you can. Professor Taylor would ask you to be conscious of the perceptions that will be radiated as a result of the meeting, and Professor Perman would want you to be caring, keep everything in a realistic context and help with clarifying the first steps of any decision process. Does that give you any food for thought?"

"Plenty," I said. "I hope I can remember all of that. I will devise a suitable coaching form as soon as I can. As a separate point, you have shown me how to use the work of all the professors. It is almost like having a team behind me. How should I use your views though?"

"You will have to decide that afterwards," said the professor. "Now, I need to ask you another question, similar to the question on delegation. How will you know you are coaching well?"

"I would know that I am doing the right things," I said, and then remembering the earlier discussion on delegation. "I would ask the person being coached what they thought about how good I was at coaching them, and I would check that the work was completed well."

"What you are building here," said the professor, "is a monthly coaching framework. Coaching can, of course, occur at any time in between. The trick is to make staff quickly aware of any issues that come to your attention and then help them. If something has gone wrong, the first step is to discover whether the staff member appreciates what has gone wrong. They would not have intended deliberately to have things go wrong, so you can't blame them, but you can help them with their awareness of the situation and what to do about it. It seems to me that you have something to work on here which will take you forward, so I think it is time to pass on to the subject of empowerment."

She looked at me to make sure that I was OK to move on. I nodded.

"You have already given me a clue on how you might perceive that word." she continued. "You consider empowerment a technique to reduce the number of managers! Do you think that increasing empowerment has any value to managers?"

"It must have some," I said. "An empowered person is more capable of taking initiative, of getting on with work where they might otherwise have had to wait for authorisation, is potentially more motivated. To me, it is the practices of increasing empowerment that are questionable. I have heard it being used as an excuse to give people more responsibility, a small salary increase, limited training, all on top of a high existing workload. Then the manager is taken out, and the staff remaining have to cope. The result is more stress, potentially more mistakes, and the staff members eventually leave to get better jobs. A friend of mine told me that, once they had taken out most of the managers in the nineties, their company realised that they had lost considerable expertise. Any additional savings were wiped out by errors and reduced productivity, especially when someone left and had to be replaced. There was also a higher liability in facing stress claims. I gather, in several instances, managers had to be re-hired once this was understood."

"That sounds like irresponsible empowerment," said the professor. "There is a better way. Some Swiss researchers came up with the notion that good empowerment was dependent on the *direction* given about what needed to be done, the amount of *autonomy* given to do it, and the *support* needed to help the individual. The researchers came up with a formula for empowerment as follows."

She wrote on a piece of paper in front of her and turned it round so I could see. On it was the formula below.

Empowerment *equals* direction *multiplied by* autonomy *multiplied by* support or, $E = D \star A \star S$.

"Notice the multiplication sign," said the professor. "What this means, is that if there is no direction, or no autonomy, or no support, we have a zero. If you multiply anything with a zero, then the result is zero. In the example you mentioned support would seem to be zero. Therefore empowerment is zero. Leading companies have used this approach to help them practice empowerment arrangements more responsibly. Then they recognised that you could give direction, give autonomy, and give support but still not get the result you wanted. They identified that the enthusiasm and the leadership of the managers was also crucial. As a consequence, they expanded the formula to read – Empowerment *equals* direction *multiplied by* autonomy *multiplied by* support *multiplied by* enthusiasm transferred, or $E = D \star A \star S \star E$."

"I can understand the message of having the various components present," I said, "but can you do anything practical with such a measure?"

"If you are measuring something, then you must be seeking to understand or improve that something," said the professor. "What you might want to know is whether there was anything you could do to increase empowerment levels. Your own observations may tell you whether someone is acting as if they are empowered, but there's only one person who can tell you whether they are actually empowered. That is the person you are endeavouring to empower. To measure empowerment precisely may not have much meaning, but you can use a measure to assist your employee in communicating how they feel about your ability to empower them and what you can do to increase their empowerment levels. Imagine you had a different scale for each of direction, autonomy, support and enthusiasm transferred. Each scale would go from zero to 10, something similar to this." She scribbled on another piece of paper, and turned it round. "This is what it would look like for direction."

Direction										
0	1	2	3	4	5	6	7	8	9	10
There is none	My boss gives direction in an ad hoc way		My boss does this in a passive way		My boss is OK at giving me direction		My boss is good at giving direction		My boss is excellent at giving direction	

"So, presumably," I said, "zero means that I have no direction and ten means I am well directed."

"Yes," said the professor, "and there are several contributory factors involved in giving direction. You need to set the direction in relation to the organisation's context and attributes. Some importance needs to be given to any responsibility that you give to a member of staff. You need to set targets and end results that are appropriate. You need to make sure the organisation's values are embedded in what you're asking your staff member to do. You need to be clear on what you require. Professor Bergamon is very hot on that." I nodded. "You need to check the employee's understanding. You need to give some feedback and slight redirections, if things are not working out as you would hope. This is all about you doing things and the employee can give you feedback on how well you do them."

"Is this approach true for autonomy, support and enthusiasm transferred?" I asked.

"Yes," said the professor. "The same is true of those as well. Each can be broken down into activities that you would have to do, to make sure your staff member is empowered. You are then asking the staff member to score you on how you do."

"I am not sure they would be willing to do that," I said. "They may not be willing to tell me how well I have scored for fear of upsetting me, or, they may feel that I will get my own back by using the reward system, or, they may simply be too shy."

"Any of those could apply," replied the professor. "Some people will give you direct feedback and a specific score. Most, however, will indicate your score area. The actual score does not matter very much."

"So why do it?" I interjected, in as polite a way as I could.

"What really matters is what you, as their manager, need to do, to increase their empowerment. The measure is simply a device to help with that discussion." She opened a drawer in a desk and took out a stapled document. "Why not have a go with this version and see what you get out of it." She handed me a document. "How empowered are you?" she prompted.

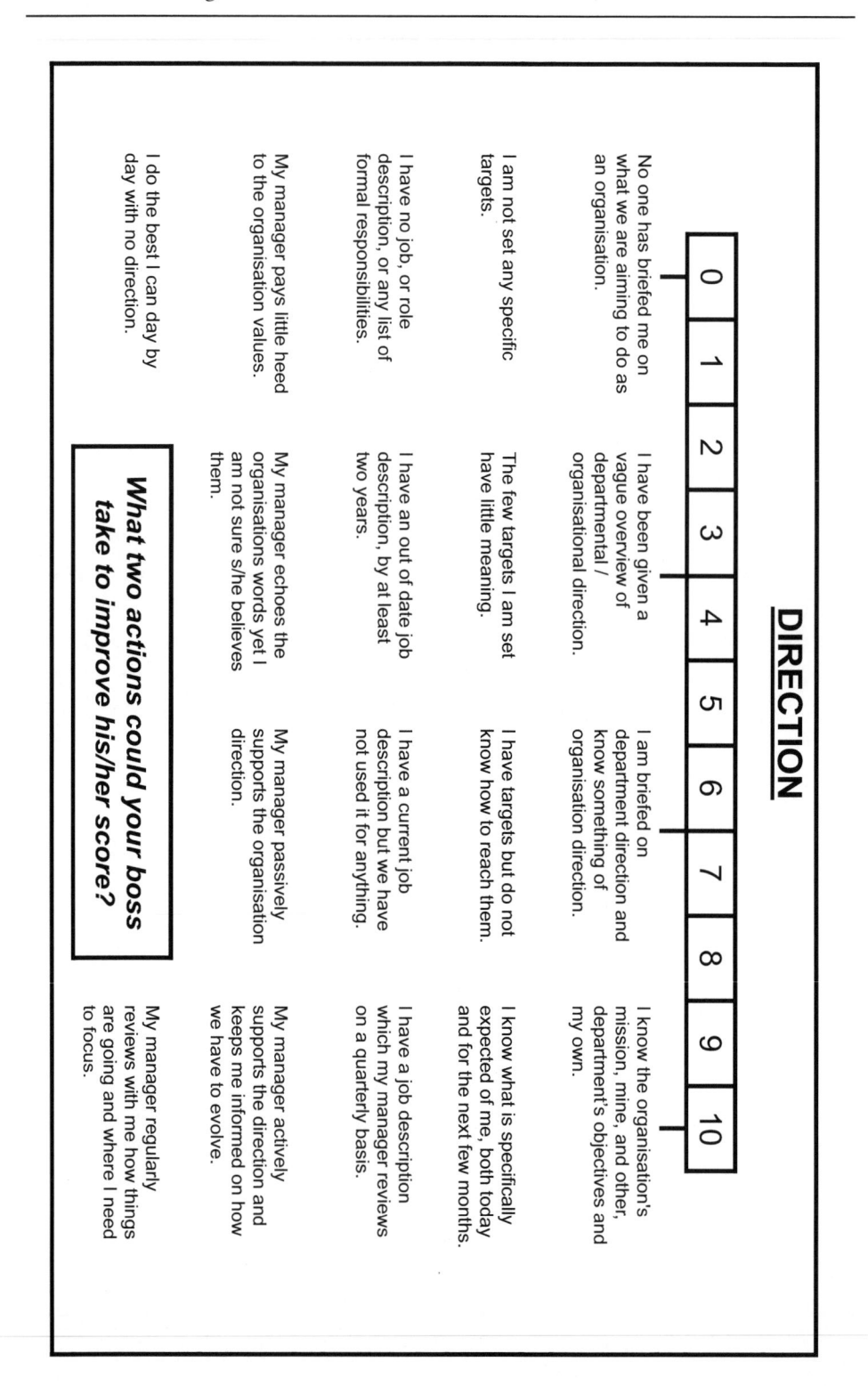

DIRECTION

| 0 | 1 | 2 | 3 | 4 | 5 | 6 | 7 | 8 | 9 | 10 |

0 — No one has briefed me on what we are aiming to do as an organisation.

2 — I have been given a vague overview of departmental / organisational direction.

5 — I am briefed on department direction and know something of organisation direction.

8 — I know the organisation's mission, mine, and other department's objectives and my own.

---

0 — I am not set any specific targets.

3 — The few targets I am set have little meaning.

5 — I have targets but do not know how to reach them.

8 — I know what is specifically expected of me, both today and for the next few months.

---

0 — I have no job, or role description, or any list of formal responsibilities.

3 — I have an out of date job description, by at least two years.

5 — I have a current job description but we have not used it for anything.

8 — I have a job description which my manager reviews on a quarterly basis.

---

0 — My manager pays little heed to the organisation values.

3 — My manager echoes the organisations words yet I am not sure s/he believes them.

5 — My manager passively supports the organisation direction.

8 — My manager actively supports the direction and keeps me informed on how we have to evolve.

---

0 — I do the best I can day by day with no direction.

8 — My manager regularly reviews with me how things are going and where I need to focus.

> **What two actions could your boss take to improve his/her score?**

AUTONOMY

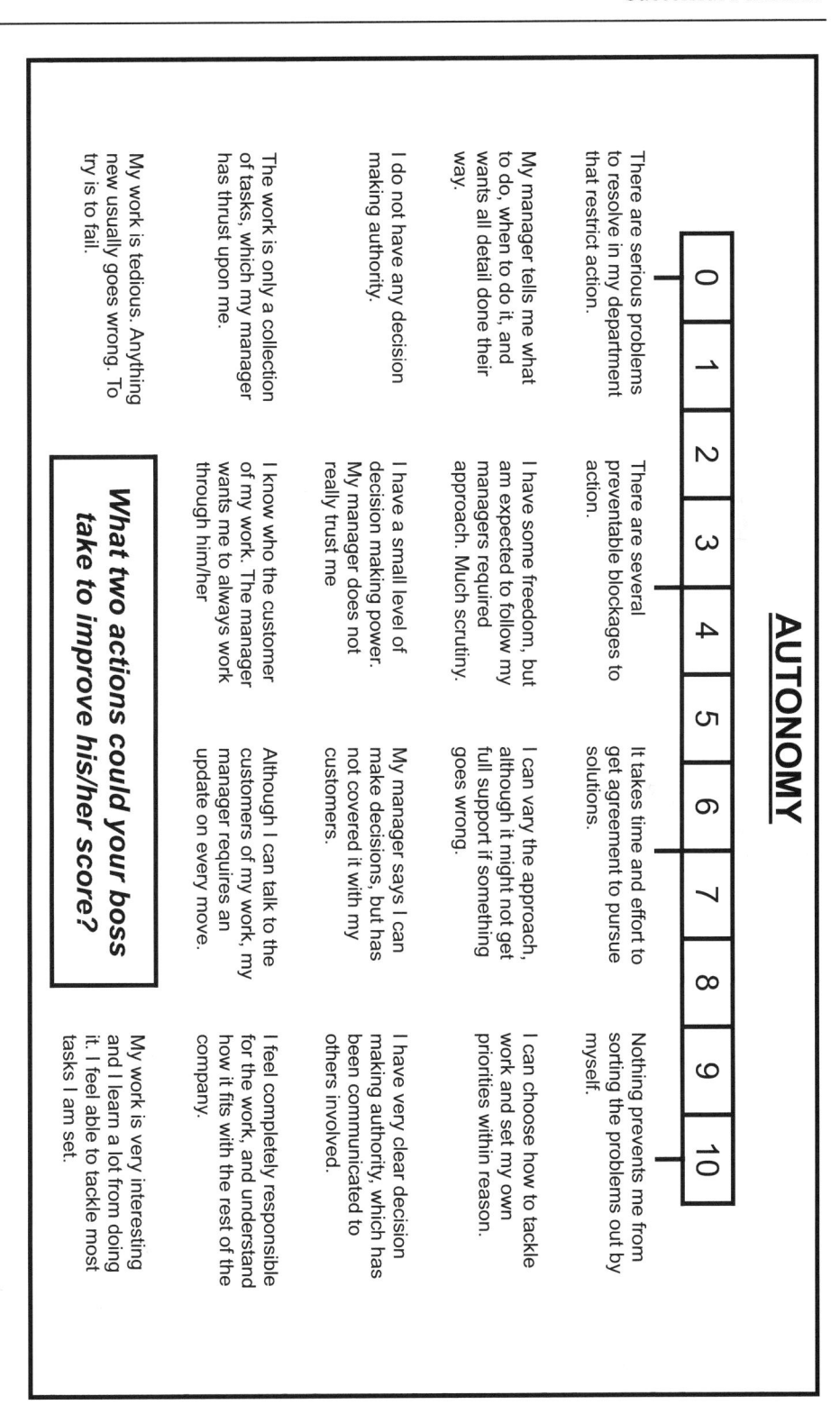

| 0 | 1 | 2 | 3 | 4 | 5 | 6 | 7 | 8 | 9 | 10 |

0 — There are serious problems to resolve in my department that restrict action.

1 — There are several preventable blockages to action.

2 — It takes time and effort to get agreement to pursue solutions.

3 — Nothing prevents me from sorting the problems out by myself.

4 — My manager tells me what to do, when to do it, and wants all detail done their way.

5 — I have some freedom, but am expected to follow my managers required approach. Much scrutiny.

6 — I can vary the approach, although it might not get full support if something goes wrong.

7 — I can choose how to tackle work and set my own priorities within reason.

8 — I do not have any decision making authority.

9 — I have a small level of decision making power. My manager does not really trust me.

10 — My manager says I can make decisions, but has not covered it with my customers.

11 — I have very clear decision making authority, which has been communicated to others involved.

12 — The work is only a collection of tasks, which my manager has thrust upon me.

13 — I know who the customer of my work. The manager wants me to always work through him/her

14 — Although I can talk to the customers of my work, my manager requires an update on every move.

15 — I feel completely responsible for the work, and understand how it fits with the rest of the company.

16 — My work is tedious. Anything new usually goes wrong. To try is to fail.

17 — My work is very interesting and I learn a lot from doing it. I feel able to tackle most tasks I am set.

What two actions could your boss take to improve his/her score?

193

The Time Advantage

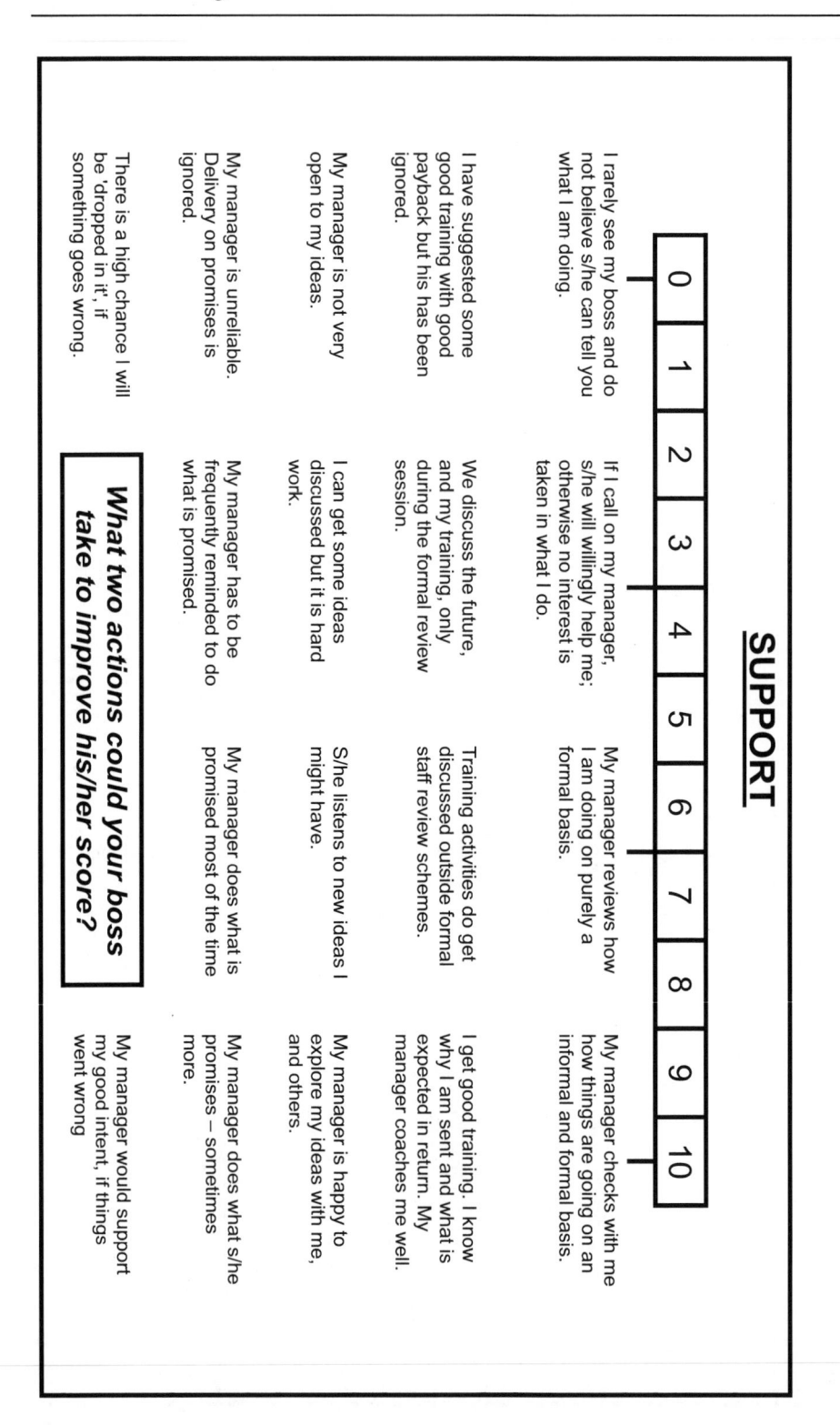

SUPPORT

| 0 | 1 | 2 | 3 | 4 | 5 | 6 | 7 | 8 | 9 | 10 |

Score	Low (0)	Middle (5)	High (10)
	I rarely see my boss and do not believe s/he can tell you what I am doing.	If I call on my manager, s/he will willingly help me; otherwise no interest is taken in what I do.	My manager reviews how I am doing on purely a formal basis.	My manager checks with me how things are going on an informal and formal basis.
	I have suggested some good training with good payback but his has been ignored.	We discuss the future, and my training, only during the formal review session.	Training activities do get discussed outside formal staff review schemes.	I get good training. I know why I am sent and what is expected in return. My manager coaches me well.
	My manager is not very open to my ideas.	I can get some ideas discussed but it is hard work.	S/he listens to new ideas I might have.	My manager is happy to explore my ideas with me, and others.
	My manager is unreliable. Delivery on promises is ignored.	My manager has to be frequently reminded to do what is promised.	My manager does what is promised most of the time	My manager does what s/he promises – sometimes more.
	There is a high chance I will be 'dropped in it', if something goes wrong.			My manager would support my good intent, if things went wrong

What two actions could your boss take to improve his/her score?

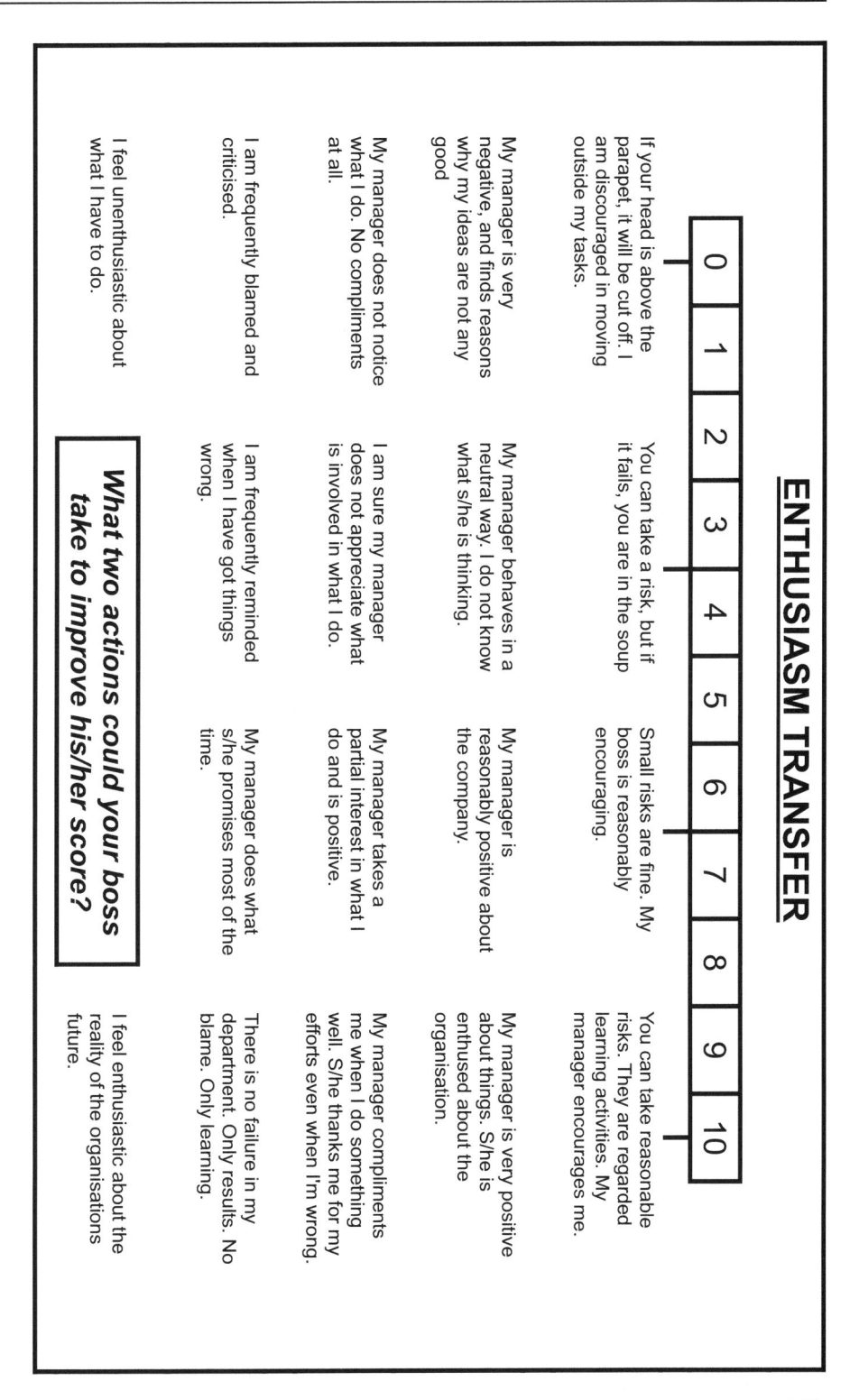

ENTHUSIASM TRANSFER

| 0 | 1 | 2 | 3 | 4 | 5 | 6 | 7 | 8 | 9 | 10 |

0 — If your head is above the parapet, it will be cut off. I am discouraged in moving outside my tasks.

2 — You can take a risk, but if it fails, you are in the soup.

5 — Small risks are fine. My boss is reasonably encouraging.

10 — You can take reasonable risks. They are regarded as learning activities. My manager encourages me.

0 — My manager is very negative, and finds reasons why my ideas are not any good.

3 — My manager behaves in a neutral way. I do not know what s/he is thinking.

6 — My manager is reasonably positive about the company.

10 — My manager is very positive about things. S/he is enthused about the organisation.

0 — My manager does not notice what I do. No compliments at all.

4 — I am sure my manager does not appreciate what is involved in what I do.

6 — My manager takes a partial interest in what I do and is positive.

10 — My manager compliments me when I do something well. S/he thanks me for my efforts even when I'm wrong.

0 — I am frequently blamed and criticised.

4 — I am frequently reminded when I have got things wrong.

7 — My manager does what s/he promises most of the time.

10 — There is no failure in my department. Only results. No blame. Only learning.

0 — I feel unenthusiastic about what I have to do.

10 — I feel enthusiastic about the reality of the organisations future.

What two actions could your boss take to improve his/her score?

I looked through the document. "This is more straightforward than I thought it would be," I said. "If I blend some of the items together, I can arrive at scores which show my boss is only halfway in everything. I can also suggest some things that she could do to improve her score."

"Hopefully, that means you have noticed the box on the bottom of the page?" queried the professor. "Just concentrate on two suggestions for your boss, rather than overload her. An overloaded boss is not likely to concentrate on getting specific things right for you, if you overload them with feedback. Now, let me ask you a question 'If your boss was able to implement the suggestions, would that save you time and allow you to produce better results?'"

"Yes, in my circumstances, I would say that is true, without a doubt."

"Do you think your staff would say the same thing of you?" asked the professor.

I was struck with the cleverness of this approach. Get me to think about my gripes with my boss, then examine whether my staff have the same gripes about me.

"Maybe," I replied, "I had better find out and this questionnaire can help me. I have no difficulty with giving it to them and asking for their feedback. However, I am a bit unsure about how to give feedback to my boss."

"You could show this particular set of measures to your boss on Monday," said professor, "as an example of one of the things that you have learnt. You don't have to give it a special emphasis. She might just be curious enough to ask you how you think they are doing. If she is not curious about it, you can ask her opinion of it. I am sure you will find a way to get her talking about it. We have now completed what I had in mind for this afternoon. I suggest that I take you back down to reception, and if you have any questions, I can answer them on the way."

I tidied up my notes and put them in my bag. As we were leaving the room, I said to the professor, "You have given me a formula for working out empowerment. Have you got any other formulae of a similar nature?"

"You mean a formula in an area of management, which has several independent factors that can be multiplied together, and, if one of them is zero everything falls apart?"

I nodded. She looked at me with a twinkle in her eye. "There are a few." she said. "I think I'm going to give you the fun of discovering them for yourself. It is also quite a fun thing for a team to do if they are contemplating a project, or reviewing their meetings. All I am going to do is simply point out that in management there should be an inspiring purpose, a good set of processes, adequate resources, good leadership, excellent communications, and well trained people, who work together well. If one of those is close to zero you can imagine what that might mean. If you develop any good measures, let me know. For now, I will just wish you good luck, and a safe journey. I won't be far behind you in time, but will be in miles – I travel on a trusted bicycle that is now 25 years old!"

"Thank you professor," I said. "I will be back in touch, possibly with a measure!"

"I look forward to it," said the professor. By this time we were back downstairs. She shook my hand and then departed, with a wave and a smile.

I went over to the administrative office, which thankfully was still open, and organised myself a taxi.

The taxi arrived very quickly, within five minutes and took me to an Inn on the south of the city. The taxi may have arrived quickly, but the journey took me half an hour through the rush hour.

I felt the professor had given me quite a lot of help, even though I may need some more of it in the future. In spite of all the people friendly pictures around her room, I felt that she had been heavily assertive with me, and perhaps not as friendly as some of the other professors. My organisational arrangements had been severely challenged. However, I had been given some specific materials I could use for delegation, coaching and empowerment. If I can improve on these areas, and still retain the same team, it would make a beneficial change. It would take an investment of my time to get a return on that time.

There was one thing I particularly liked however. The professor had shown me how to use some of the learning that I had got from the other professors. That seemed pretty powerful. If I was going to start something, I could ask myself what the other professors would be advising given their own particular view on time management. My secret helpers, I thought.

I was staying the night at an inn called 'The Water Bearer'. In retrospect, I think I could have travelled back to London that evening. Still, an evening of relaxation might be a good thing.

Given a previous night's experience, I looked at the pub sign carefully before I went in. It was very much what you would expect. It featured a man with a wooden beam across his back and a bucket of water, at each end of the beam. The only slight surprise was that he appeared to be carrying his load at night. There was a stream of stars going across to the horizon behind him. What I did not appreciate is that the sign had a strange, and greater significance. It was not until much later that I fully appreciated this.

The landlord was cheerful enough, and took me up to a decent room, complete with a desk where I could work. I decided that I would give Mary an early ring on her mobile, to update her. I also wanted to start planning the rest of the weekend, given that we would be working together on Sunday afternoon to improve our capability with office software.

When Mary answered the phone, she immediately enquired about the two professors I had met earlier in the day.

I explained that Professor Bergamon was all about increasing capability and staff motivation, and Professor Thieffer was about organising staff in a way that maximised their contribution and gained useful feedback from them. I told Mary about the formula for empowerment and some of the techniques that I had learnt.

"Some of those techniques sound very good," said Mary. "I wish my manager was more aware all of them, particularly the CAT acronym. In some ways the two professors seem related in what they do. Both are dealing with people issues. If I put these together with what the other professors have been through with you, you have covered a lot about leadership and management as well as just learning about saving time. I also sense that there is a slight analytical approach to what all the professors advocate. I suppose we ought to expect that as professors will be analytical experts almost by definition. Have you worked out the connection between all of the professors yet?"

"Not yet," I said, "but they do refer to each other as ex-colleagues, and they clearly know each other."

"Perhaps you could ask Professor Holmes that question, and make sure you run through all the professors before you meet him. You may notice what I have noticed." said Mary. "If I remember rightly, you're seeing him tomorrow afternoon. Tomorrow evening you can tell us about it. There is a small group of us from the Plough going to the Thai restaurant near Teddington. Would you like to join in."

"That's fine by me," I said. "Give me a call tomorrow when you have finished tomorrow with Professor Holmes and I'll confirm arrangements," said Mary. "Remember to think about some snappy sayings to summarise each professor." We then rounded off the telephone call.

My first job was to complete my action notes for my time with Professor Thieffer, as follows:-

	Action List	Time scale
1	Turn organisation upside down and fit to work flow.	1-2 months
2	Define and consider alternative ways of organising.	1-3 months
3	Review general capabilities of staff.	1-2 months
4	Set out expectations of flexibility.	0-4 weeks
5	Consult HR on adjusting reward system.	0-4 weeks
6	Train some of my staff on what I do.	1-3 months
7	Get some feedback on delegation using the professor's suggestions.	1-3 months
8	Build a coaching framework as suggested and get feedback.	1-3 months
9	Introduce an empowerment feedback process as suggested.	6-12 months
10	Make sure my boss knows of the feedback forms	0-4 weeks
11	Work out what other formulae might work.	Ongoing

I went down to the bar and enjoyed a pleasant bar meal. I then went back to my room and started thinking about a snappy phrase for each of the professor's teachings. It was not that easy. The good thing about doing this was that I had to review what I had learnt.

I came up with something for half of them, as follows –

Professor Taylor – *It is not what you know, it is how you are known*

Professor Soljer – *Time work is clockwork.*

Professor Bergamon - *Time does not stand still.*

Professor Thieffer – *Your time is my time.*

I thought I was being a bit unkind to Professor Thieffer. In essence this is what delegation, coaching and empowerment is all about – getting time back from my staff after investing in them heavily, so I can then use my time more productively!

I did not get very much further. So I switched on the TV and relaxed. The weekend was not far away.

Readers notes:

Did you notice the continuing activity connection with the last professor?

Are you aware of the sports team with the aggressive sounding nickname?

Can you produce any short snappy sayings for the other professors?

There is more evidence here that the professors all know each other. How might this be possible given their subject areas? All will be revealed later. Have you worked out the larger pattern between the professors that Mary spotted? Maybe the plumstone connection in the next chapter will help you?

Have you discovered a good third acronym for TIME yet that describes a third lever to time saving?

Events will start happening very quickly from now on and there are some geographical connections, so make sure you note in the next chapter where John is going to meet Professor Holmes.

Chapter 12

Friday Morning

'The Plumstone Connection.'

I had a good night's sleep and woke up a fraction before the alarm went off. Not being under too much time pressure, I switched it off completely, when I should have, in retrospect, put it into 'snooze' mode.

My purpose was to have a gentle snooze thinking about the connections between all the professors and Professor Holmes. How did all of these people know each other? Some of them work in a field quite unrelated to management, or physics. I decided I would ask Professor Holmes when I see him in the afternoon. Having made that decision, I then relaxed too much, and fell back to sleep.

When I awoke properly, I realised I had not allowed myself very much time before the pre-arranged taxi would arrive to take me back to the station. Quickly dressing, I walked down the stairs to the bar, where a self-service breakfast arrangement was laid out for cereals, and fruit. The landlord was there and asked me if I would like a full English breakfast, but, regretfully, I had to decline the offer, saying that I was short of time. I told him that I would just have some fruit, toast, and coffee.

There was a range of fruit on offer - orange segments, grapefruit segments, apricot halves, and some prunes. It is rare that I have prunes, so I decided to go for those with a small amount of muesli on top.

Sometimes it is amazing how your mind wanders when you are eating on your own. Mine was no exception. I kept on thinking about the professors as individuals and how I might summarise, in a pithy statement, the work of those that I had not managed to complete the previous night.

I enjoyed the prunes. I had eight of them to make up for the fact that I was not having a full breakfast. This gave me a total of eight prune stones on my plate. That is a coincidence, I thought. I have eight stones and I visited eight professors. I arranged the stones in four sets of two representing the fact that I had seen two professors on each of the other days of the week. I was musing whether there were any connections between each day's events, when a stranger came down for breakfast and started talking to the landlord.

It transpired that this person had an interview later on that day. At first, I did not take much notice, but then the stranger said to the landlord, "I do hope I get this job. It is a bit of a risk for me. It is a definite change of career."

For some reason, my ears pricked up. I was still looking at the prune stones.

I heard the landlord say, "I know what you mean. In my childhood, everyone suggested that I should go into the services. That is exactly what I did, but when I came out, I did not know what to do and after a couple of false starts, I ended up running a pub. I will never become a rich man running a pub, I will continue as a poor man, unless my trade falls away. Then, I will have to change career to a beggar," he said, with a laugh.

"If turning into a beggar doesn't work," said the stranger with a laugh of his own, "you will have to join the criminal profession. It is a bit overcrowded at the moment though!"

The landlord laughed even more, but clearly could not think of a clever reply. "Let's stick to our chosen careers," he said. Then pointing to the strangers place setting, he asked "Now, what's yours going to be...?"

"A pint," quipped the stranger with a smile.

"Not allowed to someone going to an interview," said the landlord, with another laugh. "I better go and do some eggs for you."

Funny, I thought to myself, this talk of careers reminded me of all the advice given to me when I was a child. I was going to be...

Then it hit me. Crikey! I looked at the prune stones. How could this be possible? There was a connection here between the professors.

I pushed all the stones to one side of the breakfast bowl and then moved them to the other side, one by one. I then slowly moved them back again, one by one. The pattern was definitely there. I knew it better with plum stones. However prunes were dried plums. I remember staring into the empty corner of the room. How could connection exist? How many people would actually recognise this pattern? It was really odd. The spellings may not be the same, but the pattern was there. Definitely there! The plum stone connection existed.

I moved the stones slowly back across the plate again. And then back to where they were, one by one. "Do I have to pinch myself?" I wondered. "Is this a dream?"

"Are the prunes alright, sir?" asked the landlord, breaking into my consciousness.

I looked up. "You have been moving those stones around in a very strange way, for a little while now," he said, "Is everything alright?"

"Yes," I said quietly. I looked at my watch. It was time to get a move on. "I have just realised something," I said, "and I really now have to move. Can you have the bill ready for when I come down? I'm going to have to go straight up now to get ready."

"No problem, sir," said the landlord. I quickly made my way upstairs. My attention was now focused on getting ready for the taxi, so I could catch the train in time.

A few minutes later, I was ready. Unfortunately, the taxi was not. It was a few minutes late. That was compounded further by traffic problems on the way to the station. The end result was that I only just caught the train.

It took me several minutes of the journey to become calm again.

I started off by checking that I had the directions to Professor Holmes' rooms that were just north of the Euston Road. Getting to the right tube station was easy. It then seemed pretty straight forward from there. Professor Holmes's directions were quite detailed, but the main message was simple. Come out of the tube station on the west side, walk up the road 100 yards, look out for Hudson's restaurant on the left hand side and, it is the door before that. Just press the buzzer against the name S.R. Holmes. This all seemed pretty clear. I wondered what the 'S' stood for in Professor Holmes's name.

Professor Holmes was likely to ask me about my experience, so I started thinking about how I would summarise my last four days. After a quarter of an hour I turned my attention back to snappy sayings of each professor and came up with the following: –

Professor Tinker – *T.I.M.E. means technically improving my expertise.*

Professor Sayler – *How do you know you're spending your time well?*

Professor Richmond – *Spending time without purpose is purposefully wasting time.*

Professor Perman – *Time management is more a question of attitude.*

None of these are the pithy sayings that I think Mary would like me to discover. Perhaps I will do better in the next few days. I did, however, refine my expressions for two of the other professors as follows: –

Professor Taylor – *You are what you appear to be!*

Professor Bergamon – *Time does not stand still, only people do!*

I also wondered whether I should rewrite Professor Thieffer's saying as 'Your time is my time; my time is your time'. These were clearly evolutions of previous thoughts. Perhaps there is a law of thinking, I mused. Your thoughts get better the more you think about them! I think Mary would take the view that thoughts get better, the more you share them and that could be a more time-saving approach. Perhaps both are right although maybe this is a little philosophical. They do say a problem shared is a problem halved. Talking to other people about your problems or what you are minded to do is probably a good idea. The word 'minded' seems a useful word for consultation, if it is used in such a way as ' I am minded to..., what do you think?'.

I really liked what Professor Thieffer did, when she demonstrated that each of the professor's views could help in the very specific situation of coaching. There were certainly differences between the professors, but it did seem that some of their views could fit together.

Take the view of Professor Tinker and Professor Richmond. If technology is part of the means to an end. Professor Tinker gets you thinking of the means and Professor Richmond gets you thinking of the end.

Take the view of Professor Soljer and Professor Taylor. Professor Soljer's approach looked after the detail, so you can concentrate on Professor Taylor's approach of managing the messages.

Take the view of Professor Bergamon and Professor Thieffer. Professor Bergamon was very keen to move you forward. Professor Thieffer was very keen to learn how it was working out for your staff.

I quickly drew an 8 x 8 matrix to test out the synergies between each of the professors. I put a list of the eight professors across the top, and the same list down the side. Synergies seem to work for every pairing, within the matrix.

Suddenly it dawned on me. Every approach was complimentary to every other approach. What they were doing was laying down not only the foundations of good time management, but also the foundations of good general management and leadership. Perhaps I was thinking too narrowly about time management. Good managers would also be good with time.

The coffee trolley arrived in our carriage. I decided I would think of something else and enjoy a cup of coffee.

As I was sipping my coffee, my mind went back to the acronym 'TIME'. I came up with a couple more alternatives, and one personal resolution. The alternatives were: –

1. Teamwork inspires more effort.

2. Travel increases my education.

The personal resolution was ' Turn in much earlier'! Perhaps, I will find an even better one soon. Although I did like 'Teamwork inspires more effort'. It is a good catch phrase to use around the office, and suggests we, as the team, get together about an issue. As I was thinking about this, another similar expression came to mind. Teamwork is more effective.

My first thought was that this was another example of Professors Tinkers habitual think patterns. Once you start thinking down one track you continue until you get inspired by something else. Then it struck me that this was an important acronym. Like training and technology, teamwork was an important lever to get things done quickly and save time. Maybe this is what Professor Tinker had in mind when he set me the challenge. This was something to put in my letter to him about how I was doing!

The train slowed and stopped in the middle of the countryside well before we entered London. I thought it might be pausing to let another train clear the line ahead. I looked out the window.

We had stopped by a small field covered in low rough grass. There were plenty of rabbits out munching the grass. They did not seem at all worried about the presence of the train. I was pleased that the carriage had relatively clean windows so I could see what was going on. In the corner of the field was a young girl just walking along the far hedgerow.

Suddenly, I spotted a white rabbit. It bounded across the grass in a series of hops, hardly stopping at all. All the other rabbits seemed happy munching away. This one seemed very determined to keep moving. I noticed the young girl had seen it too. The white rabbit crossed most of the field and then dashed down a large hole. The young girl by this time was running towards it, disturbing the other rabbits who scattered and went down some of their holes.

The train gave a jolt and slowly started moving. I watched the young girl approach the hole, but in spite of looking back as best I could, I lost sight of her before she reached it. I had this strange feeling that all was not as it seemed, that there was a connection to time, or timelessness in what I had just witnessed. I wondered what the girl would do when she got to the hole.

The train reached its normal speed and my attention came back to the inside of the carriage. I decided to run through in my mind what I would tell Professor Holmes.

Readers notes:

Have you an idea on what the young girl in the countryside might have been called?

You are now coming to an important chapter.

Watch out for Professor Holmes's assistant. Then work out how her full name relates to the activity connections between the professors.

Have you ever had to go back to work after a period away? Professor Holmes helps John with this situation?

Is all as it seems or is there something vaguely historic in this coming chapter?

What is the famous cricket ground nearby?

Something magical is about to take place and one of a few connections between the professors is about to be revealed.

Chapter 13

Everything, but the pipe

'Timely Performance!'

The train arrived on time in Kings Cross. I followed Professor Holmes' instructions, and took the Circle line going west, getting out three stations later.

I am beginning to form an interest in stations. As I went through the ticket barrier, I noticed I was facing what looks like a ticket office, but was, in the past, according to the engravings on the wall, a well-known shop. I turned right into the concourse and then right again and followed the concourse passageway as it took me to the left and out onto the street. There were clear signs to a nearby famous cricket ground. I walked up the street about 100 yards, looking out for the residential properties at the far end on the left and easily found the door before Hudson's Restaurant. I pressed the appropriate buzzer for the professor.

After a couple of moments, I heard the professor's voice say, "Hello."

"It's John Watson, Professor," I said.

"Come on in, John. Come up the stairs and go into the first room on your left, where you can wait. I'm just saying goodbye to somebody at the moment, so I will be with you very shortly."

I followed his easy instruction and found myself in a comfortable living room facing the road.

There were a large number of books on bookshelves to my right and there were some relaxing leather chairs in the centre of the room. I put my airline shoulder bag down, out of the way, and, with my curiosity getting the better of me, I walked over to a small cupboard, on which there were several photographs.

Most of these were of the professor when the professor was considerably younger. There were a couple of the professor playing a violin. He was obviously multi-talented. There was also one picture of a group of approximately ten people in their academic gowns. One of these was the professor, who must have been thirty years younger at the time of the photograph. The others seemed to be a group of students. Strangely, I thought I recognized one of them.

I picked up the frame to look at the picture closely. Then I recognised the students. They were younger versions of all the professors that I had met in the last week. Professor Taylor had a beard even in those days. Professor Tinker was even thinner than he is today. The girls all had haircuts that were in fashion at the time and clearly out of fashion now. However, if you looked at the faces, they were clearly Professors Perman, Bergamon and Thieffer. Here was evidence of how the professors knew each other.

At that moment, I heard a noise of someone going down the stairs. I heard the professor say, "See you next week, Penny." Within a few seconds the door to the living room opened. In came Professor Holmes.

"Good afternoon, John," he said, in a good humour, "Sorry to have kept you. There was something I wanted my assistant to do next week and we were just finishing as you arrived." He then noticed I had been looking at the photographs. "Ah, I see you have found the picture of one of my old tutorial groups."

"Does that mean they all studied physics," I asked politely, and in good humour as well.

"For the first degree, yes it does," he replied. "At the end of that degree, they all went their different ways – half went to do a PhD straight away, although Roger Sayler, Cathy Thieffer, Annie Bergamon, and Dick Taylor went out into industry, for a couple of years or so, before studying a management degree. I have managed to keep in touch with them all these years. They are a very special group. This will explain why you have met them over the last week, rather than anybody else."

"How did they get interested in time management?" I asked.

"Their interest in time management started a long time ago. Our subject, physics, has a lot to do with time, as well as order and disorder. There was a debate during one seminar that started it all. This was about how the laws of physics might apply to human beings. The debate ranged from the quantum mechanics of crowds to entropy in organisations. The question of how people spend time came up time and again. At that stage, it was simply some fun. Ever since then though, they have carried some interest in how to make best use of time and have taken it much more seriously. Mind you, it should not be a big surprise that physicists get involved in management matters. There are physicists, who are management gurus, and directors of companies. However, our session this afternoon, should not be about how useful physics is to management, but about how useful the views you have heard are to business."

"That's interesting," I said. "Before we leave this subject, professor, are you aware that there is a pattern that connects what I have done this last week, to the subject of prune stones or plum stones?"

"Ah, yes," said the professor with a chuckle, "I wondered if you would spot that. A pattern emerged a few years ago when two of the ladies changed their name. This drew attention to the pattern. Before that nobody recognized it, even though most of it existed. I wonder if you can understand why that should be. Perhaps, you can work it out by thinking about the way academics deal with the names of their students."

I thought for a moment. "Academics will normally be dealing with lists of names. Those lists will be in alphabetical order. The lists will be used for registration purposes, and for recording marks and results. As I think of this, with one exception, you will always be dealing with the pattern in reverse and it would also be interspersed among other names. Therefore, it was not easy to recognise."

"Precisely, uh...uh". The professor seemed to be struggling to remember my name. He paused and started again. "Precisely, John. It would be elementary to spot the pattern if the names were in order, but not if they are not and you are not looking for a pattern. So let's now move back to this afternoon. Over the next three quarters of an hour, I would like to discover how you got on with the other professors. After then, I have arranged for Jane to meet you, and give you her views on how you could be spending your time. Three of the professors during the week, thought it important that you met Jane as she had a rather different view to the ones they were giving you. I believe they are right. However, first things first, give me a summary of your week."

I spent the next twenty minutes outlining the detail of my visits and what I thought I had learnt. I particularly emphasised the way Professor Thieffer had given me a way of integrating a number of the professors' work together. I also told him about the matrix I had drawn up on the train journey back to London, and how I had concluded that all the ideas were complimentary.

As I completed my story, the professor looked away for a moment, then drew his attention back to me. "How many of their ideas were you using before you started your visits this week?" he asked.

"A few," I replied, "but mostly in an ad hoc way. I do have a few lists. I have a bring forward system on my electronic diary. I was delegating some things, However, there were a much larger number of new things I learnt, as well better ways to do existing things. There was one thing that I could have asked them all, although I did not think of it during my visits. I would have been interested to know what would they recommend to someone who has to do a lot of multitasking."

"Knowing them as you do now," said the professor, "What do you think they would have said, if you had asked them that question?"

I thought for a moment. "Professor Tinker would probably have encouraged me to think of the nature of the tasks and whether I could standardise responses or simplify them. He would have advocated better use of training and technology to deal with them. He would probably also have advised that I publish a frequently asked questions list to those who require tasks from my department so they can either empower themselves to do the work or reduce the level of the overall need from us. Professor Taylor would have said that I should list the issues involved in multitasking and take the courage to attack them, but to do so from a position of strength and good organisation. Professor Soljer, I am pretty sure, would have said that I ought to plan time to review how I, and my department, are dealing with multiple tasks and also I ought to plan uninterrupted time for them to be organised and dealt with properly. Professor Sayler would emphasise that I measure the inputs and the processes I have been using to deal with those inputs, so I could manage them better. I think he would also say that I should have a good system of prioritisation. How am I doing?"

The professor was smiling. "I'm interested in what you think the other professors would say. Carry on," he said.

"Right," I said slowly. "Professor Richmond would want to be sure that I am taking on tasks that are in my ownership and contribute to my purpose. He would also expect me to create a very specific challenge to dealing with specific groups of tasks, if that became an issue. I think he would also expect me to search for some innovative solutions to a question like ' how can I find more resources to do a specific series of tasks?' Moving on to Professor Perman, I think that she would look at my habits of agreeing to do work, turning work down, prioritising work, remembering all the tasks I have etc. She would then help me find a resolution to change how I do things so I could make some improvements. Professor Bergman would keep my spirits up and keep energy flowing into the achievement of every task, as well as seeking to ensure that the capability of my team was increasing to handle a larger number of tasks. Professor Theiffer would challenge whether the way I have organised my department is best for handling a large range of inputs. She would also have suggested that I arrange for the staff to do more through empowerment and delegation."

"That's pretty good," said Professor. "If you think further about it you would probably find the Professor Soljer would also advocate deferring items that involve reviewing procedures to when you have planned to review those procedures. Professor Richmond would also suggest that you are very clear on the nature of the task that you're being asked to do, and the priority and importance that it has for the person requesting it. In that way, you can be clear on expectations and challenge when, and how your services can be delivered. You would need to challenge in the nicest possible way of course! Multitasking is nothing new. The expression multitasking is new. I would simply say that managers have always had too much to do. Some of them like having too much to do as it distracts them from other things they don't want to do. Others are ambitious to do more and consequently take on extra activities sometimes to the detriment. A coach like Professor Perman can be a very good at helping individuals adjust to multitasking. If you wanted to you could work out what you think she might ask you and then talk that through with someone else to see if that helps you find any easy resolutions."

"Come on Professor," I said. "Managers these days have to do a lot more. Since the days of empowerment there are less managers employed to manage, and there are far more regulations."

"And managers have far more tools to help them in the form of computers, communication devices, web forums and information sources," said the Professor. "My point is that the mental challenge for any manager who has any sense of ambition is the same as it always was and the solutions lie where they always did in the amount of management managers choose to exercise over their time and activities. Talking of time that brings me nicely to the question of what you intend to do when you get back on Monday?"

"That's quite a problem," I said. "There will be a lot of e-mails to go through. There will be some correspondence. My boss will want me and my team will want me. Other managers will want me. Forms will have to be completed, people telephoned, customers telephoned. It is the usual re-entry problem that everyone dreads, after they have been away a week or more. It will take some time, before I can get round to implementing any of the things that I have learnt from this week. Normally, if I go away, I can log on to the company's server with my laptop and, at least keep on top of some of it. I have not done so this week, and I'm reluctant to do it this weekend. I am beginning to feel that I need to strike a better balance between work time and my time"

"It sounds to me," said the professor, "that you are going to let the world control you."

"That's the way it is," I said, "when you have customers." It was a bit of a cheeky remark.

"But you have told me about lots of other things, as well as about your customers," observed the professor, "and you will not be very effective, if you try and do the impossible. Your first step must be to get control of your time on Monday. Have you got access to your diary via your laptop?"

"Yes," I replied.

"That makes things easier," said the professor, "although similar principles would work, even if you had no such access. Book a meeting for a briefing with your boss late on in the day. Tell her that you will give her a full brief of what happened, and could she give you a briefing, at the same time, on current priorities. That action might prevent your boss giving you things right away. If you are an early riser, do this on Monday morning first thing. If you are a late riser, do it on Sunday evening. I would like to think of you keeping Sundays clear for the future, but on this one occasion it may be worthwhile to take an action. I also suggest you book a meeting with your team in the afternoon, and tell them something of the trip, as a whole. You could perhaps go on to suggest that the team meets fortnightly to consider some of the main themes. Use of technology would be a good starting point. This will put you in control of your afternoon. In your morning, you need to get organised. Can you work from home first thing?"

"I would normally say 'yes' to this," I said, "but I cannot get to my voicemails, and there might be something urgent there."

"It looks like you have a training need on voicemails," said the professor. "You either need to get them diverted to your mobile voicemail or learn how to access them directly. Better still, give someone else access to your voicemail, so they can do things in your absence. I would still suggest you avoid the temptation to go in for your voicemails. Send the message to the team and tell them that you'll be in later in the morning, as you'll be going through your e-mails at home before you come in. If there's anything urgent, they can call you at home. If you find anything urgent, in your e-mails, then you can give them a call. Make sure your boss knows what you're doing, just in case. When you get the opportunity to look at your diary, book some time in, as Professor Soljer would, to start planning the new practices that you will be initiating."

The professor got out of his chair as if to stretch himself. He went to the window, briefly looked outside. There was the sound of horses from the street below. The professor turned around to face me.

"Strange, as it may seem," he said, "you are at a turning point. The easiest thing to do, would be to start back on Monday, with all your old habits, on the basis that you will be able to plan in the new ones eventually. I am suggesting that you need to change habits straight away, otherwise you may never change them. The opportunity is now. People will understand if you change things now in a radical way. They will know you've been investigating new ways to manage time. If you do not make a change directly on your return, you may have to be much more incremental, and that runs the risk of not making much change at all."

He moved back to his chair and sat down. Looking at me, he continued, "I fear that you may be finding this assertive. My other fear, is that unless, you assert yourself about how you intend to manage your time, much of the real productivity, you could gain from the last week will be lost. Does this make sense?"

I paused. "I could answer meekly that I understand you, professor," I said, "You have some good ideas. In my organisation, words are not usually enough, actions need to be taken. I am going to commit myself to taking three actions on my first day. I need to think through which ones to choose and I will do that by Monday. Whether they are the same actions that you suggest. Only time will tell, so to speak! There will definitely be three actions taken."

"Thank you," said the professor, "I will leave that to you. I would like to move on to a different subject. Based on your experience, what general techniques do you think managers need to know in order to manage time efficiently in organisations?"

"If I simply take the experience of last week," I said, "it could be argued that each of the professors is saying that you need to be good in certain areas of competence, not necessarily any specific technique, although techniques help and are worth knowing. I guess the crunch point is that techniques are not always applicable. It would depend on the organisation. Good competence in key subjects will lead you to find and deploy appropriate techniques that work."

I got out a piece of paper and made a list of competences as below, talking it through with the professor as I did so. When I finished, I handed the list to the professor.

Professor	Strong Area of Competence
T	Training for productivity. Technology utilisation. Search for innovation.

T	Valuing Time. Managing Perceptions. Being an exemplar of organising.
S	Standardising Routines. Diary management. Event Management. Checklists.
S	Measuring how good a manager you are. Benchmarking against others.
R	Clarity of purpose. Awareness of holdbacks. Engagement. problem solving.
P	Awareness of own attitudes to time. Personal blocks to productivity.
B	Learning cultures Communication. Motivational Practices.
T	Job design. Delegation. Coaching. Empowerment.

"I think you are onto something here which might be more generally useful," said the Professor, " Making this list has probably been a benefit to you as well. You could look back at the topic and remember what the relevant professor might have said about it. This probably makes a very good summary of your week in a technical sense."

"There are some things missing," I said, "which we would need to include if we were to increase the general competence of managers at saving time. For instance, the management of meetings, the management of e-mails, archiving and more motivation practices. I suspect there is also more detail that the professors could tell me, if I had spent more time with them.

"Acknowledged." said the professor. "I know that you only scratched the surface with all of them. I also believe that some of their work is useful at a corporate level. Still, one step at a time. What would you suggest we do with all the learning you have got so far? In what ways can you use this to educate managers more generally?"

"One way," I said, "is that managers undergo what I experienced this week, without having to repeat the visits that I did. To do this, I could write a book on my experience, just as it happened, and they could discover the techniques that are useful to them. Some managers will already know a fair bit, others will know very little. A book gives them a choice of deciding what they want to learn and apply."

"That would seem a good step," said the professor. "I now have another question for you. To what extent, is the organisation, as a whole, responsible for improving time management, as opposed to the individual manager?"

"That's an interesting question," I said, "The organisational responsibility is to create a climate in which work can be done efficiently, and effectively. There are areas within organisations that can already manage time particularly well. For instance if you have a professional production, or logistics operation, some of the work processes will be very time efficient. The general management approaches may be less so."

"What about the responsibility of IT departments?" asked the professor.

"It could also be argued that IT departments are used by organisations to save time. However, this only occurs for processes that can be streamlined and standardised on a large scale. Generally speaking, I would say that organisations focus too much on budget costs and have very little focus on time. As a consequence, they give little attention to valuing time, unless of course, like solicitors, they are actually selling time. It has been the case in my company that a great cost of time has been incurred in saving a very small amount of money."

"So who would be responsible for that sort of occurrence?" asked the professor.

"Ultimately, the top team," I replied. "The reality, from my perspective, is that organisations approach time management in a piecemeal way. If you go on a course about time management, it is all about very basic personal management, not about managing departmental time, or even managing organisational time. OK, there will be other training courses which have an

Everything, but the pipe

impact on how managers manage time e.g. professional management qualifications, teamwork exercises etc. and there are some paper and computer business and project time systems out there to improve planning, but the overall approach is still piecemeal."

"My summary from what you are saying," said the professor, "is that organisations do not focus on time as much as cost and there may be an awareness gap to fill. It also strikes me from what you have said that there is a gap for training courses for managers with an emphasis on proper time management."

"I think top teams also need to take this matter more seriously," I said. "Managers themselves cannot do everything. If managers are responsible for making the best use of people's time, then the organisation should promote common approaches and invest heavily in internal management development. Helping managers get together to review best approaches within their organisations would be a good starting point. It needs to happen in my organisation."

"What do you think top teams should do?" asked the professor.

"I think there is a need for them, as a team, to measure how well they are currently managing organisation time," I said. "Once they know where they are, they can take action to improve their capability of managing organisational time well."

"I think you have found another output that you need to make based on what you have learnt. We should discuss how top teams can save organisational time again," said the professor. "However it is important to do first things first. What you need to do is to implement what you have learnt and discover the tricks of the trade at a practical level. Then there is probably potential for another book, or a checklist, or a measure, which will have a greater chance of producing good results for top teams."

At that moment, the doorbell rang. The professor asked me to hold on for a moment whilst he got up to electronically release the downstairs door. He then left the room to greet Jane.

219

Readers notes:

Can you recall what the other professors said about Jane?

In the next chapter there are several surprises, an interesting explanation of how the pubs are connected, famous buildings, a fleeting mystery guest appearance, a continuation of the theme that connects the professors, a couple of hippopotami, and a great deal of laughter. John also works out the connection between the restaurants. And, of course there are some big challenges, perhaps the biggest challenges, to how you spend your time!

There is lots more including including black holes, a chronosphage, grasshoppers and punts.

Remember where John and Jane are located and fasten your safety belts for a journey through time. If you have a map of London, it may be helpful for the journey although it is not essential.

Chapter 14
The Tenth Professor
It only takes a laugh!

I heard a woman's voice apologise for being slightly late, and then I heard footsteps on the stairs. I only heard two people coming up the stairs. I had anticipated there might be two visitors with the professor, based on what a couple of the professors had said earlier in the week.

The professor brought Jane into the room. She was an attractive woman, probably a little younger than me, although she was of similar height and had flowing brown hair. "Jane," said the professor, "let me introduce you to John Watson."

I got up. "I'm pleased to meet you, Jane. You come highly recommended," I said.

"I have heard a fair bit about you too." she said, shaking my hand.

Professor Holmes continued, "Jane is a rising star, and is about to become a professor herself. We are already calling her a professor," he said jokingly. "Her expertise is that good. Before you ask, John, she is a special type of physicist and she comes from…"

"The land of punt wars," said Jane interrupting in a very good humoured way, and smiling at the professor, as she did so.

"That gives rise to at least one question," I said. "What is the speciality you study?"

Jane smiled, "Dark matter, but I think we will keep that off the agenda this afternoon."

"Not a problem," I said, with a grin. "I'm used to directors considering matters in the dark, and most of the information I send them seems to go into a black hole!"

"I think we are in for a lively afternoon," said Jane. She turned to Professor Holmes. "Richard, it is a very nice afternoon out there. I thought John and myself could go for a walk in the park, as I pass on to him what few gems I can offer him. How would that suit you?"

"Might I suggest going one step further," said Professor Holmes. "I have got to go out shortly. Why don't you start, and end, in the sunshine. I can then leave to do what I have to do, and both John and yourself can return to your respective destinations, when you have finished."

"That's fine by me," said Jane. "How about you John?"

"Not a problem," I replied. "Professor, I will give some more thought to what we discussed and will talk to you, again after I have completed my surprise re-entry back to work."

"I know you will," he said. "Just out of interest, Jane will be able to talk to you about a certain grasshopper in her fair city, which is a real time eater. Chronosphage they call it. Might be of interest!"

We shook hands. I picked up my shoulder bag and followed Jane towards the door of the room, past the hat stand with just a deerstalker cap upon it, down the stairs, and out into the street. She was right. It had turned into a lovely afternoon.

"The park is about fifty yards further up the street," said Jane. We walked in that direction and crossed a couple of roads towards the park entrance.

As we were walking, Jane asked, "How did you get on with Richard?"

"He seems to be keen on the big picture," I said. "He is also keen for me to implement what I have already learnt and then to meet him again to take a more corporate approach on time management."

"He's also very astute," said Jane, "He notices far more about a person than you would think possible. He can sum them up very quickly and he is normally proved right. He also uses his influence in a very subtle way. You will probably be doing exactly what he expects you to do. Needless to say he was a very talented physicist. Before he retired, he was the one tutor that everyone wanted to have. Mind you, they say that good professors never die. I can confirm they don't fade away either! I still learn a lot from him."

When we reached the park, there was a lake immediately in front of us. "Let's go to the left," said Jane. We started walking along the side of the lake.

There were a large number of ducks and geese on the lake. There were also a large number of Canadian geese nestling, in the grassland, on the land side of the path. I could also hear some seagulls. The view down the lakeside was superb in the sunshine.

"This is like an oasis," I said to Jane. "To think that we are so close to the centre of London."

I noticed a heron standing on a drain cover protruding from the lake. I pointed it out to Jane.

"A statue," she said with a smile.

She seemed to be right. There was no movement at all. The bird just stood there. It was very convincing as a statue. Even the colours of the bird, as we came near it, seemed lifelike. It was a well-designed immovable object. We must have walked within fifteen feet of it.

"Unbelievable," I commented. We walked past the heron. I looked back. Suddenly, it moved! It was real.

"A robot," said Jane, with a twinkle in her eye. "Not everything is as it seems."

"A robot simulator," I said. I stopped and turned round to have another good look at the heron. It very slowly opened its wings, and then leaning forward, it pulled its wings right open and took off.

Looking back and taking in the wider scene, the only evidence of London was a large tower, rising above the trees. "To think, with all those large buildings in central London, all we can see is just one." I turned back to Jane.

"You are getting a bit carried away," she said. "It is good to appreciate what is around you though. Have you had a good week?"

"Yes," I replied. "The professors have been very good, although I have had some strange experiences away from the universities. Each place I stayed had something peculiar about it."

"Tell me more" said Jane. "I'm intrigued."

I told her about the pub called the Hunter with three lights on the hunter's belt and the landlord's comments about light pollution and M42, not the M42.

"That's unusual but also easy for me to explain," said Jane. "Orion is the name of a hunter. The three lights on his belt represent three stars that make up Orion's belt. Below the belt is Orion's sword. Its' shape is defined by the famous Great Orion Nebula, a massive nearby star formation, otherwise known as *M42*. Your landlord was an astronomer! What was strange about the other places you visited?"

"The next pub was The Swan. It too had a strange pub sign, but stranger still was a bio-robotics boffin I met. He seemed to be in a world of his own." I told Jane the full story and how the boffin went on about a beta Cygni."

"That is also interesting," said Jane. This time, it is not so much the landlord that knows about astronomy, but your boffin. The double star Albireo, otherwise known as *beta-Cygni*, marks the head of the swan constellation and it is a showpiece of the sky."

"I think my story is getting stranger by the moment," I said. "My next pub does have a connection to stars. It was called the water carrier and portrayed someone at night carrying water. In the background were stars."

"Aquarius is otherwise known as the water carrier. It is characterised by a stream of stars reaching to the horizon, said Jane. "Are there any other pubs you have been to recently?

Only a couple of local ones," I said, "The Great Bear and the Plough."

"The Great Bear is Ursa Major," said Jane," ...and the Plough you will know about anyway."

"Oh no!" I said. "I have just realised that we could not see a Northern entertainer, a northern star, perform at the Plough, because it was raining heavily!"

"Strange world and interesting coincidences," said Jane. "Mind you, if they keep on happening to you we will have to create a law called Watson's law. John Watson can only be found in pubs with a stellar connection!"

We came to the end of the lake, and turned right towards a bridge. I looked back over my shoulder and saw the top of a building above the trees. It was the only other building visible apart from the tower at the other end of the lake. Jane saw me looking. "Changing times," she said.

"Not part of our history," I said, "but may be an important part of the future."

We walked across the bridge and up the other side into a large open area. Ahead of us was a long straight path.

"We are here for the purpose of discussing time management," said Jane. "The only problem is that I do not know what the professors have said to you about that purpose."

That re-focused me. I found it a little surprising, as I expected her to be clear on what she would be telling me.

"They did not actually say," I said. "They simply stressed that I ought to meet you."

"I suspect then," said Jane, "they want me to give you the answer to life, the universe, and everything."

"That makes me feel all sixes and sevens," I looked into her eyes, and smiled.

"Very few people would know what you're talking about with that comment," she said, looking back at me.

"It is in the guide," I replied, in mock protestation.

"But not everyone is a hitch hiker," she said.

"Although everyone has access to a search engine," I said. "So what is the answer to life, the universe, and everything?"

"It is the one that makes sense to us as individuals," she said. "All the other professors are very focused on how to do better within a work context. So when I meet them, I am interested in challenging them about the purpose of knowing how to do things better. I am not interested in the answers of more profit, less waiting times, and that sort of thing. I am interested in the higher purpose of more profit, less waiting times etc. It is more a question of how we relate those activities to the aims that we have as a society. Lots of people, go about their daily lives without a thought about the longer term future either for themselves, or for society as a whole. Most governments tend to be reactive to situations and do not look beyond the next election."

Turning to me, she asked "How do you see your future, John?"

This question reminded me of what my boss asked at my annual performance appraisal. "Ultimately, I see myself getting a bigger job, and possibly settling down with a family," I said. "I have, perhaps, not been as aggressive as some in pursuing a career. However, I have worked hard. I tend to see my contribution to society as coming through my work."

"If your work is ethical, and somebody wants it for an ethical purpose, then there is no doubt you are making a contribution," said Jane. "The question you then have to ask is what is your work making a contribution to, in a general sense."

"That is the sort of question that I leave others to work out," I said.

"You make my point," said Jane. "You live by certain principles. You elect politicians to represent your principles in society. What I believe, is that we, as individuals, should have a view on the principles and purpose that any government might be proposing for us. The point I'm coming round to is that part of the time, we have available to us, should be dedicated to creating a society that we want and not leaving it to politicians and pressure groups. Businessmen need to play their part, rather than focussing on business and then relaxing."

"So what you are saying," I summarised, "is that part of our efforts during any day, any week, should be dedicated to building society up, or turning it round, depending on your views of the future."

"Yes. That is the key message. You cannot have a view on everything, but you should be clear what you believe in, and be prepared to influence any politician, or maybe even the population at large, to go your way. Having no involvement, leaves the world open to vested interests. It allows situations to creep up on us, which can radically change the nature of our society. There are situations that clearly have crept up on us:-- global warming, drunken behaviour, immigration to name but a few. There are also situations that are creeping up now, such as, future energy shortages, demographic changes, pension provision. Focusing on your work alone, will not provide the solutions to some of these problems. Can we therefore agree that life is not all about work, and work is not all about life?"

"In principle, I agree," I replied. "I also agree that we should make time for those things that are important to us as individuals, but it is difficult to do everything, isn't it?

"I believe there are other zones in our lives," replied Jane, "apart from the work zone. We should organise ourselves to give each one adequate attention. To me this is about overall time management, and not just time management at work. If you were not working, John, what would you be doing, on the basis that you have enough money on which to survive." she asked.

"Apart from having a good holiday, visiting places, doing things I hadn't done before, and catching up with old friends, I have not got much of an answer," I admitted.

"Maybe that is a question that should linger with you," said Jane. "Let me tell you what a well respected professor once said to me about how to structure your life. He said you should consider that your life has two major areas. There is the area in which you earn your living through exercising expertise, and there is the area of your interests, in which you follow through those things of personal interest to you. He then considered what you could be doing under each of the headings, Expertise and Interests. Each of those headings he broke down into other general activities. He then designed a questionnaire so people could reflect on how they spent their time. Are you with me so far?"

"I think I know the sort of questionnaires as work-life balance questionnaires," I said, " which by design, show that you spend too much time working, and not enough on other aspects of your life. Am I being too cynical?"

"You are," said Jane. "Many of those questionnaires that I have seen, just look at the simple balance of 'work' and 'life'. The difference that the professor came up with is how you should distribute your time, whilst you are at work and when you're not. This is far more controversial, but the good thing about working through something that is controversial, is that it helps you to form your own views about what you should, and could be doing."

"I am happy to have a look at such a questionnaire and I hope it is better than some I have seen," I said.

"It just so happens that I have a copy of his basic model with me," said Jane. "I'll show you when we stop."

We walked in silence for a while. We passed some cricket nets, and entered a glade of trees. We came to a point where a number of paths came together, although ours continued straight ahead and down a dip. We continued walking, past an athletic track on the left hand side, and went over a canal bridge. From the other side of the bridge, we crossed diagonally over a road to another park. We took a pathway to the left, passed a blue police box, and climbed gently up the slope of a hill.

As we walked up the slope, Jane asked, "Do you have a family?"

"No, I am single," I replied. "Do you?"

I was expecting her to talk about her son, so the answer that came back surprised me.

"I am the same," she said. "If you have a family, sometimes family members are useful to talk to about the future, sometimes friends are, and sometimes people at work are. It is important that you have someone you can trust as a mentor."

"I am lucky," I said, "I do have an informal 'non work' mentor who gives very sensible advice, both when I need it, and when I don't." I added a humorous tone to my voice here.

"That's good," she said.

We stopped for a moment, to catch our breath. I looked across the park and then noticed something I had not noticed before. There were street lights along every path, including the path up to the top of the hill. I had not noticed them in the park that we had just been through. I mentioned this to Jane. She thought it might be because they closed the other park at night and not this one. It seemed a rational explanation.

We carried on walking. The path led us to the top of a small hill. There was a glorious view of London from here. You could see the London Eye, St Paul's Cathedral, and the BT Tower. The Gherkin was slightly hidden, and Canary Wharf was in the distance. You could, however, see the top of St Stephen's clocktower, which has a much more famous name.

We sat down on the grass at the top of the hill admiring the view. I was relieved to put down my airline shoulder bag, whose weight was just beginning to make itself noticed.

I started thinking about Jane's son. I am sure I had heard Professor Taylor correctly when he referred to him. Yet Jane had said she had no family of her own. Strange!

Suddenly my thoughts were disturbed by the noise of someone running behind me. A man in his thirties had come up the hill from the other side. He stopped a few yards from us and peered intently into the distance with his left hand shielding his eyes. A young woman came running from the same direction and joined him and looked in the same direction.

"What is it, Doctor?" I heard her ask the man.

"I can sense he is out there" replied the man.

"Who, Doctor?" said the young woman.

"An unwelcome time traveller. Quick," he said, turning away from us and starting to run down the path we had just come up. I may have missed exactly what he said next as he had started running, but is sounded like "We have no time to lose. Back to the car, Dizz".

There are some funny Christian names around I thought. Could this be someone called Dizzie? Dizzie, if that was her name, ran after the doctor.

"A doctor in a hurry," said Jane.

"Proper doctors don't hurry. They have patients," I quipped.

"So let me test your patience," said Jane. "Here is the basic version of the Expertise – Interests questionnaire". She passed over an A4 sheet, she had taken from her shoulder bag.

I studied it for a couple of minutes.

Expertise – Interests Analysis

No	Expertise	No activity	Passive	Ad hoc	Maintenance	Active	Strongly active	Very Unhappy	Slightly Unhappy	OK	Pleasure	Strong Pleasure
1	A General Functional area											
2	A Specialist area within a Function											
3	A second Specialist area											
4	A general skill at an expert level											
5	An ability to influence change											
6	Relationships with others											
7	An ability to innovate and initiate											
8	Co-ordination expertise											
9	Business / Professional networking											
10	Involvement in other end markets											
	Interests			Activity Evidence						Satisfaction from what you do		
1	You (looking after yourself)											
2	Your Family											
3	Your Friends											
4	Your Assets											
5	A physical activity											
6	A special Interest (hobby or knowledge)											
7	A conviction calling (political or religious)											
8	A contribution to society											
9	A local community affiliation											
10	A further affiliation (local or national)											

"I think I need some help with some of the headings," I said, "What is a local community affiliation?"

"Do you belong to a local club, or any other local group of people?" asked Jane, "The rationale behind the section is that the professor suggests that you ought to be mixing with people other than immediate friends and family. There's another section which is simply called 'A further affiliation'. This can be another local, or national club, or interest group, or voluntary activity that allows you to mix with a different set of people."

"Understood," I said, "So the scoring is about whether I can evidence any activity in these areas, and then whether I derive satisfaction from that activity?"

"Yes," said Jane. "Notice the questionnaire does not ask you how much activity you do in terms of hours or minutes. It just asks you about the nature of the activity. Notice too, that there is no overall score. This is very much a discussion document."

"I have some other points to clarify," I said. "Can you tell me under the expertise heading what would be a special general skill?"

"This could be a skill at doing presentations, at problem solving, at practising a particular management technique," replied Jane, "The rationale here is that you have a skill not just related to your functional know-how, and the ability to influence and relate to other people. So to give you an example on the various headings, a lawyer would have expertise in the geographical area where they do business. That is their market. Their functional area is the law and they would be expected to keep on top of it in a general sense. A specialist area could be probate law. A general skill could be use of Excel spreadsheets, in which they have advanced expertise."

"Why is there a second specialist area mentioned?" I asked.

"The professor believed that you should not just have one area of expertise on which your career rested. He suggested there should be another area, albeit within the same functional area. This may be useful if problems emerge with a market for your first area of expertise."

"Take my position," I said, "My market would be my company's market.

I have an active expertise in that, particularly as I meet customers. My functional area would be customer service. My specialist area would be the expertise I have with the company products. I am not sure what my second specialist area would be. I am also not sure my general skill would be. I actively seek to improve my ability to influence and I can provide evidence of that. I suppose I just maintain my ability to form relationships. I can evidence my wish to learn a general skill, in a strongly active way, because I'm talking to you, Jane. Networking is an ad hoc activity for me. How am I doing?

"Pretty good," said Jane, "Your special general skill might well develop into time management, but that is the future, perhaps."

"On the personal side, under interests, I'm struggling a bit," I said, "Can you talk me through the meaning of the headings, 'You' and 'Your assets'?"

"'You' is about looking after yourself," said Jane, "Someone who is active, would be interested in what they eat, their weight, their physical fitness, their well being. 'Your assets' is about how you look after those things you own. This might include a house, stocks and shares, cars etc. If you simply react to things going wrong in your house, and the rest of the house is a mess, it would suggest that there is very little evidence that you are looking after this asset well."

"Is it possible," I asked, "to have an overlap between the various categories? I am a sports fan. I have an active knowledge of a high level in the abilities of the players, the rules of the game, the operation of the leagues etc. Does this count as an affiliation, or special interest?

"There could be an overlap," Jane replied, "If you have one thing you do that spreads very thinly across two or three sections, the professor would expect you to do something else that you would also spread thinly across two or three sections. Alternatively, if you count what you said as one of two things, then you have to find something else for the other thing.

"I think this takes us to what the heart of the questionnaire is all about. It is not a rigorous questionnaire. It is a simple prompt for thinking and discussion. It may, or may not matter that you have no evidence in a particular area. The professor simply advises that you should stop from time to time and ask yourself what are you doing in the various segments.

If the answer is nothing, then you should ask yourself, whether you are happy with that. If not, you should ask yourself how you can rebalance your time. So lets go back to the structure of the questionnaire. Are you happy that you know what to do with the satisfaction scores?"

"I think so," I replied, "I suspect there will be correlations between those things I'm interested in, and my satisfaction of those interests. I guess if that wasn't so, I should be talking to somebody about it. So broadly, I am happy with the scoring system," I said, "It may take me a little while to decide what to do with it, once I have scored it. For instance, work can be sometimes pleasurable, sometimes painful, but it's more or less OK, which is where I think my scoring is."

"There could be a number of features about the score," said Jane. "It may be that a context is not very energising for you. It may be that your personality verges towards being neutral most of the time. It may be that you do not consider that you can have fun at work. That could be an attitude, which you will be able to change. You will know which it is. The idea of the model is to challenge you. If you have not thought about things in this way before, or even from while, it could be valuable simply to review what you do. It is only by having a rounded picture, that you can know what is of overall importance to you. It could well have implications for you about how you use your time in, and out of, work. Ideally, you could run through this, and then discuss the outcome with somebody else."

"Thanks. I would like to fill this out and give it some further thought," I said. "Have you a contact number that I could discuss it over the phone with you, if you are willing."

"Yes, of course," she replied. She reached into her bag, pulled out a business card and passed it over.

I took the business card and looked at it. The first thing I noticed was that I had correctly guessed the name of the University where the punt wars occurred. It was also the city of the bicycle. Then I noticed something else.

What followed was one of those strange experiences. It starts with a half laugh of surprise, and then, as the totality of what has happened flows over you, you burst out laughing. That is exactly what happened to me. "I can't believe this," I managed to get out.

"What's wrong?" asked Jane. I looked at her, and her facial expression made me laugh all the more.

When I had recovered slightly, I said to Jane, "You know you said to me that you had no family of your own." She nodded. "I have just realised that I had been making a colossal assumption." I told her how the words of the other professors had led me to think in a certain way, when it was totally logical to think in a very different way.

She started laughing, saying "And you thought…." She could not contain herself and started laughing as well, which set me off again. Even though both of us managed to stop laughing for the odd few moments, just looking at each other again, set us off again. Other people must have thought we were mad!

That incident changed the whole tone of the afternoon. No longer would we be discussing detailed aspects of time management. Instead we engaged in natural, humorous interchanges about ourselves.

It took us quite a while to walk down the hill. I got slightly confused at the bottom as I could not remember where I had seen the blue Police Box. I could not see it where I thought it was. Jane was not interested. I was more interested in talking and walking with her so we crossed to the lower park retracing the way we came. We stopped at the canal bridge. Interestingly, I noticed, when looking south-east, that there were a couple of hippos on the right hand bank. There was s a good reason for them to be there. A couple of canal boats cruised towards us, and we waved merrily to the people on them, who returned the wave.

We took a slightly different way back. We passed the HUB in the middle of the large green space. A thought suddenly struck me. If the HUB was something different to what it actually was, then it would have a connection with virtually all of the professors, either in something they said, or something they did, or in something that was around them. And this included Professor Holmes! An activity connection. How strange!

Having passed the HUB, we made our way to Queen Mary's Gardens.

This is a wonderful place, with a number of secluded spots, fragrant rose gardens, large waterfalls. A delightful place to get to know somebody else.

I learnt a lot about Jane that afternoon, as she undoubtedly learnt a lot about me. Although we had to go different ways, we agreed we would meet again. She decided she would walk east towards the mainline station to get her home, and I walked west back towards the Tube station to head to my home. What an afternoon! I forgot to ask her about the grasshopper! Maybe next time.

Just before leaving the park, on the way back to the station, I found a park bench, where I could phone Mary, before she left work. I also found a scrap of paper for taking any notes about when to meet later on.

As I was waiting to get through, I started doodling on the piece of paper. I constructed the word TIME in a three-dimensional way, as part of the doodle.

After about a minute, I heard Mary's voice, "This is Mary Evans. How can I help you?"

Her switchboard had clearly not told her who was calling. I started to say "Mary", but then looking at my piece of paper and seeing the word 'TIME', I suddenly realised what Mary was talking about when she had left me the puzzles on Monday evening. I would never have got that, without actually hearing her now.

I heard Mary say, "Is that you, John? Are you there?"

I regained my powers of speech. "Yes, Mary. I have just worked out the answer to one of the puzzles you set me on Monday. You gave it away in your introduction."

"What about the other puzzle?" she asked, "Does our visit tonight to a Thai restaurant help?"

"Uh, I don't think so," I said slowly, looking down to my piece of paper. "Is it something to do with different nationalities?"

"That's the wrong approach," she said. "Connect your thinking back to the restaurant where we were on Monday."

"Just a moment," I said slowly. I looked at the doodle of the word 'time' and drew a line slowly underneath the T and I. As I did so, the penny dropped. "I would *not* dream of doing such a thing."

"I should hope not," said Mary, "You have solved the puzzle. Changing subject, everything seems OK for tonight. Are you ready to take down the details?"

"Yes," I said. "I am looking forward to an enjoyable night out to follow my enjoyable afternoon. It has been quite fun in a strange sort of way. I met this professor, who is not quite a professor. She believed I should have a bit of fun inside, and outside work. Go ahead with the details."

I took the details down. Then Mary added, "Why don't we have some fun tonight? The others know what you have been doing, but not where you have been. How about disguising the places and letting them work them out as you tell us what you have been up to?"

"OK," I said. "You will have to forewarn them that there is a little competition and I will do the best I can to make a mystery of my travels."

We said goodbye. I put my piece of paper in the bag and made my way back to the underground station.

<u>Readers Notes</u>

Have you worked out why John and Jane burst out laughing? Is there a son involved? If you do not know, there is a further clue in the next chapter?

Have you identified the famous buildings? What is famous about St. Stephens clocktower?

Are you independently able to work out what a Chronosphage is, and where this one is located. What would be its relationship relationship to a grasshopper and the passage of time?

What do you make of the reference to the Guide?

Who was the mystery guest (British readers only!)? Can you explain the confusion over the blue police box?

What were a couple of hippopotami doing on the river bank? Maybe a map would help.

What is the HUB? You may have to look this up! Better still if you live nearby, you could walk the route that John and Jane took.

If you are still puzzling about the connection between the restaurants that John and Mary have been discussing, why not do a doodle as John did?

Have you worked out John's favourite sport. There is an easy final clue coming!

The story is not over yet. How is John going to tackle his Monday morning? What exactly is his relationship to Mary? Why might John refer to Eel Pie? Sit back and enjoy an interesting reality in the final chapter.

Chapter 15
The Turning Point
'Time for Change.'

Friday night was a success. The others managed to work out the eight cities that I had visited. I had to give them a clue about one city being about a group of people, a fireman, pouring rain and an hourglass.

Saturday was not so successful. It was an 'away' match for my team, and it was a late kick-off. I managed to do a few chores in the morning, before setting out to join other supporters taking local pre-arranged coaches up to the match.

Mary does not come to 'away' matches, but I know a lot of the other supporters by sight. I wondered if any of them will miss me if I'm not here. This may not be a sufficient strength of affiliation that Jane's old professor would have advised. Perhaps I ought to take more of a personal interest in some of the supporters that I travel with!

As always, there is a light-hearted humour on travelling to an 'away' fixture. The mood on the way back, however, is governed by how the team performs. On this Saturday, they lost badly. Teamwork behind the scrum fell apart. We couldn't even blame the referee. Our tickets meant that we had no cover on our stand, and it rained. The late kick-off also meant that the last part of the game was played under floodlights. All of this meant we got soaked on a dreary late afternoon and had nothing to celebrate. The mood was sombre on the way back.

We got back to the local coach stop well past 10 pm, and I decided to go straight home. It was just over a twenty minute walk away.

Arriving at my house, I opened the front door and switched on the light. The house felt a bit empty. I did live there alone, although up to last year I had a lodger, who also turned into a good friend. When he got promoted in his company and left, I decided to have a break before getting another lodger. It couldn't be a long break, because the income really did help pay the bills!

A dreary match followed by an empty house. My mood was pretty low, and in some ways I felt vulnerable. What is to become of me long term, I wondered.

I went to bed, listened to some soporific music on the radio, and drifted off to sleep.

Unusually, I woke up in the middle of the night as a result of a dream. I cannot remember the details, but I do remember it was a relay race and involved all the professors. Professor Taylor had a baton, which he passed to Professor Perman, which she in turn, after a lightning run, passed to Professor Tinker, who just happened to be on a bicycle! Weird! I drifted back to sleep again.

I woke up quite early the next morning feeling much fresher. The sun was shining around the curtain and the air itself felt fresh. Normally I would linger in bed on a Sunday morning, but on this occasion I felt motivated to get up and make a list of what I had to do. Mary was coming round later in the day to go through the features of standard office software and I wanted to be prepared.

As I sat at the kitchen table with my coffee and a half completed activity list in front of me, I remembered fragments of the dream. I found myself thinking about Professor Taylor, and Professor Soljer. Time for a tidy up routine, I thought.

I started work, but then other ideas crossed my mind and I started to rearrange the furniture. I looked around the room and concluded that a change was needed. I thought about Professor Perman's change model and then looked at my watch. There would be plenty of time to do it!

Time for action. I locked up the house and drove to Bayswater Road. On the north side of a couple of London parks, there are paintings for sale hung on the road side of the park railings. There are also normally some artists present who can do portraits, and a couple who can do a simple watercolour painting on the spot.

I found a big picture I liked, and I asked a watercolour painter to do two simple smaller pictures for me. It did not take as long as expected.

I returned home, put the pictures in their places, rearranged a few more things and made myself a sandwich for lunch.

Mary was due at 2 pm., and on the dot, the doorbell rang.

She came into the house, and walked into the living room. "I can see you have made some changes," she said, after a pause. "I like the new picture. It's much more your style. Your old picture was pleasant, but did not have any real message to offer to those who saw it."

"Time for a change," I said.

"Have you been thinking about Professor Taylor?" Mary asked.

"Yes, in a roundabout way. I have also been thinking about what Jane told me."

"You better brief me more about what you did last Friday," said Mary.

I went into the detail of what happened that Friday afternoon. When I explained what happened on the hill as I saw Jane's business card, Mary burst out laughing.

"That's the best case of mistaken identity that I have heard for a long-time," she said, after I finished my story. "I have also taken the point that one of the things Jane was saying to you is that you should look after yourself and your assets. Combine that with Professor Taylor's comment that your first loyalty is to yourself, and I can see that you have been influenced, whether you fully know it or not. That's good!

"I'm going to change the subject now," Mary went on, "from admiring your house to what we are going to do this afternoon. Otherwise we'll find some very good reasons not to start."

Mary had bought her laptop, so we positioned ourselves side-by-side and went through the toolbars on the office software. It was an interesting way to learn – it was like parallel 'hands on' learning, and it worked very well. I learnt quite a few things that I did not know, and refreshed my ability to do things that I only half remembered. There were a number of areas I discovered where I could better use the software at work.

After about an hour and a half, Mary suggested we had a break and go for a walk to the river.

"You're not after a short walk then?" I said to Mary.

"Let's make it energising," she said.

It was quite a blustery day outside, so we took our coats, walked to the park, and then through the park down to the path by the river.

We stopped at the river and looked across to the other bank. All you could see across the other side was countryside. The river is quite wide at this point. On a sunny day, rowing boats and canoes are often evident. That was not the case today.

"Eel pie and ham?" I asked Mary.

"I prefer the other way today," said Mary. We turned to the left and walked along the path. They were a few other people also out for a Sunday afternoon walk. There were also a few cyclists of varying age groups who appeared from time to time.

As we walked along the river path, Mary asked, "Are you all set for tomorrow?"

"I am mentally well prepared," I replied. "Late this evening I am going to fix a couple of diary dates via my laptop, so as to give me a morning at home to clear my e-mails. I am not going touch the e-mails themselves until the morning. Even when I do get into the e-mails, I am going to put them in different categories – information, replies required, action required, future meeting topics etc. I am going to go through the lot before I start replying, unless it is a simple yes or no. This will help me quantify what I have to do, before I set about doing it in detail. I will have a team meeting in the afternoon, and I intend to give the team the task of improving the way we use technology. I will do it in a way that uses the sort of questions that Professor Richmond recommended. Once they are briefed on that I am going to set them a task on setting the purpose of the department to see whether we can agree something similar to what Professor Richmond suggested. It will be a much better outcome if I can get them engaged with it. I also intend to plan my diary using some of the tips from Professor Soljer."

"That sounds good," said Mary. "What happens if it doesn't work out that way? Perhaps they'll be something in your e-mails that means you have another urgent task to do first."

"Maybe," I replied. "I may have to put up with a temporary distraction on the first day, but the second and third day will give me the opportunity to get some decent planning into place. Oh! I forgot to mention that at the end of the first day, I am going to readjust my desk and workspace, not only to improve the physical way I gather and process information, but also to radiate some of the messages that I want to radiate."

"That also sounds good," said Mary. We then walked in silence for a while, up to Glover's Island.

"Whilst I remember," said Mary, "I have done some investigation on voice dictation. Those who have the confidence to use it, and persevere when they start, say it makes a terrific difference. There seems to be a general consensus, that you should go for the wireless version, as the headphones, can hurt your head after a while. The point was also made that if you are in the middle of dictating and have to get up, the wireless version means you do not have to remember to unplug the headphones."

"I'd like to have a go at that next weekend," I said. "If I get some software next Friday evening, would you be willing to help me to set it up on the Sunday?"

"Certainly," replied Mary. "It could help with my work quite significantly too. It is a slow process doing all my reports. If I could speed that up, I could search out more interesting work."

The scenic houses of Richmond were beginning to appear on the hill on bank. It would not be long before we reached the bridge.

"Are you going to be able to achieve the objectives you agreed with your company?" asked Mary.

"I have no problem with those," I replied. "Technology will help us. Professor Richmond gave me a process to get the issues out into the open so they can be dealt with, and he also suggested that I might publicly monitor how quickly other departments react to our needs. That's exactly what I am going to do."

When we reached the bridge, we had to turn left up a slipway, which brought us to a pedestrian crossing. We crossed over the road and walked up the bridge to a little bay in the bridge wall just beyond the apex. We leant against the wall and both of us gazed downstream past Corporation Island to the next bridge in the distance. On our right, was a wonderfully terraced area with plenty of space for the public to walk, and sit, on a sunny afternoon. There was also a rowing boat hire centre at this point.

I could feel the wind on my cheeks, as I leant against the bridge wall. It would seem to be growing in strength. There were a lot of wind ripples on the water.

"I've just decided what I'm doing on Tuesday evenings," I said to Mary.

As she turned to look me, I continued, "I am going to go swimming straight after work. I have a vague recollection lane swimming starts at six, so I'm going to arrange to do that. I'll be leaving the office earlier that day from now on."

"Decisions seem to be coming thick and fast," said Mary. "You will have to make sure you establish that pattern for it to become useful to you in the long term. I seem to recall that you liked swimming in days gone by. The good thing is that you are returning to something you like doing."

"Professor Holmes said I am at a turning point. Looks like I am turning backwards in time to times gone by!" I said jokingly.

Mary did not reply. She returned her gaze to the river. I did as well. We must have spent a good two minutes just observing what was before us, and noticing what was happening around us. I could feel the wind continue to strengthen more on my cheeks.

"John," said Mary, still staring out over the river, "you are no longer at *a* turning point. You are at *the* turning point. You are turning even now. You should remember this place and this day. You are no longer the same 'John' that you were last week."

I suppose I could have felt pleased, but I suddenly felt slightly sad, as I continued gazing up the river. I felt I was losing something; that I was leaving something that I would not be able to regain. It was one of those feelings that makes you feel vulnerable, just as the night before when I returned home and had the thought 'What is to become of me?' It was an emotional moment. Tears welled up inside me. I snivelled slightly.

Mary turned round to look at me, and I looked at her. "You are no longer the same 'John'," she said. "You are a stronger 'John'. A more confident 'John'. A 'John' who is choosing what they want to do, rather than just being a follower of circumstance. A 'John' who is being true to himself. A 'John' who is using what he learns. I like that. I will be with you all the way."

"Thanks," I muttered, rather tearfully. Mary still kept looking at me. I am sure she could sense I was feeling emotional, and could see the tear rolling down my face. Would a stream of tears add to a river of time, I wondered. I attempted to distract myself.

Suddenly, Mary backed away. Her voice changed to a firmer tone. "John, what have you been doing with your coat? Look at you."

I stopped leaning against the bridge, stood up straight and looked down at my coat. I could not see anything wrong.

"Turn around" ordered Mary.

I turned around.

"Turn around again," said Mary.

I turned around again.

"And again" said Mary.

I felt a bit confused. I started to turn and said, "Why? What's wrong?"

"Nothing," said Mary, with a laugh. "It's just that one good turn deserves another!" She then turned round, and ran to the apex of the bridge

245

and down the other side to the pedestrian crossing.

"Oh, no!" I said to myself. I had been had. However, it had worked and changed my mood. I ran after her.

"I should push you in to the river," I said catching up with her.

"Not when it's tea time," said Mary. "I think you have just proved managers are human beings as well as rational organisational people. Time to go back now, don't you think?"

"I think I've been through some sort of rite of passage," I said. "Hopefully, I am through to the other side."

We linked arms. I cannot remember when I last did this with her. It would have been many, many years ago, back in that Northern town where we both grew up.

We got back just before it started raining. After taking our coats off, we went into the kitchen. I put the kettle on.

"I can see a smiley on one of your cupboards," said Mary. "What's that it says underneath it? 'Match Me'?"

"Yes," I replied. "Why don't you try?"

Mary tried with a couple of facial contortions.

"Keep trying," I said laughing, "I'll go and fetch the camera."

She burst out laughing. "I also notice you have got a list on another cupboard door," she said, carefully avoiding the prospect of being photographed. She got up to give it a closer look. "I notice that you have headed it 'The Plumstone Collection' and I can see you've listed all the professors there including Richard Holmes and Jane. It is an interesting point that eight of them form such an interesting pattern. I spotted the possibility of that half way through your visits."

"The overall list is an aide memoire to remind me to frequently call upon the wisdom of the ten professors," I said. "I am also going to put up a list like that at work. If I ever get stuck on something, I can ask myself what each of the professors would have advised."

"Between them they probably offer you all the management guidance you will ever need," said Mary. "Richard Holmes was the coordinator. What would you say is his core guidance?"

"I'm still working on that," I said. "One of his observations was about corporate responsibility, so that will lead me to think about whether there is a corporate issue that needs fixing. For the rest of his guidance, I guess I'll know when I know."

"And Jane?" asked Mary.

"She will lead me to question whether what I'm doing is important in the whole scheme of things, and she will also make me more sensitive to looking after myself, and getting connected to other people and issues outside work."

"I notice you've written her number down on the list," said Mary with an element of cheekiness in her voice. "What is she really like?"

"Very nice," I said. "I like her. I did promise to give her a ring to give her my reaction to the questionnaire she gave me. I was thinking I might invite her down here."

"I would like to meet her," said Mary.

The kettle boiled. I poured the tea, and we sat down at the kitchen table.

"Did I tell you that I was going to write a book on all that has happened to me this week, just as it happened?" I asked Mary.

"I don't think you did," said Mary. "I hope you are going to concentrate on the professor's ideas and not put in anything about what I said."

"You will be the most important character," I said, with a smile. "You've been pulling all the strings, even the heartstrings, all along."

"I am going to insist on editing it then," said Mary," ...and proof reading the final version to make sure nothing extra creeps in. What are you going to do after you have completed the book, and presumably agreed the content with the professors?"

"What I can in the time available," I said. "There will have to be some marketing, and I can use some of the business web networks and a PR person I know, although I will be a bit limited in what I can do, as I will still have a job to do."

"We will have to cross that bridge when we come to it," said Mary. "It's important that people have an opportunity to discuss all the professors ideas, either amongst themselves, or with a knowledgeable mentor. People can read books which inspire them temporarily, but then take no action on how they work. You can learn things all your life, but it's what you do with what you learn that makes a real difference.

"When we start using the voice dictation next week," I said, "that will probably help us plan how quickly we can get to that bridge. You are right, there has to be something in the book that promotes people talking about it and using it."

"I think you should also have one resolution remaining from the past, John. Don't consider doing any work on the Saturday, including your visit reports!"

"Done!" I said.

We finished our tea. "I must go now," said Mary. "I've got things to do for next week and I am sure you have. I will just use the loo before I go."

I took the cups to the sink and Mary went to the loo. Two minutes later, there was a shout from Mary. "John, you put a smiley on the loo floor!" I smiled.

I rejoined Mary, as she was putting on her coat. "I will need to keep my eye on you," she said.

We made our way to the front door. I suddenly felt that slight feeling of loss again.

Mary turned. "Are you going to give your big sister a hug before she goes?"

We hugged. "Thanks for everything you are doing for me, big sister" I said quietly.

"Great things will come of you yet," she said. With that, she released me, opened the door, and pulled up her coat collar against the windy drizzle outside.

"Keep working on the TIME acronym" she said and walked out into the street.

I closed the door, still feeling a slight sense of loss. Everyone should have a Mary, I thought. I went back into the kitchen and saw the list of professors. She could be on that list. If Jane is half a professor, then Mary is the other half.

I had two things to do that evening. The second was to find the laptop. The first was to call Jane. I moved from a sense of loss to a sense of action and anticipation.

Jane had told me that she was sharing a flat in Cambridge, with two other people – one of them was also called Jane. The person who answered the call was not my Jane.

"Is Jane Anderson there," I asked. There was a pause whilst she was called to the phone.

"Is that Jane?" I heard her reply that it was. "It's John Watson here, Jane. We said we would get together again. Could I interest you in a special experience in my part of the world next Saturday, or the Saturday after?"

We started talking. Jane was a little unsure about whether she wanted the experience I was offering, until she heard that my sister would also be there and wanted to meet her. Then she was keen. The call ended and I had her commitment.

I feel I am starting on a new journey, and things are moving ahead nicely. In fact I am determined to push ahead. Perhaps this is the real secret to time management and adopting time saving practices. Be determined to be more productive. Now, where's that laptop?

Go back to the challenge list at the beginning of the book. If you have a solution for all the challenges, then well done! If you have not, then find another reader and find out what they think about the time management content as well as the puzzles along the way. This book exists to prompt a discussion that will help you with the greatest challenge of all - making the wealth of expertise here, and out there, relevant to the way you work, so that you will naturally implement it!

If you have enjoyed this book and learnt something from it, you may like to keep up-to-date with www.advanced-time-management.com where we will be adding additional techniques and methods over the next year.

Specifically, you may like to consider turning some of the ideas in this book into a plan of action using our **Learn what matters – measure what you do – improve how you do it** system, which is described on the website.